THE QUIET COMPANION

LOYOLA UNIVERSITY PRESS
is pleased to make
this out-of-print book
available once again
to its old friends.

This book* is a

LOYOLA

REQUEST

REPRINT

The Quiet Companion

Peter Favre, S.J., 1506 – 46

MARY PURCELL

LOYOLA UNIVERSITY PRESS
Chicago   60657

ISBN 0-8294-0377-9

A Loyola Request Reprint*

*First published 1970
Gill and Macmillan Ltd
2 Belvedere Place
Dublin I*

*Reprinted by arrangement with the author
and/or the original publisher.
This book is now sold only by
Loyola University Press.

Contents

Acknowledgments

I am deeply indebted to M. le Chanoine Coutin, keeper of the Salesian archives in Annecy, my guide on visits to Savoy and a mine of information on Favre's *patria;* also to the staff of the municipal archives in Annecy; also to the Lathuile family of Villaret, whose farmhouse adjoins the site of Favre's birthplace and whose kindness and hospitality helped one stranger to forget the cold of the Savoy Alps.

Thanks are also due to M. de Certeau, S.J., Paris, for directing me to Chanoine Coutin, for indicating some sources I might have overlooked, and for allowing me to quote from his brilliant Introduction and Notes to the French edition of Favre's *Memorial;* I thank many librarians in France, England and Ireland, especially Régine Pernoud of the Archives Nationales and the Musée de l'Histoire de France in Paris.

I am grateful, too, to the Jesuit Fathers of the Irish, Roman, French and Spanish Provinces for allowing me access to books and documents; to the monks of La Grande Chartreuse, their brethren of St Hugh's Charterhouse in Sussex and of the Carthusian Foundation in Vermont, U.S.A. for loaning books and answering queries; to Miss Grace Franks and the Fitzpatrick family of Baltimore for a rare and useful book; to Rev M. Bodkin, S.J. and C. de la Chapelle, S.J., for sustained and much needed encouragement; to officials of the French Government Travel Department, especially Mme Perraudin, until recently in the Dublin office, and her opposite number in Savoy, M. Yves.

MARY PURCELL

Introduction

PETER FAVRE and Francis Xavier, room mates at Paris University from 1525 to 1536, were the foundation stones upon which Ignatius Loyola built the Society of Jesus. The gentle and retiring Favre packed into the last seven of his forty years an incredible programme of travel and work. He was 'the Paris theologian' in the retinue of the Emperor Charles V at Worms, Spires, Ratisbon and other cities where Lutherans and Catholics met for discussions that usually ended in futility and mutual recriminations.

During the fateful years preceding the Council of Trent, Favre's assignments brought him into contact with many famous contemporaries. His writings supply interesting sidelights on the situation in Germany, particularly in the Rhineland, and stamp him as an ecumenist born four centuries too soon; his observations on men and events were perceptive and tolerant. A humanist by formation, he pleaded for calm instead of fury, conciliation instead of condemnation, and concentration on moral reform rather than on theological controversy. In 1540 Peter Favre was saying, with little hope of being heeded, what Pope John said in 1960: 'Stress what brings men together, not that which divides them'.[1] He told those who sought his counsel that the religious situation in the sixteenth century was quite different from that of early Christian times. The primitive Church preached to pagans, the policy being to bring them first to belief and afterwards to a better moral life. The correct procedure in post-Renaissance Europe was, Favre held, for the Church to set her own house in order, for self-reform, individual and collective; then, purified and renewed, the faithful, by example and kindness, might endeavour to win back those who had left the fold.

In a letter to a Jesuit friend who asked his advice on how to deal with men who had abandoned Catholicism for newer religions, Favre reveals himself. This letter, written shortly before his death in 1546, answered the query:

Remember, if we want to be of help to them, we must be careful to regard them with love, to love them in deed and in truth, and to banish from our own souls any thought that might lessen our love and esteem for them.

We have to win their good will so that they will love us and readily confide in us. This can be done by speaking familiarly with them on subjects about which we agree, and by avoiding points of discussion that might give rise to argument; for argument usually ends in one side lording it over the other. Neither should we act towards the Lutherans as though they were pagans, but rather address ourselves to a man's will, to his heart, as a means of approaching with prudence matters of faith.

Before mentioning errors of belief, try to get those who are in bad faith and who are, at the same time, leading evil lives, to abandon their vices. I once visited a Lutheran who wanted to draw me into a discussion on priestly celibacy. I set myself out to win his confidence. Then he told me that for many years he himself was living with a woman. Little by little I persuaded him to give up that life and return to his former celibacy. Meanwhile I refrained from disputing matters of faith. As soon as he ceased sinning, his errors of faith vanished and he never even mentioned them again, they being nothing more than the result of the kind of life he had been leading.

Regarding good works, which the Lutherans say are not necessary, proceed *ab ipsis operibus ad ipsam fidem,* and always speak of the things that will rouse them to good works . . . try to move their souls, so that they will develop a liking for prayer, for good works, for the Mass. It is the loss of love for prayer that has caused many to lose the faith. Assure them that with the grace of God it is possible to keep the commandments and bear the trials of life. This is one point where ardent exhortation is needed to help them recover the hope and confidence they have lost. If Luther could be got to abandon his position and place himself once more under obedience, resuming the habit he has cast off, he would by that very act cease to be a heretic and there would be no need for further theological dispute. But, oh, what fortitude of spirit, what profound humility, what

tremendous patience, what heavenly 'fire' would be needed to bring
that to pass . . .

The man who can speak with the heretics on a holy life, on
virtue and prayer, will do far more good for them than those who,
in the name of authority, set out to confound them.[2]

Writing to a Carthusian friend Favre deplored the policy of
force being adopted against Lutherans, Zwinglists, and Calvinists in so many places:

I grieve that those in power are planning, thinking of, trying no
course of action but one: the extirpation of public heretics. How
often have I not told them that this is a situation in which both
hands of the builders of the City of God are active in brandishing
the sword in the face of the enemy. Good God! Why do we not leave
at least one hand free for the immense work of reconstruction
awaiting us? Why do we not see a finger being raised to bring about
a real reformation (not in dogma or doctrine, for all is well there),
but in the moral standards of our Christian people?[3]

Not content with telling others what he considered the best
methods of *rapprochement*, Peter Favre, a man of God, prayed
constantly for the Church in crisis and for a world floundering
in an age of transition. He prayed especially for those men, his
contemporaries, who were determining the religious and
political history of his own and later times:

The Pope (Paul III), the Emperor (Charles V), the King of France
(Francis I), the King of England (Henry VIII), Luther, the Grand
Turk (Suliman the Magnificent), Bucer and Philip Melanchthon,
are eight persons for whom I mean to pray much, regardless of
their failings. My soul is saddened thinking on how harshly these
men are so often judged, and the Holy Spirit moved me to compassion for them.[4]

Such was the man who was called ' the great Peter Favre '
by no less a saint than Francis de Sales, his compatriot.

1   Willingly, to School

EVERY May, when the snow melted in the Grand-Bornand and the adjoining valleys of Savoy, the farm animals were moved up to the Alpine pastures. This annual exodus took place at Whitsuntide and the descent before the Michaelmas fairs in Annecy and Thônes. One member of each household climbed to the high meadows with the family livestock and remained there until autumn. Even children of six and seven were entrusted with the task. Reared hard and given responsibility early in life, they were quite capable of tending for an entire summer their parents' cows, sheep and goats.

Some weeks after his seventh birthday in 1513 a boy named Peter Favre was sent to the *alpage* for the first time. Like other children of Villaret, a small hamlet in the Grand-Bornand, he had been prepared for the hazards of life on the mountain. He could read the signs of settled weather or approaching storm. He had practised the giving and interpreting of the distress and danger signals peculiar to the Savoy Alps where the horns and yodellings beloved of the Swiss and Tyroleans were unknown. The need for fast action in emergency had been impressed upon him by his elders. Strident yells, shrill repeated bird-calls were not to be ignored. Such sounds might mean that someone's cow had fallen into a ravine or that bears or wolves were on the prowl, they might warn of hovering eagles or of strangers riding through a pass. Whatever the message the response had to be practical and immediate: a rush to help, a round-up of beasts, a whistling for dogs and an alerting of other shepherds, cowherds and goatherds.

Peter Favre knew the rules and conventions to be observed on the *alpage*. If he drove his few cows past a neighbour milking his goats he said 'God and St Birgitta save you', a blessing

intended for goats and for milker. Heights held dangers for
livestock and the loss of even one lamb was a serious matter for
the Bertin, Blanchet, Périssin, Pochat or Favre families. When
the bells of the valley churches rang out Peter and all the
shepherds knelt and prayed. While waiting for ruminant
animals he kept himself occupied. Spancels had to be plaited
for cows inclined to stray. Alpenstocks had to be trimmed.
Withies had to be whittled, sorted and tied in bundles for the
basket-makers.

During the summer months the boy's parents cultivated,
with patient care, the few fields and patches they had wrested
from the mountainside. Life in High Savoy was dominated by
the mountain. Its unyielding bulk confronted man at every
turn, blocking his movements and determining his mode of
existence. To emerge from its valleys he had to brave precipice,
torrent and tempest, snow and cold and treacherous glacier.
To subsist he had to reckon with the mountain and with the
long winters, white and silent, which all but buried him and
his for months for end. Up sterile slopes he carried on his back
the valley loam, spreading it on the shelves of rock where he
planted and tended plots of wheat, rye and vines. Though his
harvests were sparse and his vintages meagre, with cheese and
home-cured meat they sufficed for his frugal needs. This ceaseless pitting of himself against his native Alps bred in the
Savoyard courage, ingenuity, foresight, habitual and persever-
ing effort, a combination of tenacity and patience, the will to
win.[1]

Peter Favre's parents, Louis Favre and Marie Périssin, were
natives of the Grand-Bornand. Louis' brother, Dom Mamert
Favre, since 1508 Prior of the Carthusian Monastery of
Reposoir, some ten miles from Villaret, would be succeeded
in office by Dom Claude Périssin, Marie Favre's nephew. The
Favres and Périssins, like most of their neighbours, had several
relatives in religion. To this day the homes of those Alpine
valleys continue to furnish large contingents to the ranks of the
clergy and the religious orders.[2]

Louis Favre was not the poorest farmer in a village where no
one was wealthy and life was arduous for all. Peter described
his parents as 'very pious Catholics, good parents who reared

me in the fear of God'. The description fitted not merely his own parents but those of his companions. Four centuries later Stendhal, journeying through Savoy, found its inhabitants 'strong and faithful, upright and virtuous, uniting in themselves the qualities that go to make good soldiers with their own religious convictions'. Since France annexed Savoy in 1860 Paris officials have made periodic surveys and reports on the Departments of Savoie and Haute-Savoie.[3] The reports on Peter Favre's native valleys are almost unanimous. One stated:

The Savoyards in these parts are humble, devout folk, upright of heart and with very high moral standards. The men, though not tall, are well built. They are good looking, with superb teeth, and seem very healthy. Though they can be lively and animated in conversation, their habitual facial expression is serious. Indeed, a face in repose is so spiritual and peaceful that it resembles a sculpture. They are solid, silent, rather inclined to thought and introspection.

Another, while admitting their virtue, noted their failings:

They are a living proof that virtue unadorned, noble poverty, hard work and the simplicity of old customs can form the basis of happiness. The Savoyard does not tell you to be good but is himself the personification of goodness. The Celtic streak in them makes them warm-hearted, excessively hospitable, sometimes intemperate. They set so much store on their rights that they are forever going to law. This penchant for litigation means that there are many lawyers. In fact everyone is well-versed in law; and irony, that gift so useful in the law courts, is common to all . . . They are extremely hardworking and virtuous and have simple likes and dislikes, the latter including pretentious, lazy and gluttonous people, impostors, hypocrites and the astute who try to overreach their neighbours.

So deep was their attachment to faith, local valleys and ancient traditions that Savoyards suffered more than men of other nations when exiled from the *patria*. The obverse side of this fidelity was a stubbornness which made them resistant to change and over insistent on their rights. Their obstinacy drove them to such systematic contradiction of their rulers that one, Duke Victor-Amadeus II, exclaimed in exasperation, 'These devils of Savoyards are never content. If the good God hailed gold sequins on Savoy they would complain to Him that He had damaged their roofs'.[4] Until recent times their mountains guaranteed them a safety and isolation envied by more powerful nations. Secure within those formidable ramparts they, though few, could repel large armies. Who but the men of *Sabaudia* could boast of having closed the Alps to Caesar and opened them to Hannibal? Like other peoples whose origins are lost in antiquity they were, and are, prone to pride of race. Just as a Basque, disdaining to claim French or Spanish nationality, will always proclaim himself as Basque, so a native of Savoy will say 'I am a Savoyard', not 'I am a Frenchman'. Peter Favre, however, did not trouble to record his nationality. He lived in an age when nationality had not the importance it has since acquired. To him frontiers were man-made barriers, to be crossed as peacefully and as speedily as possible. In his eyes all men were kin and heaven their *patria* and his. There is no mention of Savoy in the laconic lines in which he records his beginnings. He gives no more than the name of his birthplace and native diocese:

I was born and baptized at Easter 1506 . . . in a village named Villaret in the Grand-Bornand. Grand-Bornand was in the diocese of Geneva which was then wholly Catholic.[5]

In 1506 Easter Monday, the day he was born, fell on 13 April. He was baptized the same day in the parish church of St Jean-de-Sixt. The custom of baptizing infants on the day of birth, though not confined to Savoy, was a custom strictly observed in that country at the time. A reason for this may have been the Confraternities of the Holy Spirit then to be found in most parishes of Geneva and Annecy dioceses. Because of these Confraternities devotion to the Spirit of God was widespread and the doctrine of His dwelling in the soul well understood, hence among the Savoyards there was a deep appreciation of Baptism, the Pentecost of the individual. A prayer often on Favre's lips during his lifetime was one he would have heard said at meetings of this Confraternity: 'Heavenly Father, in the name of Jesus, give me the Holy Spirit'.[6] The brotherhood, which included members of every family in a parish, collected portions of crops, firewood, fleeces, meat and other necessities of life from all for distribution among the needy, the sick, widows and orphans, and the aged.[7]

Peter had two younger brothers, *petit*-Louis and Jean.[8] His hard worked parents looked forward to the day when their eldest son, grown to manhood, would lighten their toil. But the boy had other ideas:

Before I was ten I had an intense desire to study, but I was a shepherd and my parents intended me for the world. Each night in bed I wept, so great was my longing to be educated.[9]

He was an intelligent child with an extraordinarily retentive memory. At an age when other children were still lisping he had absorbed everything his parents could teach him. His mother taught him his prayers, his father showed him how to be a good shepherd. Unlettered though they were, Marie and Louis Favre had clear ideas on what a child should know and how he should be trained.

On Sundays and feasts Peter Favre went to Mass in the parish church of St Jean-de-Sixt, where he heard the *curé's* sermons and religious instructions. At seven he could repeat these homilies verbatim and deliver them with effect. The same feat, performed a century later in Rome by the young cleric destined for fame under the name Richelieu, was considered so marvellous an achievement that the Pope rewarded it with a bishopric.[10] The future Cardinal was then twenty-one. Seven year old Favre had in his humbler environment his own admirers and his own rewards. His companions used to make him stand on a boulder and preach while they played congregation to his *curé*. This game, a serious and decorous affair, fascinated older people too. Grown-ups who stopped to listen paid dues, in the shape of berries, nuts and apples, to the earnest if diminutive preacher.[11]

Peter himself makes no mention of this but refers more than once to his 'continuous and immoderate desire for study and learning'.[12] His parents came to know that it was he, not *petit*-Louis or Jean, who cried himself to sleep each night. They knew that his tears were not caused by his constant toothache, which he bore stoically,[13] but by his hankering after education and their refusal to send him to school.

If they wondered at his longing for schooling they would have ascribed it to the influence of the Carthusian relatives, or to Guillaume Fichet, the local boy who had become a legend in the seven valleys. Peter had visited Reposoir and had seen the white-robed, silent monks. He had been shown and had handled printed books. More than likely he had preached a sermon to Dom Mamert and Dom Claude and they, educated men, had fired him with the desire for learning. From his grandparents and their cronies he heard of Fichet, the Petit-Bornand shepherd lad who went to school at La Roche, from there to Avignon and thence to Paris where he rose to be Rector of the Sorbonne.* In later years when he himself was a student in Paris Favre learned more about his compatriot. It was Fichet who, during his term as librarian in the University, introduced printing to Paris. His fame in the schools, however, was not due to that innovation but to the long fight he waged against the debasement of Latin. 'The deformation of the texts and the copyists' endless errors' were anathema to him, 'a scourge which is causing the Latin tongue, and the Sorbonne, to relapse into barbarism'. No doubt the copyists' errors spurred him into sending to Germany for printers and printing presses.[14]

While visits to Reposoir, the Fichet story, or both may have kindled in Favre the yearning for education, a more likely cause for his desire and his subsequent grief at its frustration lay in himself. Children of exceptional ability, aware of their latent powers, are usually eager to learn and fret if denied the opportunity of exercising and developing their minds. Peter Favre was that kind of boy. But he was also endowed with the tenacity of the Savoyard. Although the refusal of his request caused him tears he kept on asking. Finally the parents gave in. Their *volte-face* is thought to have been due to the two

*Fichet's term as Rector was brief. When Louis XI, 'King Spider', proposed arming the students, the Rector opposed the project strenuously. Called to the royal presence and asked why he had dared to defy the king's mandate he defended himself with courage. The matter was dropped but soon afterwards Fichet found himself appointed to lead an embassy first to Burgundy, then to Milan, and a new Rector was found for the Sorbonne.

Carthusians who took Peter's part. Peter reports his parents' surrender thus:

> In spite of themselves my parents agreed to send me to school. Then, seeing my progress, they allowed me to continue studying . . . Besides, God made me very inept and quite useless for anything else.[15]

Two old men from Grand-Bornand who claimed to have known Favre as a child gave evidence at the preliminary enquiry into his life and virtue in 1596. Louis Blanchet, then in his eightieth year, testified that Peter, 'at the age of six or seven, took no pleasure in playing with his companions, but devoted himself to nobler occupations, occupations far beyond those usual to children of his years. He was much esteemed, especially by his own age group whom he reproved for their faults.' Jean Pochat, another octogenarian, said that Peter Favre was regarded as 'already a very holy person, even at the age of seven or eight, being devout, abstemious and modest. He fasted twice a week.'[16]

These statements, both of which have been repeated and embellished over and over since 1596, will bear closer examination. The two witnesses were ten years younger than Favre and could not possibly have known him when he was seven. They were, in 1596, at an age when people tend to confuse reality with wishful thinking and memories with hearsay. For years they had listened to the gossip—gossip that became more exaggerated as time went on—of a small village.

The aged Blanchet's assertion that Favre as a child was disinclined to join in his companions' games and that he reproved their faults is completely out of character. Peter could never have grown to be the lovable person he was in adult life unless he had had a normal childhood and boyhood. Pochat's remark that Favre fasted twice a week and was very abstemious carries even less weight. Jews, Christians and Mohammedans fast, and allow their children to fast, for devotional reasons or to comply with regulations of their religion. Peter may have appeared abstemious to old Pochat but he himself once confessed to having had, in his late twenties, great difficulty in weaning himself from the pleasures of the table.

2

The evidence of these two ancients reminiscing about Peter Favre fifty years after his death was on a par with evidence of other witnesses called before similar tribunals during the last four centuries. It was regarded as unthinkable that a holy person could ever have been a child like other children. Happily, more reliable witnesses came forward to prove that Favre was the most understanding and accessible of men. It was a matter of wonder to him that he could never remember having had an enemy.[18] The man who advised his fellows not to let their minds dwell on the evil of others, but rather to find excuses for the offenders and to put the best interpretation possible on their offences was unlikely to have been a child who took it upon himself to correct his little friends. It is still more unlikely that his playmates, thus rebuked, would have held him in high esteen, as Blanchet declared. Peter tells us that, while still very young, he formed the habit of calling himself to task. Those who make a practice of looking for and correcting their own faults seldom have the time or the temerity to notice or rebuke the shortcomings of others.

We may take it that Peter Favre entered fully into the games and pastimes of the other shepherds. Life on the high pastures was not all work. The children chased and caught young marmots, tamed them and taught them tricks. Boys tried their skill with slings or at pole-vaulting. Everybody sang. Shepherding was a task favourable to singing. When the first weeks of the *alpage* and the novelty of living away from home paled, the long days became monotonous and the youngsters, scattered over wide areas with their flocks, grew lonely. Then one would begin to sing in a high, clear voice and all within hearing would take up the refrain. They imitated the bells with the *Bin-Bin-Bin-bin-bin* chorus. *The Wily Shepherdess*, *The Flock Saved from the Wolf*, and *My Father had Five Hundred Sheep* were firm favourites. When all raised their voices in *Houp-la-la, the Dragon's Daughter*, the chamois on the high peaks, more fearful of noise than of humans, leaped frantically from ledge to ledge. There were religious songs and chants, too. On Fridays *The Plaint of the Passion* was sung, on Saturdays a song for Our Lady and St Catherine:

Catherine was the daughter,
The High-King's daughter,
Ave Maria! Sancta Catherina.[19]

During the summer of 1516, happy in the knowledge that after Michaelmas he was to be sent to school, Peter Favre would have joined in all the songs and games. Despite his persistent toothache, when *The Dragon's Daughter* drew echoes from far and near, he would have taken up the chorus and *Houp-la-la*-ed with the rest.

*　　　*　　　*

Thônes*, six miles from Villaret, a walled town with three gates, had a hospital, hospices for travellers, a fortified castle and tower, but no school. The hospital chaplain, however, augmented his salary by teaching reading and writing. After seven months tuition Peter Favre 'was well able to read and write and had a knowledge of grammar. He made remarkable progress, passing out all the other scholars'.[20] Books being scarce, extra reading matter was provided by extracts translated from the Geneva missal by the teacher. The star pupil, young Favre, must have been especially pleased when a collect invoking the aid of St Apollonia against the toothache was given as an item of required reading. He memorized it and said it often. Quarter of a century later, on the feast of St Apollonia, he recalled this practice and its sequel: 'From that time on I suffered no more from toothache'.†[21]

A priest named Mamert Périssin lived in Thônes. His name suggests that he was a relative but there is no evidence that the Grand-Bornand boy stayed with him. Peter's astounding prowess as a walker in later years, when he crossed and re-

*Thônes girls and cherries were immortalised by Rousseau in *Idylle des Cerises*. The lane where the young philosopher, perched in a cherry tree, found inspiration, may still be traversed.

†St Apollonia, martyred in Alexandria in the third century, was tortured by having all her teeth torn out before her execution. The collect in the fourteenth century Geneva missal reads: O God, who by a special privilege hast adorned Thy holy Virgin and Martyr, Apollonia, with the gift and merit of banishing toothache from those who suffer it: grant to us who ask, trusting in her, that through her we may obtain a healing remedy, through Christ our Lord, Amen.

crossed Europe on foot, indicates that in youth he got much
practice in walking on all sorts of terrain and in all kinds of
weather. To walk twelve miles a day might deter modern
pupils used to twentieth century transport, but students of
other times, especially students eager to learn, took such
journeys, literally speaking, in their stride.

Peter was in Thônes in May 1517 when a Bishop deputising
for the Bishop of Geneva came to the town on episcopal visitation. The principal church was being rebuilt and the clergy
were told to have it ready for consecration by mid-summer, to
put back any church furniture they had appropriated for their
own use during the rebuilding period, and to present in future
quarterly inventories of church furnishings and revenues.
Stained glass windows, a Blessed Sacrament lamp and missals
were needed. The first Mass should begin at sunrise, 'that is,
four o'clock in summer and six in winter'. One abuse not
corrected since the previous visitation was mentioned. Fairs
and markets were still being held in the graveyard, consecrated
ground, and townsfolk met there to chat, disturbing the clergy
when they were chanting Divine Office. All in all, in the
southern end of Geneva diocese the people were not as de-
praved or their priests as lax as the Reformers claimed.

Having been present for the Rogation Processions the
visitor noted some individuals who slipped away as the processions moved off. He exhorted each family to send at least
one adult representative to church processions. As the Thônes
Rogation Procession covered a traditional route almost fifteen
miles long across the mountains, it must have been regarded
by many as an endurance test, a forced march to be dodged if
possible. Peter Favre would not have dodged it, for the procession not only passed his parents' door, but stopped in
Villaret, that being one of the official points where the pro-
cessionists halted for refreshments.[22]

Before leaving Thônes the visiting prelate tonsured fourteen
youths, three of them from the Grand-Bornand. Favre, barely
turned eleven, could not have been one, but he would have
been present at the ceremony. Later that summer when
shepherding, a task he resumed in the long vacation, he made
a personal pact with God:

In my twelfth year, being in a field with my flocks . . . I promised God always to guard chastity.[23]

Thônes, the initial test, was so successful that his parents decided, in 1517, to let him go further afield. They sent him to La Roche where, seventy years before, Guillaume Fichet had studied. La Roche, twelve miles from Villaret, was on the highway that had once been the old Roman road running north from Annecy to Geneva. The town was on the marches of the Counts of Geneva, vassals of the Duke of Savoy, vassals whose allegiance to the reigning Duke, the weak Charles III, was just then wearing thin.

Hundreds of pupils flocked to La Roche that autumn, news having percolated through the valleys that the famous Peter Velliard had come there to teach. A great teacher, Velliard was also a holy priest, so holy that after his death Favre prayed to him and made a point of visiting Velliard's grave when passing through Savoy in later years, 'for I count him as a saint, though he is not canonized'. Earlier in 1517, the printing presses of Geneva had run off Master Velliard's only published work, a Complete Letter-Writer. His method proceeded from the Salutation and Introduction, via the Narration, Petition or Reply to the Conclusion, Signature and Address. Besides the usual subjects then taught, Velliard taught the classics 'in such a way as to make them seem like the Gospels', said Favre. Peter displayed an unusual flair for Greek and later found himself at a considerable advantage in Paris University when his acquaintance with Aristotle stood him in good stead. The students of Velliard were also encouraged to apply their minds to abstruse problems of theology and philosophy, problems that had long before engaged the attention of Aquinas, Peter the Lombard and other schoolmen.[24]

In the three-hundred-page copy book he took away with him when he left La Roche in 1525 Favre had summarized what he had learned. Here and there the pages were embellished with drawings of alpine flowers, human faces and the hieroglyphics that then passed for signatures. His uncle, Dom Mamert Favre, Prior of Reposoir, died three years before he left La Roche. The next Prior was Dom Claude Périssin, Peter's first cousin, and the friendship between them, evident in their letters of later years, suggests that as a young student Peter had frequently visited Reposoir. Wherever his journeyings took him in the last crowded decade of his life he seemed to gravitate naturally to the Carthusians and not the least of the bonds that knit him to Ignatius Loyola was their mutual love and esteem for the sons of St Bruno.

But Paris and its University as yet lay far ahead. In that autumn of 1517 news of epoch-making events in Germany was brought to La Roche by travellers riding south from Geneva. At Hallowe'en an Augustinian named Martin Luther had nailed his ninety-five theses to the doors of the College chapel in Wittenberg. Luther was then thirty-four. Some weeks later a Swiss priest of the same age, Ulrich Zwingli, told the dumb-founded pilgrims at Einseideln, the shrine of which he was custodian, that religious practices were useless and that he had buried the relics to prevent people from venerating them. In Picardy, hundreds of miles north of Savoy, a boy three years Favre's junior was distinguishing himself at school. The facility with which he grasped, absorbed, and pigeon-holed in memory all he was taught astounded the savants of the town of Noyon. His name was John Calvin.

The world beginning to open to Peter Favre was still to a large extent medieval. Christendom had dissolved into a plurality of nations, yet the social structure of the preceding centuries was little changed. Throughout Europe there was unity of faith, a unity upheld by rulers if for no other reason than that it formed a firm foundation for unity in the kingdom. Although a growing independence of Papal and Church authority was in evidence, the practice whereby the Church handed over to the secular arm for punishment those who denied the faith still held, though, outside Spain, it had more or less fallen into abeyance. Soon it was to get a new lease of life when Catholic princes would hunt down and destroy Lutherans, Calvinists and other dissenters, while rulers favouring the Reformers would prove themselves equally adept at per-secuting and slaying Catholics. Statesmen and politicians intent on removing opponents were to find it convenient to do so in the name of religion, and often came to persuade themselves that by such deeds of violence they were doing a service to God.

Throughout large areas of Europe conditions were similar to those obtaining in Thônes at the time of the episcopal visitation in 1517. Records of the passing scene left by contemporary travellers show that there was little scepticism and no general revolt against Christian teaching and principles. Festivals, sacred as well as profane, might be sometimes marked by grossness, immorality and brutality but on the whole life was anchored in a profound if not always well instructed faith. Denial of dogma, sacrilege, failure to receive the sacraments at Easter, prolonged absence from Mass were rare. Rarer still and held in universal abhorrence was suicide. Even in Renaissance Italy among the inbred nobility—those powerful families who had come to regard the Papacy as their special preserve and manipulated Papal elections in the most shameless and calculating manner—suicide was rare and when it occurred was due more to the corrupt milieu than to any weakening of faith. Atheism was unheard of. If old superstitions and pagan customs revived in places, the revival was mainly the result of ignorance and lack of instruction; it was also due to the example set by the aristocratic and educated classes who consulted astrologers, sought the services of sorcerers and dabbled in black magic.

Very little news of the outside world filtered into the Grand-Bornand but in La Roche, a border town on a main highway, every traveller had a tale to tell. Peter Favre was there at a time when events happened in Savoy that were later to have repercussions far beyond that country's frontiers. Charles III of Savoy, uncle to Francis I, the young king of France, was an indolent ruler. The French and the Savoyards agreed that he should have been the woman and his sister, the formidable Louise of Savoy whose indomitable determination and patience set her son on the French throne, the man. Charles, a bachelor past his first youth, sighed for faraway Infantas with huge dowries. This mirage beckoned him since 1514, when Manuel the Fortunate of Portugal sent an embassy to Rome advertising his country's position as a maritime and colonial power and himself as the wealthiest ruler in the West. Europe gaped at the three hundred mules laden with the splendour of Ind, at the ambassadors' jewels and silks and stirrups of solid gold, at the panthers that could dance and the Hindu elephant that had been taught to genuflect to St Peter's statue, at the sacks allegedly crammed with ivories, perfumes, ostrich eggs and fantastic trinkets, at the exotic fruits and birds and the strange beasts. The cavalcade had bemused Duke Charles, as had the rumours of the Lisbon coffers bulging with gold, fortunes for the Infantas. To a friend who observed that foreign princesses with large dowries had been known to scorn and ruin the men they wed Charles turned a deaf ear.

During Favre's first years in La Roche a Savoy embassy was in Lisbon seeking the Infanta Beatrix as a bride for the Duke. Other ambassadors from more powerful princes were in Lisbon on a similar mission. The Savoyards were at first cold-shouldered. Was it fitting that a king's daughter should wed a mere Duke? How could a princess from a sun-drenched land exist in cold Savoy? But the Savoyards were tenacious. They exaggerated their master's avuncular influence on the French king. They assured Manuel that Francis, victor of Marignano, was certain to win the election for Emperor of the Holy Roman Empire. Luckily, they had won the princess and got the contracts signed before the news came that Charles the Hapsburg had won the election. Two more years elapsed before Manuel could be persuaded to actually part with his daughter and her dowry. But the Duke of Savoy, in no hurry to marry, did not fret. Perhaps he had a premonition of what was to come.

Beatrix disembarked at Nice, then a Savoy possession, in 1521. As the Duke's friend had warned, the beautiful but haughty seventeen-year-old regarded her marriage as a disastrous come-down. She despised her bridegroom—more than twice her age—and his small alpine kingdom, and sulked from the moment she set foot ashore. Charles, fearful lest Chambéry, his ducal capital, might not please her, took her to Turin, the first city in his Piedmont domains. She belittled Turin and let it be known that all Italy had to offer was as nothing to what she had left behind in Portugal.

Later Charles persuaded his Duchess to accompany him on a tour of Savoy. The Savoyards turned out in strength to welcome her, as their forebears had welcomed other princesses —Yolande of France, Anne of Cyprus, Bonne of Bourbon—

come to wed former Dukes. But Beatrix, sullen and contemptuous, ignored them. From Chambéry the ducal procession went to other towns, passing La Roche on the way to or from Geneva, seventeen miles farther north. Velliard's scholars were out to cheer the cavalcade. Peter Favre was then at school in La Roche. He can hardly have imagined, as he watched the ruler of Savoy ride by, that twenty years ahead he would refer to the Duke as 'my spiritual son'.*

Geneva, a free city, though not actually belonging to Savoy, looked to the Dukes to fortify it, protect it and fight its battles. Having heard that neither Turin nor Chambéry had impressed 'Madame Beatrix' the Genevois determined to show her how their cultured and wealthy city received kings' daughters. They hung the walls with her colours, white and tan. Poets composed verses in Latin and Portuguese which were set to music and practised by choirs. Pageants and tourneys were rehearsed for an entire month and much money was spent on elaborate preparations and decorations. Unfortunately for Savoy the Duchess reserved her most disdainful manners for Geneva. She scarcely glanced at the floral arches and made it plain that the pageants and choral items bored her. When presented with gifts of superb craftsmanship she and her Portuguese ladies 'were heard to sigh for Lisbon with its four hundred and thirty goldsmiths'. The Genevois, mortified and seething with resentment, said nothing, but when the Duke and his lady rode out the drawbridge went up, never again to be lowered to allow a prince of the House of Savoy enter Geneva.

In 1525 Beatrix's head was completely turned by the news that her sister Isabella was to wed the Emperor, Charles V. 'She now regarded herself as imperial, only sister to an Empress, and Savoy and its Duke fit for nothing only dragging at the

---

*Favre always had a warm corner in his heart for 'my prince' and Ignatius and the early Jesuits seem to have twitted him for his devotion to 'Charles the Unfortunate'. Beatrix, whose meddling helped to bring about the Duke's ruin, died in 1538; all their children but one died young. Charles' brother-in-law the Emperor annexed his lands on the Italian side of the Alps, while his nephew the French king and the Swiss, between them, despoiled him of the remainder of his duchy. As a Prince of the Holy Roman Empire he attended the Diet of Ratisbon in 1541 and appealed to the Electors and other Imperial Princes for justice. He got promises but little else, and did not live to see his son return to a free Savoy as its Duke. At Ratisbon he met Favre whom he took as his confessor.

Emperor's chariot wheel'. She went to reside permanently in Turin, to be near Milan, an imperial city. Worse still, she began to meddle in high politics, a dangerous activity for a feather-brained young woman closely related by marriage to the protagonists in the struggle for power, Francis I and Charles V.[25]

While Beatrix was thus complicating life for her mild and easy-going husband, Peter Favre was preparing to leave Savoy. He had completed his course at La Roche and was to go to Paris University. Opinion is divided as to whether his first year in Paris was paid for by his parents or by the monks of Reposoir or whether he was there on a scholarship, but he seems to have been on a bourse from 1526 on. Intelligence, application and tenacity had taken him a long way in ten years, from Villaret to Paris, from shepherd's field to lecture hall.

For Savoy and France 1525 had been a fateful year. The Duke had been his nephew's ally at Pavia and all during spring and summer survivors straggled home in twos and threes to tell the tale of horror and woe. René of Savoy, brother of Charles III, had been killed in the battle, together with half the paladins of France and ten thousand of the mighty army that had marched so hopefully through Savoy the previous year on the way to Italy. The French king had been made prisoner and taken to Madrid where the Emperor held him captive. It seemed as though France must disappear as a European power. But the Regent, Louise of Savoy, was at the helm of state. When she read her son's letter with the famous phrase 'nothing is left to me save life and honour' she did not waste time lamenting. She wrote to the Emperor and got her brother of Savoy to do likewise. She calmed the disaffected lords and captains, saw that a new army was raised and trained, wrote to the Pope, to Venice, to Suliman the Magnificent and to Henry VIII. She incited the Sultan to attack Austria, an Imperial possession, and blew upon the English monarch's envy of the Emperor so that the rift already between the two widened. She intrigued with Wolsey, turning a blind eye to his designs on Picardy in her efforts to bring about an alliance between France and England.

In Germany there was religious and social turmoil. The

Peasants' War had spread from the Black Forest to the provinces on every side before finally collapsing in a welter of blood. Prussia, Saxony, Hesse, Mecklenburg and many Imperial cities had gone over to the Reformers. Luther went through a form of marriage with Catherine de Bora, one of several nuns who had been persuaded to leave their convents and disregard their vows. Zwingli, already left Einseideln for Zurich, where his preaching attracted great congregations, followed up the suppression of images by banning the celebration of Mass. Pope Clement VII, a Medici, indecisive and lacking in courage, had departed from his usual policy of neutrality and supported the French at Pavia. When the incredible happened 'the Pope was as one dead, his terror being increased by the rejoicing of the Spaniards and the Colonnas in his household'. Colonna and Orsini fought in the streets of Rome while the Romans blamed the Pope for the fighting, the floods, the famine and the ever-recurrent plague. An English girl of seventeen, lady-in-waiting to a dowager Duchess of Savoy, the widowed Margaret of Austria, returned to London where she began to attract the notice of court and king. Her name was Anne Boleyn. 1525 was certainly an eventful year. But for Peter Favre it was significant in that it was the year he was leaving Savoy for Paris and its University.

2 The Ste-Barbe Students

GOING by Geneva and crossing the Juras through the Pass of Faucilles good walkers could cover the distance between Savoy and Paris in a week. They travelled in groups for greater safety, sleeping the first night in the Benedictine guest house at Saint-Claude, the next at Cluny, and the following nights in similar hospices at Vézelay—pilgrimage shrine of the Magdalen—Auxerre, Sens and Fontainebleau. In September 1525 Peter Favre, then in his twentieth year, joined others going to Paris either by this route or a longer road that took them through Citeaux and Dijon to the source of the Seine, which river they followed for the rest of the way.

'At the age of nineteen I left my own country and came to Paris.'[1] He says no more about what must have been for him a memorable event. Though he makes no mention of the leave-taking, first and hardest of the many that were to be his lot, a phrase in a letter written years later is significant, 'It is the Holy Spirit who helps the heart to bear exile from the *patria*'.[2] A Savoyard, he was as prone to nostalgia as his compatriot who wrote in 1805:

. . . Here, six hundred leagues from my native land, thoughts of the family, memories of childhood, ravage me with grief. . . . I still see my mother walk into my room, my mother with her holy face, and as I pen these words I weep like a child.[3]

Villaret, with its seven 'hearths', had been left seventy-seven leagues behind when Paris, a city of five hundred streets, ten thousand dwellings and some three hundred thousand inhabitants, came in sight. Before the travellers reached the great moat, thirty yards wide, that encircled the walls, those familiar with the capital would have drawn their companions' attention to certain landmarks. Half a mile outside the south-east gate stood the Chartreuse of Vauvert, for Peter Favre a reminder of Reposoir. In the years ahead he would often traverse the pathway leading to this haven. Razed during the Revolution and long since replaced by the Luxembourg Gardens and part of the Boul'Mich', Vauvert had been built by St Louis on a spot shunned by medieval Paris because the place was believed to be haunted by demons. As this legend persisted into the sixteenth century the monastery did not attract many visitors, so the Carthusians were assured of the silence and solitude essential to their way of life.

Travellers from Savoy entered Paris by the Porte Saint-Jacques and then found themselves in the street of the same name. This main thoroughfare was lined on both sides with bookshops, taverns, pastry shops, colleges, convents, mansions of the great, and shops selling such mundane trappings of scholarship as gowns, shoes, ferules and regents' bonnets. Only the rue St-Jacques and the rue St-Etienne des Grés could take two carriages abreast. In other one-way streets drivers of wagons and coaches exchanged words and blows sooner than yield right of way. In the many streets too narrow for vehicular traffic mounted riders lorded it over pedestrians, crowding them against the walls and bespattering them with the filth which lay thick upon the ground. Peter Favre's first long journey ended in one of these noisome lanes. It opened off the rue Sept-Voies, now the rue de Valette, and was called the Street of the Dogs. The main building in the Street of the Dogs was Peter's college, the Ste-Barbe.

He was on the left bank of the Seine, in the south east sector of the city where a labyrinth of streets wound in and out through the jumble of buildings crowded together in the Latin Quarter. The University was not centralized but functioned through almost fifty separate colleges. The various Orders—Jacobins (Dominicans), Cordeliers (Franciscans), Mathurins (Trinitarians), Bernardines, Augustinians, Carmelites, Cluniacs, Benedictines and others—had their own colleges where their novices pursued their studies while at the same time serving their apprenticeship to the religious life. There were, too, the colleges already venerable in 1525, the Sorbonne, the St-Victor, the Ste-Geneviève, where memories of Bernard and Abelard, Aquinas and Duns Scotus, lingered. There was the Picardy where Dante saw, in fact or in imagination, Siger de Brabant *leggendo nelo vico degli strami:*

— reading in the straw-strewn lane,
And not escaping envy when he argued for truth.[4]

More than thirty other colleges, some new and prosperous like the Ste-Barbe, some old and famous like its rival and nearest neighbour, the Montaigu, were also in the University enclave.

Twenty years before Favre's arrival in Paris determined efforts had been made to reform French 'abbeys, churches, convents, universities, colleges and cathedral chapters', many of which had fallen into deplorable laxity. A Papal Legate, backed by royal authority and empowered to act without delay and with whatever severity he deemed necessary, began his mission in Paris by visiting the Jacobins. Two attempts having failed to induce the young Dominicans, some three hundred strong, to wear their Order's habit and refrain from roving the streets at will, the King's archers were called in. Immediately 'a thousand scholars from all over the Latin Quarter, each with a weapon concealed beneath his long gown' ran to the aid of the Jacobins. All day long the tide of battle rolled up and down the rue St-Jacques until finally 'these friarlets' were evicted. A few days later, when they and their supporters tried to retake the convent by assault, property was damaged and innocent people injured. The citizens, hitherto inclined to side with the students, now joined the authorities and helped to run the rioters out of Paris. Then the Dominican superiors took things in hand. They sent down 120 of their brethren and, by riding the remainder on a tight rein, brought the college back to discipline and order. The rules, particularly those concerning poverty, were rigidly enforced and by 1525 the Jacobins were in high repute for their exemplary lives as for their learning.[5]

The Legate was not so successful with other colleges run by religious. Having heard of the Dominicans' revolt and its sequel the Cordeliers decided to adopt different tactics. When the reforming prelates entered their convent the assembled friars, facing them, began to chant, *O Lord, judge us not according to our offences,* and similarly appropriate versicles and antiphons. This chanting they kept up for more than four hours and would not desist, not even when ordered to do so in the name of the King. Next day a hundred archers arrived and found the friars disposed to repeat their performance. 'This time there was no difficulty in silencing them. Burlesque having failed, the Cordeliers tried argument and finally pathos, indulging in much weeping and wailing'. The Legate, however, was adamant. Ringleaders and other refractory characters were severely dealt with. His task was hampered by 'that hundred-headed monster, the Paris populace'. Foreseeing a drop in profits if customers and potential customers were lost to them, owners of taverns, pastryshops, gaming houses and less reputable establishments opposed collegiate reform tooth and nail.[6]

Long before the Papal Legate descended on the Jacobins and similar religious colleges, the Montaigu had known a greater reform and reformer. Jan Standonck, a Fleming who had studied in the Ste-Barbe, became Rector of the Montaigu at a time when that college was at a very low ebb. Dedicated to religious, moral and educational reform Standonck was a man of iron for whom every day was a fast day and hairshirts and other instruments of penance among the necessities of life. Under his rule the all but defunct Montaigu got a new lease of life, a resurgence of learning following on the reform of manners.

The students, not being cast in the Rector's calibre, found the reformation hard going. Erasmus later revenged the miseries he suffered by enumerating the trials he and others who survived the regime endured: scurvy, fleas, hard beds and harder blows, stale herrings, rotten eggs and sour wine. Rabelais, writing in similar vein, described the daily routine of a *Montacutien* from four in the morning to eight or nine at night. Even then the wretched scholar could not be sure of his sleep, being liable to be called to the rooftop at some unearthly hour to contemplate the heavens, watch for comets, study the positions, oppositions and conjunctions of the stars and consider what all this might portend. Satirists, however, have been known to exaggerate. Certainly the Montaigu's most famous theologian, the Scot John Mair, had little use for star-gazing and star-gazers. To him astrology was not a science, *valde hoc studium abhorreo*, and the astrologers he knew 'men of much fantasy and little devotion'. Standonck was succeeded in the Montaigu by Beda, who inherited his passion for reform. With Beda as Rector and Mair as its leading professor the college continued to flourish. Despite Erasmus' assertion that many promising students died, went mad or blind, or contracted leprosy during their first year there the fact remains that students of other colleges clamoured for admission and wept when refused. Within a generation the number of the Montaigu's students increased four-fold and during that period its registers included the names of Vives, Erasmus, Buchanan, John Calvin, Rabelais and Ignatius Loyola.

By contrast with the Montaigu the Ste-Barbe was comparatively new. It had always been in high repute for learning. The fact that it had given the Montaigu such men as Mair and Standonck was proof that Peter Favre's college had no need of reform. It had amenities, unknown in other colleges, which it owed to the generous patronage of the Portuguese kings. Manuel the Fortunate and after him John III thought it good policy to demonstrate to Paris and the world, through the moneys lavished on the Ste-Barbe, the colonial wealth of Portugal. The Rector, Diogo de Gouvea, most of the regents and the majority of the students were Portuguese. Peter Favre enrolled in the Ste-Barbe at a time when the rejuvenated Montaigu seemed likely to outstrip it in scholarship, a situation which caused constant rivalry and occasional hostilities between *Barbistes* and *Montacutiens*. Traditional opinions were upheld in the Montaigu while the Ste-Barbe professors flew the humanist flag. Portuguese and Spaniards, partisans of the Emperor, predominated in the Ste-Barbe while French nationals were in the majority in the Montaigu. From 1524, when King Francis marched away to fight the Imperial armies in Italy, until his return from captivity in 1526, relations between the students of the two colleges were particularly strained.

The principal of the Ste-Barbe, de Gouvea, was 'vigilant and able, a very grave man of the highest probity, one who knew how to enkindle in the young the fire of emulation'. He became Rector at a time when an exceptionally gifted group of students enrolled in the Ste-Barbe, 'all of them perfectionists, students who needed no pushing or urging, being only too eager to do better than their masters'. The college was almost a de Gouvea fief, most of the auxiliary posts being filled by the Rector's relatives. Four of his nephews, brilliant men, were regents. Another cousin was bursar while two de Rodriguez nephews and four other de Gouvea relatives were among the students. Simon de Rodriguez, with whom Favre was to be closely connected in later years, had a scholarship paid for by the Portuguese king.[7]

Peter was a paying student for his first year at least. In 1526 King John III established no less than fifty bourses in the Ste-Barbe, not all of which went to Portuguese students. Subjects of King John's brothers-in-law, the Emperor Charles V and Charles III, Duke of Savoy, are likely to have been among those who profited by this munificence. Before Favre was a year at college his proficiency in Greek had been noted. 'The regents, when in doubt as to how a certain passage in Aristotle should be rendered, referred the matter to Master Peter Favre'. With this distinction to his credit he was high on the list of those qualifying for bourses reserved for students other than Portuguese.

Arrived at his college Favre's first task would have been to present himself and his credentials to Jacques de Gouvea, the then bursar, and make arrangements for board and lodging. He was sure of a roof and food, unlike the *martinets*, students who worked their way through college and who had the run of the Latin Quarter. Such a poor scholar might be on the roll of one college and attend lectures there, act as valet to a regent or wealthy student in another in return for lecture fees, serve in the kitchen or refectory of a third where he got meals and a bed—small wonder that the *martinets* were the heroes and ringleaders of so many student revels, riots and revolts.

Whether a student lodged in a college or in some house nearby he signed—as did the landlord or bursar giving him

3

bed and board—a legal document setting forth in detail the obligations of each party. One such document signed by five students and one Pierre Rouable who lived 'opposite the Cocqueret College, at the Sign of Saint Sebastian' gives an idea of how Paris students of Favre's time made arrangements at the start of a term:

We . . . have made this bargain with honest Pierre Rouable . . . He is to let us have a small furnished room near the Seine, to see that it is kept clean and that our laundry is done. He is to supply us with food, good meat, bread and wine for two meals, dinner and supper. Half a *cestier* of wine for each of us at each meal, with sufficient bread, also good potage. On fast days four herrings each or other fish of our choosing, the same for supper together with some good pea-soup, fried beans or similar of our choosing.
Also each Sunday he is to supply us with six clean white serviettes apiece. Aforesaid food, lodging and entertainment to be supplied to us from 1st January to the end of Paschaltide for the total sum of 23 francs and 15 silver *dousains*. This sum we will pay on the last day of Paschaltide or sooner if we think fit, each of us five being responsible for his own share, to wit, 4 francs and 15 silver *dousains*. This deed and present bargain being signed by us in the presence of monsigneur maistre Michiel de Feste, Nicholas Barbier, etc. etc. Holy Innocents Day, last Feast of Noel.[8]

One of the professors then in the Ste-Barbe was George Buchanan, later to be the tutor of Mary Queen of Scots and later still to win fame as a Presbyterian leader. A committed Erasmist and a writer of elegant Latin verse, Buchanan's carping manner earned him few friends. He saw only the worst side of his students and was never done enumerating their faults:

While their professor shouts himself hoarse these lazy idlers sleep or think of their pleasures. One, absent, will get a friend to answer his name at roll-call. Another has lost his shoes, a third, entranced by the sight of his slippers, has eyes only for his feet. This fellow is sick, that one writing to his parents. There is no remedy but the rod . . . Then we have the loafers from the town (here he is referring to the *martinets*). They announce their arrival by the clatter of their hobnailed shoes . . . They grumble because notices of the courses are not posted up at every street corner . . . Others are scandalized if a professor does not read out of a big bulky tome all full of marginal glosses. They kick up and make a tumult and take themselves off to sanctuaries like the Montaigu and other colleges smelling of white-beet soup.[9]

With a surfeit of herrings on fast days and almost a pint of wine daily these five students would have been the envy of the Montaigu boarders. There the younger scholars had to make do with half a herring or an egg, the herring a long time left the sea and the egg long removed from the henhouse. The repast was washed down with cold water or a thin soup made 'from the vilest of vegetables'. Older *Montacutiens* were promoted to a whole herring, two eggs and a third of a pint of sour wine daily.

Favre found himself sharing a room in the Ste-Barbe with a young regent who had qualified that summer, Juan de la Peña, and a Basque a week younger than himself, a student who would yet go far—in every sense of the word. The Basque's name was Francis and he came from a dilapidated castle in Spain, the castle of Xavier in Spanish Navarre. The two new-comers had to undergo the usual initiation rites for first year students. One night Favre would have been the 'beano' or *bejanus*, the next night Xavier. In this ragging, a survival from medieval times, older students surrounded the new arrival, pretending to discover in him a strange beast of uncouth appearance and habits. Outrageous and insulting remarks concerning the *bejanus* were bandied about in the barbarous Latin[10] of the students.* The 'beano' then became the butt of rowdy horseplay, being blindfolded, poked, pummelled and roughly handled. One surmises that Favre submitted to the ordeal with a better grace than Xavier. He was gentle and unassuming while Francis was ambitious, inclined to haughtiness, 'claiming as his ancestors nobles and persons of great distinction and pre-eminence in the realm of Navarre'. Francis Xavier had not come to Paris to be baited as a brute beast from beyond the Pyrenees.

---

*This *argot*, known as the *lengua parisiense*, was the delight of the students and the despair of their professors. 'On all sides one heard yelled such gems as *Noli crachare super me, semper lichat suos digitos, sanguinat de naso, etc.*'

Favre and Xavier arrived at the Ste-Barbe more than a year too late for a pitched battle between that college and the Montaigu. While feelings ran high between the two colleges the students let off steam by yelling names and insults at one another from the windows overlooking the Street of the Dogs. The dirty laneway, following the unprecedented summer rains of 1523, became unbearable. Because of the foetid airs arising from it all windows of both colleges had to be closed thus depriving *Montacutiens* and *Barbistes* of an outlet for their mutual animosity. After many complaints and appeals the civic authorities had the alley paved over. This made matters worse, for the clamped down filth threatened to seep up into the Montaigu premises, already far from sanitary. The students there thought it would be a lark to help the nuisance transfer itself to the other side of the Street of the Dogs. Not much knowledge of engineering or drainage was needed to do this and the *Barbistes* emerged one morning to find their well-kept courtyards in a sorry state. The first reaction of students and regents was dismay, the next anger and a determination to return evil for evil. That night after curfew they crept down to the lane and worked quietly until dawn, slanting the paving stones and channels away from their college. To this nocturnal activity the Rector, de Gouvea, turned a blind eye.

'Next morning there was havoc in the Montaigu, all from the oldest to the youngest seething and simmering with rage'. The authorities, taking their cue from de Gouvea, gave unofficial consent to counter-attack. The *Montacutiens*, under the command of their two porters Ulysses and Orion, piled stones near the now wide open windows facing the Ste-Barbe. When night fell the *Barbistes*, suspecting that retaliation was afoot, sent Polypheme, their huge one-eyed porter, to challenge Ulysses and Orion. Polypheme's first roar of defiance was met by a hail of stones from the Montaigu windows. At once the Ste-Barbe men, who had been lying on their beds fully dressed and who had equipped themselves with safety helmets in the shape of kitchen pots and pans, ran out and began smashing the enemy's windows. The *Montacutiens*, not as reformed as was generally believed, rushed down and the battle began. The Ste-Barbe bakery was demolished, the baker flying for his life.

'You took our Ceres, now we'll take your Bacchus', yelled the *Barbistes* as they rampaged through the vineyard that supplied the sour wine of the Montaigu. By this time day was dawning and Noel Beda and de Gouvea, appalled at the destruction and the bills to be met, regretted their permissive silence. They discussed the matter later that morning and, having decided not to call the king's archers to deal with the students, or the civic authorities to replace the paving stones, sent for workmen and had drains dug. The affair had one good result in that the Street of the Dogs was less offensive from that on.[11]

The word 'reform', unfamiliar to Favre before 1525, was one he frequently heard in Paris. Our innocent from Savoy, who had known no greater transgressors than the Thônes parishioners who chatted in the graveyard or made themselves scarce when processions were getting ready to move off, must have been amazed to hear of friars who fought in the streets and who would not allow the Pope's Legate to make himself heard. The Ste-Barbe students were rather proud of the fact that their college, unlike the Montaigu, needed no reformation. Yet, at this period their Rector's frequent absences were having an adverse effect on discipline. De Gouvea often acted as his King's ambassador at large, and more than once when he was away students and regents broke bounds at night and roved the city with other roisterers. Francis Xavier joined in some of these excursions, either out of curiosity and bravado, or just to be one of the boys, but he soon tired of the company and the adventures—often sordid—and remained with Favre in their room.

Luther's writings had been condemned by the Sorbonne in 1521 but the word 'reformation' conveyed to the Paris student of 1525 not so much the upheaval then taking place in Germany as the reform in Meaux, a bishopric about twenty miles from the French capital. Briçonnet, Bishop of Meaux, with his friend the scholar and writer Jacques Lefèvre, were leaders of a group working for a reformation to be effected within the Church and by the Church. They aimed at bringing Christians back to the Gospel, back to primitive observance of Christ's teachings. Many long overdue reforms were introduced at Meaux and the influence of the group extended beyond the boundaries of that diocese. But after some years these reformers, in their vehement reaction against abuses, leaned so dangerously from the orthodox in their writings and sermons that the Bishop was perturbed and forbade some of the preachers to enter the pulpit. The Meaux group incurred first the displeasure, then the suspicion of the Sorbonne, the fortress of orthodoxy. Until 1524, however, no proceedings were taken against them.

King Francis, his mother, and his sister Marguerite, 'queen of the humanists', had been highly sympathetic towards the Meaux reform, a work already beginning to show fruit, but the King was away from 1524 until his release from prison in 1526. Because of his absence the Regent, Louise of Savoy, had no time for anything but state cares and international affairs. Marguerite, in seclusion for some time following her husband's death, went to Spain in August 1525 to visit her brother and try to induce the Emperor to release him. Thus the Meaux group were for almost two years without their royal protectors.

In Paris Lutherans and their sympathisers, taking advantage of the Meaux reform, began at this time an open campaign against Catholicism. Posters depicting the Pope as Anti-Christ were affixed to church walls and public buildings, speakers in the streets attacked fundamental doctrines, and some adherents were won among the University students. The Sorbonne and the Parlement, finding themselves free to act, suddenly moved against all suspected of heresy. Those heard expressing unorthodox views or found selling Lutheran books and pamphlets were prosecuted and given terms of imprisonment, little care being taken to distinguish between those who sincerely advocated true reform and those who wished to break with the Church completely. The Meaux reformers got special attention, the Bishop being called before a special court. His friends, deeming it prudent to disperse, fled to Strasbourg.

Favre and Xavier, coming from remote, wholly Catholic areas of the Alpine and Pyreneean foothills, must have been confused during their first term in the Ste-Barbe, hearing their fellows debating about the Meaux reformers and the Lutheran reformers and discussing the rigorous measures taken by the Sorbonne. In their second term the two room mates witnessed the execution of a heretic.

It was compulsory for the student body to be present when a condemned heretic paid the supreme penalty. On a Saturday early in Lent all the colleges marched out to see young Guillaume Joubert, son of the King's advocate, die. He was a licentiate in law and, having made the *amende honorable* on the parvis of Notre Dame for his blasphemous utterances, he was taken in a tumbril, the long procession of students following, to 'the church of Madame Ste-Geneviève' where a similar *amende honorable* was made. Then all proceeded to the Place Maubert where his tongue was pierced, he himself strangled and his body burned. The Bourgeois, Nicolas Versoris, duly described the execution, of which he heartily approved, in his journal that night, adding, 'I myself was present'.

In France not many voices were raised in protest. The nation was preoccupied with the King's imminent release and the immense payments to be made to Spain. Erasmus, then living in Basle, was writing to men of influence on both sides in Germany, Switzerland, France and England, condemning violence, and making suggestions for resolving the religious conflict. The prince of humanists understood as few of his contemporaries that charity, not force, was needed to mend the shattered unity of Christendom. In the Ste-Barbe, an Erasmist stronghold, the censure of the Rotterdam scholar by the Sorbonne and his reply in 1526 would have been discussed with interest. The Montaigu, where he had studied, though justifiably proud of his attainments, was not of his way of thinking, but in the adjoining college the opinions of Erasmus were endlessly quoted and his writings enjoyed much popularity.

Favre was cast in the same mould. Peace-loving by nature and convinced that more good was likely to be achieved by example and persuasion than by force, he was to mirror Erasmus again and again in his attitude towards those of other faiths. Peter, who prayed daily for Suliman, the Grand Turk, was in the same tradition as Erasmus who implored Pope Leo X to abandon the idea of a crusade against the Turks:

If it is true that Christ and after Him the apostles and martyrs conquered the world through meekness, patience and holy teaching, would we not do far better to try to overcome the Turks, not by force of arms but by the holiness of our lives?[12]

Erasmus protested that heretics of his time were not being given, as in former centuries, a fair hearing. He complained of how persons were accused of heresy for the most flimsy reasons:

Formerly a man was regarded as a heretic if he deviated from the Gospel, articles of faith, or matters resting on similar authority; but nowadays they shout 'Heresy! Heresy!' for almost anything. If a man differs ever so little from St Thomas Aquinas he is a heretic . . . What is displeasing or not understood is heresy. It is heresy to know Greek. It is heresy to speak like a cultivated man.[13]

Erasmus loved to repeat the words of Isaias applied to Christ by the Evangelists: *Behold My servant, My elect . . . The bruised reed he shall not break and the smoking flax he shall not extinguish . . .*

Here there is no mention of tortuous syllogisms, of threats or thunderbolts; no reference to soldiers armed with steel, to bloody massacres or burnings. But we are told of gentleness, of kindness towards the weak . . . of a victory not won by armed might but by just judgment . . . of a victor who does not terrorise or rob those he conquers, or deal harshly with those he overcomes.[14]

This teaching, which in an age of violence stood out against force and pleaded for charity, was popular in the Ste-Barbe, where most of the regents were avowed Erasmists. Peter Favre, a Greek scholar but no heretic, imbibed these sentiments as naturally as he drank the good wines from Oporto and the Douro that graced the tables of the Ste-Barbe.

At Easter 1526 the king returned from captivity and all Paris turned out to welcome him home. By the treaty signed with the Emperor, Francis forfeited the large pension paid him annually by Naples, relinquished his rights in Flanders, abandoned his pretensions to the duchy of Milan, and sent his two young sons as hostages to take his place in the Alcázar of Madrid. Once across the frontier he announced that he had no intention of keeping a treaty made under duress. The only clause kept was the final one, for the royal children had to be handed over before their father was escorted to the French bank of the Bidoassa river.

When he heard of the trials and executions of heretics the king was angry and relations between him and the Sorbonne remained strained for some time. His sister Marguerite, soon to remarry and become Queen of Navarre, favoured and protected many Lutheran sympathisers. Her pleadings, which Francis could seldom resist, ensured that from autumn 1526 to spring 1528 there were no trials like that of Joubert.

But there were other trials which created an even greater stir in Paris during that eighteen month lull. This time the king, not the Sorbonne and Parlement, was the accuser and the offences concerned money, not religion. His treasurers, who had been congratulating themselves on the economies effected during the absence of an extravagant monarch and because, for once, France was not at war, suddenly found themselves called to task. Their accounts were scrutinized and the oldest and most honourable man among them condemned and executed on a mere pretext.* As Francis had foreseen, the others, not all so honest, were scared into paying huge sums to save themselves from a similar fate. They were fair game.

The sensation caused by the trials of the treasurers was confined to Paris, but all Europe was horrified that same year by the news of the sack of Rome. Clement VII, on hearing of the French king's return to the throne, had renewed his alliance with France. Meanwhile the Emperor's mercenaries, Spaniards, Bourbons, Germans and Tyroleans, unpaid and hungry and spoiling for fight began to mutiny in northern Italy. To pacify

*The treasurer to be made an example of was Semblançay, honest and revered treasurer of three reigns, an aged nobleman whom Francis used to address as *mon père*. The crime for which he was sentenced to be strangled and hung was trivial—the alleged acceptance of a gift of two horses and a length of velvet. A servant was bribed to swear falsely. The jury was packed. The old man was found guilty and his goods and those of all his family confiscated. This enriched Francis by almost a million gold crowns. One of Semblançay's sons, the Archbishop of Tours, dropped dead on hearing the verdict; another, a Maréchal of France, fled the country. The populace, quick to sense injustice, 'lamented and grieved and pleaded with the king'. Those charged to execute the treasurer delayed as long as they dared, hoping for a pardon to arrive at the last moment. Next day ballads about the execution at Montfaucon were sung all over Paris. Few incidents in the reign of Francis I show more clearly the ugly side of his character.

them, their officers offered to lead them to a promised land farther south where they could help themselves to rich booty. Florence and other cities managed to buy the marchers off by paying huge sums of money and handing over their stores of food and clothing. Brigands and bands of starving peasants rendered desperate by war and famine joined the ranks and all marched on Rome. On the morning of May 6 this rabble, by then completely out of control, scaled the walls and began to sack the city. The Pope, some Cardinals and Papal officials had barely time to barricade themselves inside the Castel San Angelo when the first of the attackers reached St Peter's. For the next eight days there followed an unprecedented orgy of murder, rapine, looting and destruction and *il Sacco di Roma* became a historical landmark. 'Dearly beloved son,' wrote Pope Clement to the Emperor, in a letter begging him to get the mercenaries out of the city at all costs, 'we look out upon a dead Rome, her corpse in a shroud of rags.' Coming less than nine months after the defeat at Mohacs, when Hungary lost her king and her freedom to Suliman the Magnificent, and at a time when Luther and Zwingli were gaining new and powerful adherents daily, the sack of Rome seemed to some a portent of the end of the world.

A few weeks after this event Henry VIII of England told Cardinal Wolsey that he intended to divorce his Queen, Catherine of Aragon, the Emperor's aunt. His royal conscience had given him no ease, he said, since his realization that for the past eighteen years he had been living in sin; it weighed heavily on him to recall that his marriage had been contracted in face of a canonical impediment. Not recalled or mentioned was the dispensation granted by Julius II. Neither was there mention of the king's infatuation for Anne Boleyn. Wolsey was sent to Amiens in August to confer 'with our brother in France on this most secret matter'. Francis, Henry thought, was in a position to bring pressure to bear on his ally the Pope.

While these happenings succeeded one another Peter Favre was continuing to attend lectures and disputations in the Ste-Barbe. His friend, Xavier, a promising athlete and 'one of the finest vaulters on the Ile de la Cité', spent most of his free time at the students' playing fields, the Pré-aux-Clercs. There

Barbistes and men of other colleges played tennis and *jeu-de-paume* and wrestling, while the less energetic fished, or strolled up and down 'arguing about nothing'. Favre, though not mentioned as a ball player or high jump expert, presumably spent his time as the others did. He was fair-haired, good looking, of imposing height, and so friendly and soft-spoken that he was a general favourite in his college. Yet, while his fellow-students found no trouble in deciding what careers they would follow, Peter seemed unable to come to a decision. Francis Xavier meant to seek a post as regent in the Beauvais college when he obtained his diploma, and hoped that later on his brother might succeed in obtaining a benefice for him in Pamplona diocese. But Favre felt himself completely at sea, unsure of what direction to take:

I was tossed about by every wind, one day wishing to marry, the next wanting to be a doctor, a jurist, a regent, a theologian, a poor curé, sometimes even a monk[15] . . .

On Whit Monday 1528 a statue of Our Lady was smashed and mutilated in a Paris street. Public opinion was outraged and the king, exasperated, offered a thousand gold crowns for information leading to the arrest of the culprit. For an entire fortnight processions of reparation wended their way through the city. On Tuesday, 9 June, the day of the University procession, Peter and Francis, each bearing a lighted taper, took their places among the *Barbistes*. Nearby, limping in the ranks of the Montaigu scholars, was a man of thirty-seven, a partly lame first year student named Ignatius Loyola.

Ignatius, like Xavier, was a Basque. Born in a castle south of the Pyrenees, he had been a page, later a knight, at the court of Castile, then a captain of Spain. Until his twenty-sixth year he was, according to himself, 'a man given to worldly vanities, delighting in feats of arms, being filled with a great and vain desire for fame'. Wounded in the siege of Pamplona (1521) he had to lie still for more than half a year while his fractured leg knit. Reading the only books available, a *Life* of our Lord and *Lives* of the Saints, he now found himself fired with a new ambition—to imitate such heroes of God as St Dominic and St Francis of Assisi.

With Ignatius to decide was to act. Having made a pilgrimage to Montserrat, where he surrendered his sword to Our Lady and his soul to God, he spent a year subjecting his body to severe penance and meditating on the eternal truths. With a view to helping others to a similar conversion of heart he composed the Spiritual Exercises that have since been the basis of so many missions and retreats. Not yet sure of what God required of him he set off on a pilgrimage to Jerusalem, but his goal was not there. Back in Spain he joined the small boys of Barcelona at their Latin classes and went on to the Universities of Alcalá and Salamanca. In both towns his habit of attracting followers and giving them the Spiritual Exercises drew upon him the attention of the Inquisitors and prison sentences. Finally, realizing that his attempts to advance his studies were getting him nowhere so long as he remained in Spain, he set out for Paris. Arriving there in February, 1528, he spent four terms studying Latin and grammar. 'He was a man who would begin a thousand times, when he was sure of his goal, regretting neither the time hitherto lost, nor the new labours upon which he had to embark.'[16]

The University year began on 1 October, St Remi's Day. On that date in 1529 the room in the Ste-Barbe already occupied by Favre, Xavier and de la Peña became more crowded when Ignatius Loyola moved in with them. A late starter, he had spent the previous eighteen months at the Montaigu, studying Latin with the youngest scholars. He was fifteen years older than his three room-mates and not quite unknown to them, having been at the centre of a commotion that had excited the *Barbistes* during the preceding months.

A Basque scholar, Amador, the most promising scholar not only of the Ste-Barbe but of the entire Latin Quarter, suddenly disconcerted all who knew him by becoming extraordinarily pious. He prayed and meditated all day until his fervour reached a pitch when he no longer had ears for his professors or time for the usual disputations and arguments. His charity, on a par with his piety, also went to extremes. He sold his wardrobe, item by item, giving the money it realized to the poor. His books followed his clothes. The climax came when one morning he himself was missing. There was general consternation, regents and students asking one another where he could have gone, and why, and how. The Montaigu students suffered a similar loss the same morning, their star scholar, Pedro Peralta, having vanished. Within an hour it was known that Juan de Castro, a Spanish theologian of note, was no longer in the Sorbonne.

A hundred *Barbistes*, the fleet-footed Francis Xavier no doubt among them, set off determined at all costs to find and bring back Amador. Following up a report that of late he had been often seen in the company of another Basque, a poor *Montacutien* named Ignatius who lodged in the Hospice St-Jacques, the students crossed the Seine and ran to the hospice in the rue St-Denis. The three runaways were there but when their comrades, assembled outside, yelled at them to return they calmly announced that they had renounced the world for good. This so infuriated the students that they rushed the hospice, forced the doors and marched the three back to their respective colleges. Amador, a minor, was persuaded to defer his withdrawal from the Ste-Barbe and the world until he had attained his majority.

The authorities, glad to have their brilliant student back, questioned him about his defection. He explained that he and de Castro and Peralta had experienced a real conversion following thirty days of Spiritual Exercises given them by Ignatius Loyola. It was a name de Gouvea knew, having received an application from and agreed to admit to the Ste-Barbe a Montaigu man of that name. The Rector promised, in the presence of all the regents and students, that when 'the man who had made a madman of Amador' arrived in the Ste-Barbe the following term he would be given a 'hall'. This severe public punishment and humiliation was reserved for students who raised grave disturbances or who were known to have pernicious habits. It consisted of running the gauntlet in the great hall of the college. The offender, stripped to the waist, was made run up and down between a double file of masters who belaboured him with their canes.

When this ultimatum was issued Ignatius was away. It was his custom to go to Flanders, an Imperial possession, during the long vacation to beg from the Spanish merchants there sufficient funds to tide him over the coming year. On his return he was warned of what awaited him at the Ste-Barbe. Always a man to grasp the nettle he immediately presented himself at the college and was taken to the Rector while the regents equipped themselves with canes and hurried to the hall where the *Barbistes* were gathered to witness the flogging of the man who had so changed Amador. To the amazement of all, de Gouvea and the new student emerged from their interview arm in arm, seemingly on the best of terms.* The Rector announced that he was quite satisfied with the explanation Ignatius had given of the Amador affair and there was no 'hall'.

Others were not so understanding. A Spanish theologian of the rigorist school, Dr Pedro Ortiz, patron of Peralta and de Castro, the two who had joined Amador in his flight from the world, was perturbed to hear that Ignatius Loyola had been seducing students. Though once a friend of the Meaux reformers, Ortiz had changed his opinions by 1528 and approved of the Sorbonne's methods of dealing with those who deviated from the orthodox. He found it intolerable that a Spanish captain whose reputation in Spain had been far from blameless and who had now turned up in Paris—a middle-aged scholar still trying to assimilate sufficient Latin to enable him follow the lectures of the first-year students—should be turning the heads of brilliant scholars, giving them secret instructions guaranteed to lead to conversion of life. The Doctor delated Ignatius to the Inquisition as 'an *extravagante* from Spain who was fomenting disorder in the most disquieting manner'.

This news was also relayed to Ignatius. Having had more than one experience of Inquisition procedure and penalties in Spain, he at once sought the Spanish Inquisitor in Paris, Mateo Ory, a Dominican of the St-Jacques convent. He offered to answer all enquiries but begged that his case be promptly dealt with so that he might start his Arts and Philosophy course on 1 October. The Inquisitor was as friendly as de

*This meeting was the beginning of a lasting friendship. de Gouvea remained a staunch supporter of Ignatius from that on. He it was who recommended the Society of Jesus to King John III and Pope Paul III as 'men who should be given the Indies and the vast expanse of the farthest Orient as a fitting field for their zeal'.

Gouvea and Ignatius, cleared in the eyes of authority, took his few belongings from the Montaigu to the Ste-Barbe. He bore no grudge against Ortiz and it is pleasant to record that that worthy, ten years later, made the Spiritual Exercises himself, Ignatius trudging from Rome to Monte Cassino to help him. The Doctor would have become a Jesuit 'only that his corpulency unfitted him for the labours of the Society'.

Though Ignatius stood in the good graces of the Rector of the Ste-Barbe he was far from popular with the students when he first took up residence in that college. They did not forgive him so easily for the change in Amador, and they 'regarded him as dangerous and were not slow to let him feel their aversion and contempt'. Two of his room-mates, Francis Xavier and de la Peña, did not put themselves out unduly to help him. Both seem to have delegated to Favre the task of helping the newcomer in his struggles with Aristotle. As we have seen, Favre had at this time his own struggles. His inability to come to any decision about his future made him restless and inclined to depression. He was finely strung and tended to oscillate from elation to a gentle melancholy. We shall yet see him, the supreme optimist at Worms and Spires and Ratisbon, expecting full and certain reconciliation between the Lutheran and Catholic leaders assembled in these towns for discussions, and meet him when the negotiations break down, disillusioned and down-hearted.

Apart from his uncertainty about his future Favre also suffered from scruples. He debated with himself whether he should tip the college barber a sixth or a quarter of a *sou*. He worried about his past confessions, fearing that he had not made full declaration of all his sins. Temptations of the flesh assailed him, 'suggested to me by the spirit of fornication and concerning matters about which I knew only through reading'.[17] Not all the Paris regents had the gift of old Velliard in La Roche who could make the profane authors he explained seem like the Gospels. Within Favre a man of action and a man lacking in decision pulled him this way and that.

Nothing is more helpful to such characters than a discipline which regulates life and an obedience which stabilizes. But neither can operate unless the individual is humble enough to

submit to guidance and to obey readily, convinced that God
speaks through lawful authority. Favre was humble enough to
do so. To his dying day he never ceased to thank God for so
arranging things that he should teach Ignatius about Aristotle
while Ignatius taught him about God. He tells us how Ignatius
dealt with him:

We became intimate friends, sharing the same room, table and
purse . . . He became my spiritual teacher, and gave me rules for
ascertaining the Will of God . . . He advised me to make a general
confession to Doctor de Castro and after that to go to confession and
communion weekly . . . We spent four years together in Ste-Barbe
having all things in common with others who had come to share our
way of life . . . My soul passed through the waters of vain-glory . . .
for which I sought a remedy during a long and anguished time.
I also had to conquer myself in the matter of eating and drinking;
that was a stiff battle which I did not win until I had done the
Spiritual Exercises. At that time I spent six days without eating or
drinking except for a little wine after returning from Mass. I was
also tempted to remark the shortcomings of others, to suspect and
judge others. In that matter, too, thanks be to my consoler and
master who taught me to take my first steps in fraternal charity . . .
I still suffered many temptations but Our Lord, through the
help of His angels and the light of His Holy Spirit, delivered me
each time at the very moment when, alone, I might have fallen.[18]

It is understandable that he should enjoy the good food and
wine at the Ste-Barbe. At Einseideln on days of big pilgrimages
strangers who watch the peoples of 'the Alps of the four nations',
their religious exercises completed, begin to tuck into a meal,
marvel at the appetite and capacity of these hardy mountain
folk. Favre had grown to manhood in the same hunger-
sharpening air, but in Villaret meals were frugal and monotonous. To him the food at the Ste-Barbe would have made a great
appeal and his temptation to eat and drink heartily was very
human. He seems to have been well ahead of his roommates
as regards studies, even the regent depending on him for Greek
translations. It is a sign of how he was maturing intellectually
and evidence of his inner conflicts that others sometimes grated
on him. Even his friend Ignatius occasionally irked him:

When in Paris sometimes I resented certain orders of Ignatius and I used to say to him that in France people would not stand for things that he seemed to think fitting.[19]

Doctor de Castro, the Spanish priest to whom he was sent to make his general confession, was the same who had left the Sorbonne to fly the world with Peralta and Amador. He was back there teaching theology, but later left to become a Carthusian in Valencia. The Carthusians and the early Jesuits were linked in many ways and friendships with Carthusians in different European countries stand out like signposts along Peter Favre's road of life. On Sundays he and Ignatius, with de Castro and Simon de Rodriguez, and later Xavier and others, made their way to Vauvert where they spent the day 'recollecting ourselves, reading and praying'. In Vauvert, too, they could have met the brilliant Pierre Cousturier, known as 'Sutor', one-time regent in the Ste-Barbe. During Peter's years in Paris Sutor was engaged in an interminable controversy with Erasmus, defending the Carthusian vocation and explaining its fundamental features. Alone among the Orders the Carthusians needed no reform. This they attributed to their *Si, So, Vi*, their *Silence*, their *Solitude* and their practice of remaining in their priories instead of *Visiting* the world from which they had withdrawn to intercede for it before God.[20]

The persecution of heretics, which had ceased for eighteen months, flared up again after the breaking of the statue of Our Lady. Marguerite had gone to live in Navarre, while Louise and Francis, seeing the turn events were taking in Germany, thought that the safety of France lay in relying on the forces of law and order. So the University students turned out several times during 1529 and 1530 to witness executions in the Place Maubert or the Place de Grève.

This did not have the salutary effect it was meant to have, for most of the students, particularly the arts students, made it a point of honour to attend *all* executions, of criminals as well as heretics. In fact an execution was regarded by them, as by the general public, as a gala occasion. They organized parties, collecting wine, pasties and girl friends to go to Montfaucon, the great gibbet by the Porte St-Denis, spending the day and

4

often the night there. To run alongside the carts in which the condemned were roped together and to shout pleasanteries at these unfortunates was considered the height of fun. They mocked and advised the Sergeants-at-arms, the archers and the executioners. Even the nuns of the Filles-Dieu convent at the city gate who waited to offer bread, wine, and words of consolation to the condemned, did not escape the students' witticisms. Wilder spirits got in the way of the Provost as he whipped back the crowds, interrupted the priests reciting the last prayers, yelled at the hangman as he busied himself with ropes and beams and chains, and cheered and roared when the empty carts moved on and the hanged, in their agonies, trod the air. They watched to see which soldiers, which street bullies, were preparing to make a night of it on Montfaucon. The students, too, would remain to carouse, to play grim jokes with the corpses, to fight running battles with all and sundry. So it was that the executions of Lutherans and others, though they might fill a few gentle souls with compassion, were for the majority of the students on a par with those gay occasions— criminal executions. Instead of proving a salutary warning the branding, strangling, hanging and burning of heretics were welcomed as holidays, days when classes were suspended.

Francis Xavier did not yield to Ignatius as readily as Peter Favre. He had been appointed as regent in the Beauvais college and Ignatius had to pave the way to winning his friendship by inducing students to attend Xavier's classes. Francis was great-hearted and generous, well worth waiting for. Finally, like Favre, he agreed to join Ignatius and was told of the Spiritual Exercises, the thirty-day retreat and series of meditations which Ignatius proposed to his followers. More than four years, how-ever, were to elapse before Favre, the first of the Ignatian group to do the Exercises, was allowed to begin them.

Ignatius kept him for two years like a novice, getting him to examine his conscience daily on his thoughts, words and actions . . . After-wards he got him to work diligently to extirpate his bad habits, taking them one by one. He made him begin with those who gave scandal to others or which hampered his own spiritual progress, not allowing him to fight them all together, but singly, giving special attention to those bad habits most deeply rooted.[21]

Meanwhile Peter's studies were not neglected. His three years philosophy completed he went on to study theology, intending to become a priest. The next four years passed quietly enough for the occupants of his room in the Ste-Barbe. Elsewhere the times were not uneventful: Francis I contrived to lose another army and his final hopes of regaining French possessions in Italy. Clement VII, free again, was being importuned to grant a divorce to Henry VIII. The Emperor's sister Eleanor set out for France to marry the widowed Francis; with her went the Dauphin and his brother, released after more than four years imprisonment in Spain. When in 1533 the Emperor and his court visited Bologna, the lady whose arrival made the greatest stir was Madame Beatrix, the Duchess of Savoy, last met with riding out of Geneva.

The following day, without sound of tambour or trumpet, Duke Charles came along, like a poor relation. He came only because his wife had insisted that he come. There was a splendid tournament to which the Emperor invited princes and ambassadors. Someone told the Duke of Savoy that he would be admitted to the principal tribune but that he would have to take a place behind Francis Sforza, the freebooter whom the Emperor had created Duke of Savoy. For once Charles III showed some spirit and stayed away from the tourneys. His Duchess presided at the fetes to a fanfare of trumpets which echoed in the modest room where her husband lodged.[22]

Louise of Savoy, the Duke's sister, died in 1532 and Francis I, after writing to break the news, expressed some misgivings about the attitude of Savoy, France's traditional ally. Charles III replied evasively while Beatrix replied from Turin in a tone that made it clear who was the real ruler of Savoy. The French King, quick to size up a situation, realized that the Emperor could now take Savoy whenever he wished. This would mean a France surrounded by Imperial possessions. Already her frontiers on the Pyrenees, the Juras, the Lowlands and Lorraine were blocked. All that the Emperor had to do to complete the encirclement was to place strong garrisons in Chambéry and Bourg-en-Bresse, a move which would put Lyons and Grenoble in mortal danger. Not being lacking in decision like his uncle of Savoy Francis, failing to obtain a guarantee of neutrality, sent troops to occupy towns in the Duke's territory. The Savoyards put up no resistance. The weakness and apathy of their ruler and the haughty pretensions of his Duchess had detached the people from the dynasty.[23]

Thus, when Peter Favre went to visit his family in 1533, he found Savoy a French province. He left Paris in July, not returning until the following January or February. 'I remained in Savoy for seven months,' he writes, 'My father was still living. My mother was dead.'[24] His long absence from Paris may have been due to difficulty in obtaining the documents he needed for his approaching ordination. The timid Bishop of Geneva had fled his See that summer leaving his flock to the preachers of a more radical reform than Luther's. They were waiting for John Calvin to complete his studies—he was then in Orleans—and come to make Geneva the Calvinist Rome.

Favre returned to Paris in January 1534. By that date four more Spaniards, Lainez, Salmeron, Simon de Rodriguez and Nicolas from Bobadilla had joined Ignatius and were prepared to devote their lives to promoting the greater glory of God. As Favre was now preparing for his ordination Ignatius allowed him to do the Spiritual Exercises. Although that February and March were the coldest in living memory* he withdrew from the Ste-Barbe to live like a Carthusian in a little room off the rue St-Jacques, where he did without a fire and took no food or drink except a few sips of wine in the mornings when he returned from Mass. At the end of the first week Ignatius visited him 'and found that he had eaten nothing for six days, that he slept in his shirt on the timber left him to make a fire, and that he made the meditations in the snow out in a little courtyard'. Telling Peter that he was sure he had not sinned but done something meritorious in undertaking these penances —the retreatant must have had some scruple and asked for direction on this point—Ignatius said that he would go away and pray and return in an hour's time to give a decision. When he returned he said that Favre should fast one day more, which was the time he himself had fasted when he first did the Exercises; after that he should eat and have a fire. To reinforce

*Carriages and wagons could be driven on the frozen Seine.

his decision Ignatius came laden with wood and food; he lit a fire and cooked a meal for Peter.[25]

Spiritual Exercises for the conquest of oneself and the ordering of one's life so that one's decisions are not influenced by any inordinate affections.

A method by which the soul may prepare and dispose itself to set itself free from disordered affections and, this achieved, go on to seek and find the Will of God in its regard and for its salvation.

In this sub-title of the Spiritual Exercises Ignatius defined their aim. In a note he elaborated further on their purpose:

Hardly any retreatant since Ignatius himself made these Exercises with the single-mindedness and fervour of Favre. In later years Ignatius used to say that none of the first generation of Jesuits could give the Exercises as well as Favre.[26] He certainly emerged from his thirty days retreat imbued with the conviction that in all things a man should try to discover the will of God, and having discerned it immediately do it.

On 28 February 1534 he was raised to the sub-diaconate, on Holy Saturday of the same year to the diaconate, and on 30 May 1534, the eve of Trinity Sunday, Peter Favre was ordained priest by the Bishop of Paris, Jean du Bellay.

3 Master Peter: The Paris Theologian

FOUR other students frequented the room shared by Peter Favre, Francis Xavier and Ignatius Loyola. One was Simon Rodriguez, Rector de Gouvea's nephew, a handsome Portuguese in the Ste-Barbe on one of King John's scholarships. Two Spaniards, Diego Lainez and Alfonso Salmeron, who had known Ignatius at the universities of Alcalá and Salamanca and had sought him out on their arrival in Paris, visited him often. Also in the group was a poor scholar, Nicolas Alonso, called Bobadilla because he hailed from a Spanish village of that name.

The seven spent their Sundays at Vauvert, exchanging the noisy streets of the Latin Quarter and the incessant arguments and brawls of the students for the quiet of the Carthusian cloisters. In their meetings at the Ste-Barbe they discussed the future. At Vauvert they pondered the matters discussed; they prayed and got their Carthusian friends to pray that they might know God's will and do it. Between Easter and autumn 1534 all but Xavier made the Spiritual Exercises Favre had made earlier that year and each one emerged from the thirty-day retreat fired with the desire to do great things for God.

Finally they decided to bind themselves by vows of chastity and poverty and to devote their lives to 'the greater glory of God'. A third vow was also decided upon: when their studies were completed they would undertake a pilgrimage to Jerusalem. Although the Crusades were past history the name Jerusalem still had power to stir Christian hearts. The great medieval pilgrimages had declined but the Holy City still drew the faithful, prefiguring as it did that other Jerusalem 'where the sun shall set no more, nor the moon wane.' On 22 July 1534, two months after his ordination, Favre said his first Mass:

I said my first Mass on the feast of the Blessed Mary Magdalen, my advocate and advocate of all other sinners, men and women.[1]

He was then twenty-eight. In a note written eight years later he thanks God for the graces of 1534, for 'the sublime vocation to the priesthood', for his consecration to the religious life, for having been enabled to renounce ambition, and for having succeeded, 'thanks to God and Iñigo', in overcoming his previous vacillation and arriving at a decision regarding his future. He continues:

I shall never, of my own merits, be equal to the demands of the priesthood or be worthy of God's choice. But the very recognition of this obliges me to do my utmost, physically and spiritially, to respond to his call.[2]

Three weeks after Peter's first Mass the students had a free day. 15 August, feast of Our Lady's Assumption, was a holiday for town and gown. According to the chroniclers it was a glorious morning, and shortly after sunrise the seven companions left the Street of the Dogs, crossed the Seine and made their way through the still sleeping city to Montmartre, the hill traditionally associated with the martyrdom of St Denis. Their goal was an ancient chapel some distance below the site of the present Sacré-Coeur basilica. On their way up the slopes they stopped at the Benedictine nuns' abbey to get the key of the chapel. To Favre, the only ordained priest in the group, fell the honour of saying Mass. Before receiving Holy Communion they pronounced the three vows they had resolved to take. Peter Favre, already bound to chastity since his ordination, vowed to live in poverty and to go on pilgrimage to Jerusalem. In a record of that morning's happenings he calls the chapel Notre-Dame of Montmartre, though its name in civil and episcopal documents of the time is given as *Sanctum Martyrium*. It is typical of him to omit mention of the celebrant of the Mass:

Already united by a common resolve and formed by the Exercises —all of us, that is, save Master Francis who had not yet begun them but who was one with us in our project*—we went to Notre-Dame

*Ignatius, Rodriguez and Broet later stated that Xavier's retreat was postponed because he was lecturing in the Beauvais College where he was then a regent.

on Montmartre, near Paris. There each of us vowed to leave for Jerusalem at the appointed time and, on our return, to place ourselves under obedience to the Roman Pontiff. We also vowed to begin, from a given date, 'leaving our parents and our nets', keeping only a little money for the journey.

There were present on that occasion: Iñigo, Master Francis, I, Favre, Master Bobadilla, Master Lainez, Master Salmeron and Master Simon. Jay had not arrived in Paris at that time. Jean and Paschase had not as yet been won over. We returned to the same place in 1535 and 1536 on the same feast of Our Lady in August, to confirm ourselves in these resolutions, resolutions through which we found ourselves each year making spiritual progress. During these two years (from August 1534 to August 1536) Master Jay, Master Jean Codure and Master Paschase Broet joined us.[3]

The Jay referred to was Claude Jay, a Savoyard. He had been a school-fellow of Peter's at La Roche and succeeded Velliard as principal of that school. When Favre visited his home in 1533 he met Jay and persuaded him to come to Paris to study theology. Claude arrived in the capital in the autumn of 1534 and commenced his university career as a theological student. One of his classmates was Paschase Broet, a priest from Picardy, Calvin's native province. Although Jay and Broet were six years older than Favre they took him as their spiritual guide and did the Exercises under his direction. Jean Codure, a Dauphinois student in his middle twenties 'tormented by the desire for holiness', also came to Favre seeking counsel. He, too, did the Exercises, taking forty days to complete them instead of the customary thirty. These three, drawn to the nascent Society by Peter Favre, brought the numbers to ten: two Basques, two Savoyards, two Frenchmen, three Spaniards and a Portuguese.

Jean du Bellay, the bishop of Paris who ordained Peter Favre, was a humanist. Like Erasmus, he and his diplomat brother Guillaume were opposed to religious intolerance and persecution and anxious to preserve Christian unity. They recognized the need for reform and sought to promote it by conciliation and dialogue; they also foresaw and worked to forestall the further splintering of Christendom. During 1534 Guillaume travelled to Strasbourg and other imperial cities where he met

Lutheran leaders known to favour religious peace and unity. Melanchthon in particular and to a lesser degree Bucer, desired a *rapprochement* with the Catholics. Du Bellay also visited Switzerland and made overtures to the Zwinglians but, though politely received, he was not so successful there. The followers of Zwingli rejected all compromise, but there were high hopes that Melanchthon and Bucer would meet leading Catholic theologians in Paris before the winter set in.[4]

Clement VII had died in September 1534 mourned by none more than Benvenuto Cellini, then on the road to fame. Before the artist presented his bill for the gold medals he had struck, 'with Pope Clement's head on one side and a figure representing Peace on the reverse', the Pontiff died unexpectedly. 'All my pains went for nothing,' lamented Cellini, 'but I kept up my heart with the thought that these medals had won me such fame that I was now sure of commissions from any Pope and perhaps better than hitherto.'

The new Pope, Paul III, was a patron of the arts and a protector of artists, even when they broke laws—civil, church or divine. His early life, typical of a Roman nobleman of the Renaissance, had been far from edifying. It was an age when the Medici, the Colonnas and other powerful families like his, the Farnese, strove to obtain Cardinals' hats for sons who might yet sway Papal elections or even wear the triple tiara. Alexander Farnese was a layman and in his twenty-sixth year when elevated to the Cardinalate. Twenty years later he reformed his way of life and was ordained. He was sixty-seven when elected Pope and had served under the four preceding Pontiffs. At two of four Papal conclaves he had been proposed for election only to be defeated each time by a Medici.

Catholics anxious about the situation confronting the Church felt little reassurance when they heard that Paul III began his reign by enriching and advancing his relatives. But it was soon realized that this Pope had qualities his immediate predecessors lacked. He was shrewd, intelligent, cultured, an able and experienced diplomat, far-seeing and decisive. He approved of the moves made by the du Bellay brothers to bring Catholics and Lutherans together. Francis I also supported their efforts, not because his sister the Queen of Navarre held the du Bellays in high esteem, but because it suited his political plans at that particular time.

The rapprochement of the various denominations and religious conciliation was an essential condition for the solid establishment of French influence in Germany. The (German) States would go to whoever would give them religious peace. The Emperor tried to obtain this peace by numerous colloquies and the promise of a General Council. It would be a great triumph for Francis I if he could achieve this before Charles V.[5]

The possibility of an early conference between Lutheran and Catholic theologians was no secret in court and university circles in Paris. Favre, Ignatius, Broet and Jay, attending lectures and disputations at the Sorbonne and with the Dominicans in the rue St-Jacques, would have heard of the projected meeting. An essay by Melanchton published that autumn, *Consilium ad Gallos,* suggested deep sincerity and a desire for unity on the part of the author who found good things to say even of the Papacy, an institution anathema to most of the reformers and roundly attacked by them. The publication gave rise to high hopes in Paris and was the subject of discussion in the colleges. In later years when Peter Favre found himself in the same town as Melanchthon he was very eager to meet and speak with him. This wish, never realized, could have had its origins in the autumn of 1534 when the expected visit of the Lutheran theologian was an oft debated topic among the theology students. Great things were expected of the coming conference but the happenings of 18 October put an end to preparations and hopes.

During the small hours of that day all Paris, including the Latin Quarter, was placarded with broadsheets attacking the Mass in blasphemous terms. In Orleans, Tours and other French cities similar notices fluttered at street corners. The king, rising to a new day in his magnificent Château at Amboise, found a placard nailed to the door of the royal bedchamber. Its heading, in heavy Gothic lettering, read: *The Horrible, Great and Intolerable Abuses of the Papal Mass.* Francis was appalled. He might be a cynic, a dissembler, a breaker of treaties, a Renaissance rake, but he was a believer and what he read as his gaze travelled down the placard shocked him to the core.

The initial shock absorbed, anger took its place. He raged to think that some insolent unknown had succeeded in penetrating the defence rings that protected the royal person—the sentinels, the archers, the bodyguard—to nail up insults to the Lord whose anointed he, Francis, was in the eyes of France and all the Christian world.* In the affair he saw not only denial of a fundamental Catholic doctrine but a threat to his authority and realm. Heresy, he told himself, was more strongly entrenched than he had realized. Heresy meant subversion. Subversion led to unrest and division. Everyone knew how religious disunity had torn the German States. Action, immediate and stern, was called for.

A wave of cruel repression followed. Time and again during the winter of 1534–1535 Peter Favre and his fellow students found classes suspended while they were marched out to witness burnings and torturings. The students might have been excused for not knowing who was in good or bad faith when in March 1535 they assembled on the parvis of Notre-Dame and saw that solid and firm pillar of orthodoxy, Noel Beda of the Montaigu and the Sorbonne, on his knees making the *amende honorable*. Beda's particular heresy was to have criticized the king. He said aloud and in company what more careful folk whispered— that weakness and misrule on the king's part over many years were responsible for all the trouble. Although he had powerful friends in court and in the Church he was banished to Mont St-Michel where he remained until his death.

Between October 1534 and May 1535 several hundred persons were imprisoned or exiled and twenty-five burned at the stake. In June Paul III wrote asking Francis to repeal 'this horrible law' that decreed the 'extermination of heretics' and the suppression of book printing throughout France. The good Bourgeois, who noted in his diary floods, frosts, storms, deaths, robberies, street scenes, plagues and executions and added comments on all these happenings, duly reported the contents

---

*A choirboy in the royal chapel, one of the king's household and one of the last to be suspected, was responsible for affixing the document to the door of the king's room. The unfortunate lad paid the extreme penalty.

of the Papal letter. 'His Holiness reminded the king that Our Lord when on earth was more concerned with mercy than with justice . . . and that it was a cruel thing to let a man be burned alive. He besought his Most Christian Majesty to appease his fury and rigorous justice and grant grace and pardon.'[6]

Thanks to the Pope's intervention and the mollifying influence of the du Bellays the king was prevailed upon to moderate his anger and his sudden zeal for religion. The persecution ceased. Immediately, Guillaume du Bellay set off again, armed with a safe-conduct and an invitation signed by Francis himself, to seek Melanchthon and renew the invitation to a conference with Catholic theologians in Paris. On his way Guillaume met many reformers and their sympathisers who had fled the country months before and were now venturing back from Strasbourg, Basle and other cities on the eastern frontiers of France.

One who remained at Basle that summer, completing the book that enshrined his doctrines, was John Calvin. The brilliant student of the Montaigu and the Orleans law schools had gone over to the reform a year or more previously but, finding some of the reformers' teaching unacceptable and their moral laxity repellent, he began to put his own ideas on reform and doctrine in order. Those who knew him during his years at the Montaigu and other colleges cannot have been altogether surprised when in 1535 this more logical, more radical reformer than Luther proclaimed his creed and gathered adherents:

Calvin, when at the Paris colleges, spoke little but was quick at repartee and formidable in debate. Indulgence of any kind was unknown to him . . . He saw evil on all sides and voiced his disapproval of it in bitter terms . . . It was said that the Accusative was the only Case this indefatigable delator could decline.

He fasted rigorously and his only pleasure consisted in meditating upon and speaking of religion.* Joking and levity he found quite intolerable. He had an absolute passion for work and study, a prodigious memory, rare reasoning power and a truly great literary style.[7]

While Calvin was correcting the proofs of his *magnum opus*,

---

*Doumergue, in his monumental Life of Calvin, refutes this description and calls Audin, the biographer responsible for it, an audacious pamphleteer.

The Institutes of the Christian Religion, and du Bellay posting between Paris and the imperial cities, another one-time Montaigu scholar was riding southward from Paris. It was Ignatius Loyola returning to the Basque country he had left in 1522.

. . . In Paris Iñigo suffered from gastric trouble which by this time had become chronic. Every fifteen days he had an attack that lasted for at least an hour and brought on a fever . . . The malady went from bad to worse, and none of the several remedies he tried did him any good. Finally the doctors told him that the only course open to him, if he wished to be cured, was a sojourn in his native air. The Companions, too, advised this and strongly urged him to go.[8]

Favre, Xavier and the others, thoroughly alarmed by the doctors' reports, pointed out to the leader of their little company the benefits to be expected from a stay in Spain. Ignatius could recuperate there; he could visit the families of Lainez, Salmeron, Bobadilla and Xavier. The rest cure and these visits would take at least a year. Then he could proceed by slow stages to Venice. Allowing for wars, plagues, pirates, unfavourable winds, storms and possible shipwreck—not to mention the attentions of the Inquisition which Ignatius attracted wherever he went—that would account for another year. When the Companions completed their courses they would join him in Venice. While he awaited them in that city, the usual port of embarkation for the Holy Land, he could make arrangements for the pilgrimage they had vowed to make. To strengthen their arguments they put their funds together and bought him a *quartago,* a chesnut cob. This animal, destined to find a place in Jesuit annals, was the equivalent of a modern airline ticket. Ignatius agreed to go, 'hoping to give some edification in his *patria* where formerly he had given scandal to many'. Lainez recorded that 'before leaving, Iñigo appointed good Master Peter as our oldest brother to take charge of all'.[9]

As a matter of fact Favre, made responsible for the little group dubbed 'Iniguistas' by the student body, was not at that time entitled to be called 'Master'. He and Xavier had taken the Licentiate examination in 1530 but when Francis took out his Master's Degree Peter did not do so. There was no further examination for the higher degree but candidates had to pay a stiff fee; they were also expected to tip the beadles, give presents to the regents, and wine and dine their fellow students. The expense involved was considerable, so much so that Ignatius had scruples as to whether it was consonant with his vow of poverty, and sought advice before becoming a Master of Arts. When the conferring and the junketings were over—and the bills came in—he wrote to friends in Barcelona telling them of his predicament:

This Lent I obtained my Master's Degree and alas! I had to incur expenses, heavy and unavoidable expenses that I was unable to meet. As a result I am now very much in debt.[10]

Iñigo's friends in Barcelona came to the rescue then as on former occasions. Favre waited until 1536 before paying for the honour of writing Master before *his* name. Scrupulous by nature—it will be remembered that he worried over the size of the tip to give the college barber—he would have had even more difficulty than Ignatius in reconciling expenditure that bordered on the extravagant and unjustifiable with the vow of poverty. He was also 'fearful lest I yield to vainglory'.

He had devoted more than five years to the study of theology and coached Ignatius and later the other companions in the same sacred science. He was to achieve repute as a theologian. St Peter Canisius stated that he had never 'seen or heard a more learned or profound theologian than Master Peter Favre'. The Prior of the Cologne Carthusians, Gerard Kalckbrenner, referred to him as 'the Paris theologian'. Pope Paul III, who heard Favre in a disputation the early Jesuits held one evening in his presence, nominated him as one of the theologians to the Council of Trent. But, though Peter passed the theology examination for a Master's degree, he could not wait until conferring day, for the Companions had to leave Paris earlier than they intended.

Before relating the circumstances of their departure from Paris it is interesting to note the dissimilarities in background and experience of life between Ignatius, the First Jesuit, and

Peter Favre, his first recruit and the Second Jesuit. Peter had come to Paris a youth of nineteen reared in a home protected from outside influences by a double range of Alps. Imbued with the intense faith and living traditions of the people of Savoy he had always enjoyed a sense of security, solidity, permanence. His humble birth and religious upbringing gave him a taste for simple things; he never lost his preference for the devotions his childhood had known: the feasts of Our Lord, Our Lady and the saints; relics, processions, shrines and pilgrimages; the angels who guarded individuals, households, towns and peoples.

Ignatius, when he arrived in Paris, was in his thirty-eighth year, twice as old as Peter had been when he began his studies there. Home for him had meant Loyola, a frontier castle where weapons hung always ready and where there were Loyolas just as ready to snatch them and dash away to local fray or distant wars. His youth and early manhood had been spent among the Castilian courtiers whose elegance, decorum and strict code of etiquette set standards for all Europe. He had known army service, bivouac and battle, victory and defeat, wounds, deformity, long illness and the hard-fought siege of his soul. Having sorrowed for his sins he did penance, subjecting his body to harsh treatment and his heart to immense renunciations. He had wandered seeking the will of God around the Mediterranean coasts, to Rome and to the Holy Land. He returned, still seeking God's will, and began the slow labour of learning at an age when most men had finished with schooling, in Barcelona and in the universities of Alcalá and Salamanca; he had been in and out of the courts and prisons of the Inquisition. By these tortuous ways Ignatius had come to God and eventually to Paris.

Five of the first companions were, like Ignatius himself, from beyond the Pyrenees; of these all but Bobadilla were sons of noblemen or provincial officials. Favre alone had come from a world still almost medieval in customs, in outlook and in faith.

He was initiated step by step, by the Church herself as by her schools, in the new ideas he was so soon to encounter on the frontiers of Catholicism . . . Born into a world resting firmly on the solid foundations of living traditions, he slowly came to know of the new ideas current in his time. His tolerance was compounded of sympathy for men and a certain lack of knowledge of their ideas, ideas which were to him an indication of men's weakness rather than a new force to be reckoned with. Unlike his companion Jesuits he had never sensed in his youth the fragile nature of human institutions. Experience of his own weakness, while it helped him to understand and heal errors and shortcomings of which he could diagnose the underlying cause, did not enable him to perceive, with the same clarity, their general significance.[11]

His first five years in the Ste-Barbe were devoted to the Arts course which comprised grammar, dialectic, geometry, cosmology, literature and philosophy. 'This should have given him an almost encyclopedic intellectual baggage, ranging from Hebrew vocabulary to astral influences. It also called for incessant mental gymnastics, argumentations of all kinds, attacks and defences.'[12] For the remainder of his University career (1530–1536) he studied theology. His studies, however, do not seem to have been well ordered or continuous. At one end of the rue St-Jacques he attended the disputations of the Dominicans, at the other end he heard the Cordeliers or Franciscans lecturing. He was to be found in the Sorbonne and also in the College of Navarre. For good measure he attended lectures given in his own college, the Ste-Barbe, by the Scot, Robert Wauchop—a man he was to meet in very different circumstances in future years. How then, we may ask, did he come to be regarded as an outstanding theologian?

Favre may not have been a professional theologian. He had no diploma. He had no taste for theology. But 'theologian' in the sense used (by Peter Canisius and Kalckbrenner) does not mean the rigorous science dealing with the truths of faith, but that perception of mysteries which experience yields, the wisdom imprinted by piety and matured by discernment, reflection of a particular type born of personal encounters with Jesus Christ and the moral attitudes these encounters engender . . . *Eruditio* and *pietas*, that is how William Postel characterises 'this type of very fruitful theology that is orientated towards meditation, that is based on affectivity rather than intellect' and which had its origins, he thought, 'among these *iniguistas* who were ready to go to the ends of the earth.'[13]

While Ignatius was riding away from Paris the Pope was writing to his Nuncio in that city praising the French king for his efforts 'to induce the Germans to take part in conciliatory talks', and for renewing the invitation to Melanchthon to come to Paris 'for discussions in order to prepare and facilitate the examination of issues that will be brought before the Council'. In the previous Pope's reign there had been widespread demands for a General Council but Clement VII shelved the project each time it was broached. His objections to a Council arose partly from his own indecisive character, partly from memories of the Synods of Constance and Basle and the controversies on Papal and Conciliar authority to which they had given rise, and partly from his political involvements and the fears and harassments they brought upon him. He lived in constant apprehension, if not of the Emperor, of the French King; if not of the German princes and reformers, of the Great Turk, or of Henry VIII, so persistent in his demands for a divorce. But Paul III was of different metal. From his accession he enthusiastically supported the moves for a General Council.

In Paris hopes soared when Melanchthon accepted the second invitation, but his prince, the Elector of Saxony, refused him permission to travel. In a letter to King Francis, John Frederick of Saxony said that the University of Wittenberg could not possibly spare so eminent a professor as Philip Melanchthon, even for a few months. He did not add that he himself was on the point of concluding a treaty with the Emperor, a situation in which it would have been inopportune and highly impolitic to oblige or seem to oblige the French King. Following this disappointment du Bellay invited Martin Bucer to Paris. Bucer referred him to the princes of the German States due to meet at Schmalkalden. At the meeting, although the French diplomat spoke ably and eloquently and read a carefully phrased letter from his royal master, he pleaded in vain. The princes were haughty and contemptuous. All the efforts of Guillaume and Jean—then Cardinal—du Bellay to bridge the religious chasm failed.

Closely interested in these advances and rejections were the Paris theologians, among them Peter Favre. A born optimist, who felt keen disappointment when hopes were dashed, Peter would have been more downcast than others when news of the breakdown in negotiations became known. This disappointment came when he was in charge of the Companions and at a time when every post brought bad news from Savoy. Geneva had followed the expulsion of her bishop and the renunciation of her allegiance to the House of Savoy by a ban on the Mass. Zwinglians and Lutherans from Basle invaded the city and part of Savoy. In May 1536 the people of Geneva and the occupied territories swore 'in close union and unanimously' that they wanted to live according to the reformed religion 'and to abandon all Masses and other ceremonies and papal abuses, images and idols.'

At this juncture, Francis I, realizing that the real ruler of Savoy was not his uncle, the easy-going Duke, but Madame Beatrix, saw an opportunity of thwarting the Emperor. He invaded Savoy on pretext of coming to the aid of Geneva. The Savoyards, feeling that their hereditary rulers had failed them, offered little resistance. The French King had never forgotten that Savoy had harboured Bourbon, the Constable of France who had gone over to the Emperor and played a significant part in the imperial victory at Pavia, so the duchy was now made to suffer the resentment that had long smouldered within him. His troops were allowed to pillage at will and misery crept closer to La Roche and Thônes and the little hamlets of the Grand Bornand.

A subtler ruler than Charles of Savoy would have known how to play off King and Emperor, Bernese and Genevois against one another. His two brothers, humiliated by his indecision, weakness and apathy as much as by 'the unbearable hauteur of Madame Beatrix', deserted to France. Forsaken by all, the unfortunate Duke fled to Milan where his duchess presented him to her brother-in-law the Emperor. But Caesar received him coldly. If Charles had lost his duchy in the imperial service he could have expected consideration. But what had become of the vaunted valour of Savoy? How had it been handed over to France without one real battle being fought? The Emperor, just then embarking on yet another war with France, had more to do than waste time on the French King's uncle. Duke Charles, summarily dismissed, retired to his ruined province of Piedmont and lived there in poverty but not without dignity for the remainder of his life. For more than twenty years his duchy was ruled by France and he did not live to see it won back by his son in 1559. We shall meet the Duke again, in the company of Peter Favre.

In retaliation for the French seizure of Savoy and Piedmont, the Emperor besieged Marseilles and sent armies from Flanders to the Somme where they encamped some eighty miles from Paris. Fortifications were thrown up around the capital and rationing was mentioned. Spaniards were made to feel unwelcome, so Favre and his companions decided to cut short their studies and proceed to Venice to join Ignatius. Before leaving Paris Favre took out his Master's Degree; the rumblings of war would have meant less expensive graduation parties. Ignatius, despite wars, tempests and Mediterranean pirates, had succeeded in reaching Venice early in 1536. From there he wrote to Fray Gabriel Guzman, Dominican confessor of Queen Eleanor, second wife of Francis I and sister of the Emperor, asking him to obtain a safe conduct for the *Iniguistas*.

Master Peter Favre and a group of companions will soon undertake a very arduous journey . . . Owing to the increasing troubles and wars that our miseries and sins have brought upon Christendom they may find themselves in great or very extreme difficulties. In your kindness, and for the love and glory of God who is goodness itself, . . . will you please do what you can to help them? Our mutual friend, the good Doctor de Castro, has written several letters to me from the Chartreuse of Val de Cristo near Segorbia where he is now a Carthusian monk. He made his profession this year . . .[16]

When Favre asked a professor for advice on the move he and the other *iniguistas* were contemplating he was told bluntly that it was the opinion of all the doctors in the faculty of theology 'that he was sinning mortally in risking his life going to a strange place where he could not be sure of doing nearly as much good as he was doing in Paris'. We are not told what reply, if any, Peter made. Mid-November was not the best time to tramp across Europe even in times of peace. They set out in very rainy weather to cross a continent in the throes of war. When Peter Favre went through the Porte St-Jacques for the last time one wonders did he lead his little band to Vauvert, the Chartreuse where they had spent so many quiet Sundays, to bid farewell to the white monks and ask a blessing on the long trek to Venice.

Their route led through Meaux and Verdun to Lorraine, then through Basle, Constance and Trent. It was arranged that if they met French troops the four French-speaking travellers were to do the talking; if they met imperial soldiers the five from south of the Pyrenees were to act as spokesmen. They wore broad-brimmed hats, a slight protection from the incessant rain, and their scholars' gowns. Each carried a stave and a knapsack containing a change of linen, a Bible, a passport, university parchments attesting to their degrees and, in Favre's case, Mass requisites. They wore rosaries, the livery of Our Lady's clients, around their necks. Favre does not waste words describing the journey:

We journeyed on foot, crossing Lorraine and Germany where many of the towns were already Lutheran or Zwinglian, such as Basle, Constance, etc. That winter was intensely cold and rigorous. France and Spain were at war but the Lord delivered us and preserved us from all harm. We arrived in Venice in the best of health and spirits.[17]

Lainez and Rodriguez are a little more expansive. Rodriguez, whose brothers had ridden from Paris hoping to persuade him to return, reports that they were so happy that they walked like men whose feet barely touched the earth. When held up by French or imperial patrols within the borders of France they explained that they were Paris students on a pilgrimage, a truthful answer though no doubt those not partial to Ignatius or his Order would describe it as Jesuitical. Lainez writes:

On each day the three priests among us, Master Peter, Master Claude and Master Paschase, said Mass and the rest of our group of scholars confessed and received Holy Communion. When we entered an inn we said a short prayer of thanks; we said another brief prayer when leaving. As for our meals we ate sufficient, sometimes less, never more. While on the road we prayed or meditated or spoke of holy things. In this way, although we were novice travellers, and although it rained almost every day from Paris to the frontier and snowed every foot of the way through Germany, our Lord in his goodness preserved us from dangers, making even the soldiers and the Lutherans act as our guides and be our good companions on the way . . . I remember that on the very first day one man—I don't know of what persuasion—asked passers-by 'Are these going to reform some country?'[18]

On this journey Favre made his first acquaintance with the actual Reformation. In Paris he had heard Lutheran doctrines denounced. He had been marched with his fellow students to witness burnings and torturings of those convicted or suspected of 'being Lutherans'. He had heard of, and possibly read, the works of the reformers then circulating in France. But not until the winter of 1536–1537 could he have had any idea of the reality and extent of Protestantism.

At Basle, 'the city of free thought', they could have met Nicholas Cop, not so long before a Rector in Paris and friend of the Rector of the Ste-Barbe. Calvin, another friend of Cop, had left Basle for Ferrara. The Companions visited the tomb of Erasmus in Basle Minster, for the great humanist had died a few months before. The last year of his life had been full of sorrows and trials. Worn out by work, rheumatism and disappointment, he began to die in August 1535 when news reached him that his friend More had died on the scaffold in London. 'In More's death I die somewhat myself,' he wrote to a friend, 'We were two men who had but one soul between us.'

Somewhere near Lake Constance when they were 'half dead from the cold and the misery of trudging through snowdrifts', Peter and his company stopped at an inn for the night. An ex-priest who had become a Zwinglian pastor and now had a wife and children used to spend his evenings not in the bosom of his family but in the *Gasthaus*. Arriving this particular evening to make merry with his parishioners he found nine 'Paris scholars' installed there, the rosaries they wore proclaiming where their allegiance lay. He challenged them to a debate on religious matters, a foolish gesture for a man outnumbered and outclassed by men fresh from the lectures and disputations of Paris. The poor pastor cut a sorry figure before his flock who had hoped to hear him confute the wandering scholars. Finally he lost his temper and threatened to have the travellers put in irons next day, but long before he bestirred himself the following morning Favre and his friends were miles away.[19]

On 8 January 1537 Ignatius, at his usual task of tending the sick in the Hospital of the Incurables in Venice, was told that nine strangers awaited him in the courtyard. Hurrying out as fast as his lame leg would permit he found his former roommates, Favre and Xavier, with the others. They were a bedraggled looking lot in their sodden, mud-caked gowns, the hardships of the journey showing in their tired eyes. But there was nothing that a wash, a change of clothing, a good meal and a blazing fire could not remedy. All that, and a warm welcome, Ignatius provided. It was a joyful reunion. When Ignatius introduced three new recruits from Spain Favre adjusted the balance of power by presenting Jay, Codure and Broet, subjects of the French king.

They remained in Venice until Lent began. Four of them worked at the hospital of SS John and Paul, five at the Incurables. When they left for Rome to get the papal permit necessary for their pilgrimage and to ask the Pope's blessing Ignatius remained in Venice. He feared that his presence in Rome would be no help as he was *persona non grata* with two influential persons there. One was Doctor Pedro Ortiz, last met with delating Ignatius to the Paris Inquisition as an *extravagante* who had 'seduced scholars' from orthodox paths. Ortiz was now a counsellor in the papal court. Also close to the Pope was Cardinal Carafa whose displeasure Ignatius had incurred in Venice some months previously. The Cardinal was joint founder of the Theatines, a new Order, and very proud of them. Ignatius thought that the Theatines could do more good if some adjustments were made in the rules and he wrote an honest but, for him, not very tactful letter to Carafa giving his suggestions and the reasons for them. Apart from the Cardinal's understandable vexation on receiving this missive there was another reason why Ignatius was not likely to be popular with him. During the *sacco di Roma* in 1527 Carafa had suffered much at the hands of the imperial troops and he knew that Ignatius of Loyola had once been a Spanish captain.

Peter Favre led the delegation to Rome. Ignatius had given directions: they were to explain to the Pope their plan to go on pilgrimage and obtain the necessary permits; they might also mention that they wished to devote their lives to apostolic work in the Holy Land; permission for those not yet ordained to receive Holy Orders was to be requested. As on the journey from Paris to Venice, bad weather accompanied them all the way to Rome. Few gave them alms. On one occasion they gnawed pine cones to ease their hunger pangs; on another they pawned a breviary to pay for a sea passage from Ravenna to Ancona; in Ancona they had to beg sufficient money to redeem the breviary and buy food. After making a detour to visit Our Lady's shrine in Loreto they proceeded to Rome, reaching the city on Palm Sunday, 25 March.

To their surprise Doctor Ortiz welcomed them warmly and introduced them to the Pope with whom he was in high favour.* Paul III seldom dined without having poets to recite or learned men to discourse in his presence, so on the Tuesday of Easter Week he asked the Doctor to fetch the 'Paris theologians' and have them engage in a disputation while he took his evening meal. They pleased him greatly, so much so that he declared his delight 'at seeing so much learning in conjunction with such humility'. He granted them permission to go on their pilgrimage but remarked that he doubted whether they would succeed in reaching Jerusalem. He also gave them leave to be ordained. Before they left for Venice he sent them substantial money donations, which were added to by Ortiz and other papal and Spanish dignitaries in Rome.

Back in Venice they resumed their work in the hospitals. Ignatius and seven others were ordained on 24 June. Writing to a Spanish friend in July Ignatius admitted that their chances of getting to Jerusalem were poor:

*Pedro Ortiz had defended Catherine of Aragon during the divorce proceedings that dragged on from January 1531 to January 1536 when the unhappy Queen died. When Henry VIII heard of his wife's death he dressed in yellow, put a white plume in his cap and went dancing. On the day of Catherine's funeral (Henry refused to pay for the hearse from St Paul's) Anne Boleyn had a still-born son. Four months later Cranmer declared her marriage invalid and a week later she was beheaded 'for adultery against the King'. Twelve days later Henry married Jane Seymour, once a maid-in-waiting to Catherine of Aragon.

This year, though our hopes of getting to Jerusalem were high, there in no ship and no hope of a sailing, since the Turk is on the sea with an armada. We decided to return the 260 ducats given us in Rome towards the expenses of our voyage; for we do not wish to keep the money when we cannot make the pilgrimage and we should not like people to think that we hunger and thirst for that wealth for which the worldly die. We are leaving here, two by two . . . travelling around Italy for another year, to see if there are any hopes of going to Jerusalem. Then, if it be not to the service of God our Lord that we should go there, we will wait no longer but go ahead with the work we have commenced. [20]

Some weeks after the ordinations the Companions decided to spend 'forty days in solitude, attending to nothing but prayer'. When they emerged from this retreat a message was received summoning them to Rome and at the end of autumn Favre, Ignatius and Lainez set out, travelling by Siena rather than by Loreto. This 350 mile walk was to be the last of Ignatius' long journeys in search of the will of God. Every morning he assisted at the Masses said by his two companions, but he himself waited a year and a half after his ordination before saying his first Mass. Eight miles from journey's end they came to the village now called La Storta where Ignatius had a mystical experience he referred to only twice, and in rather cryptic terms, in later years. As they proceeded on the last stage of their long walk he told his two companions that at La Storta he had heard the words, 'I will be favourable to you in Rome'. 'But,' he added, 'I am not sure what was meant; perhaps we shall be crucified there.'

They entered the city by the old Roman road, the Flaminian Way which passes in through the Porta del Popolo and continues along the Corso. The first church inside this gate was Santa Maria del Popolo and beyond that lay a slope reputed to be haunted by Nero's ghost. On they went by the Augustinian convent, where in 1510 Friar Martin Luther of Wittenberg spent a month, and into the heart of Rome. The city Peter Favre was seeing for the first time had a population of about 50,000 and had not yet recovered from the sack of the previous decade. Oxen lumbered along, drawing blocks of marble and undressed stone from the Campagna for the rebuilding of St.

Peter's and the many churches and palaces wrecked by the imperial armies. The streets were almost as crowded as the Paris Latin Quarter but not by students. Prelates and princes, ambassadors with their retinues, Italian nobles and captains with their bodyguards, officials with their servants and their servants' servants, and hangers-on of every kind went up and down without noticing the three strangers. Ignatius remarked that all the windows were closed and wondered if that meant 'contradictions'. More likely it meant that the Romans felt chilly, for winter had begun. 'We need to proceed with prudence,' continued the leader, who knew Rome of old, 'and not speak to any women'.

The Curia received them rather coldly but Paul III made them welcome and appointed Favre and Lainez lecturers in the Sapientia University. Favre's assignment included lectures on theology and the giving of commentaries on the Scripture, a hazardous task at a time when the interpretation of Holy Writ was a matter of controversy. A nobleman who owned a vineyard on the site of the present Piazza di Spagna allowed them to lodge in a hut in his vineyard. There they were joined the following May by their companions, all except Hoces who had already gone to his reward.

Seeing that this year (writes Favre) no more than last there seemed no hope of getting a passage to Jerusalem we asked for permission to preach, hear confessions etc. . . . God was good to us, for all that year we and our projects met with contradictions and trials, above all because of the enquiry we demanded.[21]

He alludes to a persecution they suffered while the Pope was away trying to make peace between the Emperor and the French King. A popular preacher gave a series of sermons that Ignatius and his followers considered heretical. Finding remonstrance useless the Companions, who now preached in several Roman pulpits, began to refute the preacher's errors in their own sermons. As might be expected, this brought a storm of abuse upon them. The preacher found an ally in a Spaniard who had once attached himself to Francis Xavier in Paris but later fell foul of the *iniguistas* and made much trouble for Ignatius in Venice. This man now spread calumnies about

Ignatius in Rome, taking care to emphasize that he had been up before the courts of the Inquisition in Spain and Paris and twice imprisoned by the Spanish Inquisitors. As the reports circulated they gained virulence and credence. Finally Ignatius, realizing that his priests could do no useful work in Rome or elsewhere until his character was cleared and the doctrine he and the Companions taught declared orthodox, demanded a full enquiry. For months it seemed that his opponents would succeed in preventing the enquiry being held. But the delay was providential. When the trial eventually took place the Inquisitors of Alcalá and Paris as well as churchmen and high civic authorities from Venice and other Italian cities happened to be in Rome. All of these had known Ignatius in former years and came forward to repudiate the charges brought against him. 'Far from deserving any infamous judgment' ran the findings of the tribunal conducting the enquiry, 'the life and teaching of Ignatius and his companions is praiseworthy, and the same holds for the Spiritual Exercises they give to others.'[22]

That same year John III of Portugal wrote to de Gouvea, Rector of the Ste-Barbe in Paris, asking him to recommend zealous priests for the Portuguese colonies in India and the east. In his reply de Gouvea suggested that the king should apply to the Company of Jesus in Rome:

. . . The principal among them is Master Peter Favre, a learned man of very holy life, and another, Iñigo . . . If these men can be got to go to the east it will be an inestimable advantage. . . . It is sufficient to write to Master Simon Rodriguez (de Gouvea's own nephew) and to Master Peter Favre and to Iñigo, as the others follow the decisions of these three.[23]

de Gouvea also wrote to the Company in Rome mentioning King John's request. Favre replied in the name of all stating that 'despite the great harvest to be reaped in Rome' they were inclined to go to the Indies but that the matter was one to be decided between the King and the Pope. When His Holiness asked them to go they would be ready to obey.

Meanwhile no ship left for the Holy Land. The Grand Turk's henchman, Barbarossa, whose pirate fleet was spreading terror along the southern coasts of Europe, had hemmed in the port of Venice, permitting neither merchantman nor pilgrim ship to put out to sea. When Francis I abandoned his Turkish allies to sign peace with the Emperor the Companions again thought of their vow to go to Jerusalem. One evening as four of them debated while the Pope dined, Paul III asked, 'Why are you so anxious to go to Jerusalem? If you wish to do good work for God and the Church you will find a Jerusalem here.'[24] Following this, they placed themselves unreservedly at the Pontiff's disposal and within the next year the Society of Jesus came into being as a religious Order. In May 1539 Peter Favre and Lainez were sent from Rome on their first mission. Though he did not know it, Peter would never again meet Codure or Broet or Salmeron or his countryman, Claude Jay. Never again would he see his room-mate of the Ste-Barbe, Francis Xavier.

4 The Watch on the Rhine

DURING the summer of 1539 Paul III, asked to send some exemplary priests to Parma, sent Favre and Lainez. The Parma 'Legation', forming the central sector of the papal states strung across northern Italy from Genoa to Venice, was administered by a papal legate and was noted then as now for its cheese, its fruit, and a perfume distilled from violets. The Parmesans were used to wars and changes of rulers. Disputes between rival nobles and neighbouring towns were frequent. Even priests went about armed and took part in these feuds.

On the plea that punitive measures were necessary to subdue rebel lords in the papal states, Pier Luigi Farnese, the Pope's nephew,* overran the Legation in 1537. Having burned and plundered at will he appropriated to his own use the palace of Parma's former dukes. The citizens' hatred for Pier Luigi extended to all his family and, when the Pontiff broke a journey to visit him, one of the papal retinue, the Master of the Stables, was assassinated. This incident took place the year before Favre and his companion arrived in Parma. They travelled from Rome with the newly appointed Cardinal Legate, Filonardi, a prelate absolutely dedicated to Church reform and only too well aware that religion had become almost a byword throughout the Legation. He it was who had requested the Pope for 'two priests of reformed life' to accompany him as he set out to shepherd the flock of Christ entrusted to him.

At first only a few of the more curious came to hear the 'preachers from Rome' when they expounded the Scriptures

*Paul III, though raised to the cardinalate at twenty-six, was a layman, and a far from edifying one, until his forty-sixth year. His 'nephews' were his illegitimate sons. Pier Luigi, a true Renaissance *condottiere*, was murdered by a clique of nobles in 1547.

on Sundays and feastdays. Before long the numbers increased but, as sermons were then usually preached in Latin, the return to God of an entire city within a year cannot be attributed to pulpit eloquence. Favre and Lainez declared that the tremendous and rapid change for the better, which amazed them more than anyone, was due under God to the Spiritual Exercises. The more intimate person-to-person talks in the vernacular to small groups and to individuals, all of whom relayed the Exercises to other groups and individuals, proved highly effective. The Jesuits' confessionals were besieged by Parmesans coming to accuse themselves before God with the humility and sorrow of the Prodigal: *Father, I have sinned . . . I am not worthy to be called thy son.*

Lainez, more expansive than Favre, reported to Ignatius some months after their arrival on their fully occupied days:

Thank God we can say truthfully that in this city we need not examine ourselves on idleness. Often it happens, even in carnival time, that we begin to hear confessions by candlelight in the mornings and we are still at the same work until an hour or more past midnight—and that without stopping except to take a meal. Even then we have many interruptions. The communions increase daily. As I say, Master Favre and myself are all the time hearing confessions and giving the Exercises. Besides this, Master Peter studies as much as ever. As for me, not many hours of the night remain for saying my office, snatching a meal, resting, not to mention trying to glance at, or rather give a thought to the sermons that bear so much fruit—more fruit than can be imagined or described.[1]

Undoubtedly Lainez was the better preacher but Peter Favre was 'the specialist of the confessional'. His natural gentleness and kindness, his eagerness to put others at their ease, his winning manner and ready sympathy drew all Parma to him. Some who came had a lifetime of sins to confess, some had a lifetime of careless confessions to undo. He took time to talk with each one. Those who did the Exercises were patiently helped to make a general confession, to be truly contrite and resolved to repair the past by a complete conversion of life. They were advised not to be content 'with a self-examination on the commandments and the seven capital sins' but to look deeper, to discover beneath the surface of the soul the root cause of its spiritual ills. The converted were urged to confess frequently and were helped to plan a spiritual programme suited to their circumstances, responsibilities and capacities.

Four years later Favre wrote a long letter to young Jesuits in Cologne instructing them how to act when hearing confessions. The final paragraphs show his high concept of the role of confessor:

Above all, seek the aid of the Holy Spirit, an aid that is readily given to those who earnestly pray for it. When hearing confessions be mild and gentle. Never permit yourselves to speak sharply or show repugnance, no matter how uncouth the penitent. Let us take care not to become bored with this sublime and sacred task, we who represent Christ taking away the sins of the world. Let us take care that no sinner who comes to confession (that source of so much good), who kneels before us to be tried, exhorted and judged, faces an ordeal when he approaches us, the vicars of the gentle Christ. Let us beware of acting the haughty disdainful pharisee, or the angry impatient judge. In fine let us do our utmost to ensure that every penitent leaving the confessional will freely return there.[2]

Master Peter's converts were certainly not afraid to return to him. In fact, for the remainder of his life he was to spend most of his time hearing the confessions of those who became his regular penitents. His letter to his younger brethren concludes with a reprimand to confessors who believed that the converted should be treated with increasing severity:

Why should we be so austere? Do we not realize that God regards it a great thing that anyone should come to us for frequent and regular confession? It is a great thing, indeed, that a penitent should bare his soul to you. But it is a far greater thing that he looks forward to your admonishments. For he finds this humbling, but if he did not come to confession he would not have this opportunity of exercising humility and other concurrent virtues. *Charity is patient, is kind . . . believes all things, hopes all things, bears all things, sustains all things. Charity never falls away.*[3]

During 1539 Italy experienced the worst famine of the century. The Parmesans, their territory already laid waste by Pier Luigi's soldiery, suffered terribly. Country people barely able to walk dragged themselves to the cities and towns where they begged, sickened and died in the streets. Favre's heart was wrung at the sight of their misery and his inability to relieve it. In a letter to Xavier he wrote:

There are in this city 6,500 beggars, 3,000 of them strangers from the surrounding countryside, and many of these persons of property who have been reduced to begging the necessities of life. We have not been able to do much for them as in Parma we do not beg from door to door* and our numbers are reduced to one. (Lainez had left Parma for a brief period to preach in Piacenza and to give the Spiritual Exercises in several monasteries and convents). Perhaps if we had a flair for business and if we had not such a harvest to be reaped of persons wishing to serve God our Lord, we could concern ourselves more with this problem.[4]

Three years later the plight of other beggars in a Rhineland town reminded Peter of those he had seen in Parma and he reproached himself for not having exerted himself more on their behalf. In October 1542 he wrote in his journal:

On the vigil of the apostles, Simon and Jude, I rose in the silence of the night to pray. I was stongly inspired to do all I could to procure a hospital for the sick poor who wander about this town of Mainz, a hospital into which they could be gathered, welcomed, cared for, and their ailments treated. I saw very clearly how often I had been negligent, unheeding, wanting in care for those others I saw, not so long ago, covered with sores, and in what an indifferent, half-hearted way I sometimes helped them. True, I had not the means to assist them, but I could have induced others to do so; I could have gone from door to door begging for them and thus eased their misery a little more than I did. I could have gone to the church authorities there, to the doctors and surgeons, to the lords and magistrates of that and other towns where the sick poor and many others suffer such wretchedness.[5]

*During the terrible winter of 1538–1539 the Jesuits in Rome 'begged and collected money and bread in all quarters. They made herb stews and searched for the poor in the streets and piazzas and fetched them to their own little house . . . There they washed their feet, doctored their ills and sores . . . sometimes putting the sick in their own beds, they themselves sleeping on the floors. They begged hay, fuel and food from their friends and carried such alms home on their backs through the city. Sometimes as many as three hundred were crowded into the Fathers' house, all being fed and comforted.' (MHSI: *Rod.Comment*, 554 ff.)

A young Spanish priest, Jeronimo Domenech, who had
known the *iniguistas* in Paris, met them again in Rome. Through
the influence of an uncle Jeronimo was appointed to a secre-
tarial post in the Curia. Before taking up this position he
decided to do a post graduate course in Paris and to make the
Exercises which so many of the Roman clergy were making
under Jesuit direction. He told Xavier, then acting as secretary
to Ignatius, that he wanted to do the Exercises before leaving
for Paris. As his journey led through Parma he was given a
letter for Favre with instructions from Ignatius: the young
priest was to be given the Exercises; he was of Jesuit calibre
and might be won for the Order. By December 1539 Jeronimo
had abandoned his prospects in Rome and was working with
Favre and Lainez in Parma. He seems to have caught the art
of giving the Exercises from Peter Favre. Years later, when
assessing the merits of the early Jesuits as retreat givers,
Ignatius used to say, 'No one excelled Favre in giving the
Exercises; after him came Salmeron, then Domenech and
Francis of Villanova.'[6]

In his breezy reports to Rome Lainez mentions Domenech's
part in the conversation of Parma:

Domenech gives the Exercises to fourteen or more . . . many of
those who do them give them to others, some to ten, some to
fourteen. As soon as one brood is fully fledged another is hatching,
and so it goes on until we see our *children's children to the fourth
generation.*[7]

As might be expected, the uncle who had obtained the
Curia post for Jeronimo Domenech was much put out at that
young man's change of direction. He hastened from Rome,
breathing fire and slaughterings. Favre, awaiting instructions
from Ignatius on the attitude to be adopted towards the angry
uncle, took the precaution of sending Domenech to give the
Exercises in a town ten miles from Parma. When the uncle
arrived he had Lainez and Favre summoned before the
Cardinal Legate and complained bitterly to Filonardi about
how his nephew had been enticed from a promising career by
the two Jesuits and inveigled into their Order. The cardinal,
however, 'said that he liked our Order better than any and

that if he had a nephew like this young priest, to whom he wished well, he would direct him to us before any other.' The cardinal also advised the uncle to do the Exercises himself.[8]

Favre was dispatched to fetch Domenech. He found him giving the Exercises to the townfolk. This good work had to be interrupted, for Favre had promised the uncle a meeting with his nephew next day.

We returned next day, but the uncle had left for Pavia to visit a lady whom everyone says is a saint. He is due back in four days time . . . If she does not come up to his expectations we can show him one here in Parma who has had nothing to eat or drink except the Blessed Sacrament for five months past . . . I think that the uncle will content himself now with getting Domenech to agree to go to Paris, and complete his course there, which is what his (Jeronimo's) father wishes.[9]

Eventually the uncle did the Exercises and became a firm friend of the Jesuits. Thanks to Favre, Lainez and Domenech, several young men from Parma and its environs entered the Society, among them Antonio Criminali, the first Jesuit martyr; Landini, the future apostle of Corsica; Ugoletti, a noted musician; Francisco Palmio and his brother, big Benito, whose candour delighted Ignatius as much as his prodigious capacity for food.*

On the second day of April 1540 Favre left Parma for Brescia, a Lombardy town some fifty miles away, to visit another candidate for the ranks. This aspirant's family strongly opposed his intention of joining the Jesuits and treated him rather cruelly. He fell ill, so ill that his life was despaired of. Favre arrived when the patient, having survived the crisis, began to show signs of improvement; he remained in Brescia thirteen days, by the end of which time the youth's family had withdrawn their opposition to his vocation. Peter's absence from

---

*Ignatius kept the ever hungry Benito beside him in the refectory and plied the young giant with the food he himself, constantly ailing, was unable to eat. Benito was an eloquent preacher, 'and well aware of the fact'. Once he told a devout old lady who was very fond of listening to sermons that he was to preach in a certain church on a certain day and invited her to come and hear him. The story reached Ignatius and tickled him greatly. After that, whenever he assigned a task to Benito he would say, 'Now Benito, if you do this well for me I promise to round up crowds of old ladies to attend your sermons.' MHSI: *Scripta S. Ig.* (I), 495–6).

Parma deprived him of a last meeting with Francis Xavier. Xavier, on his way to the Portuguese Indies, was travelling to Lisbon with the ambassador of King John III. After reporting to Ignatius on his journey to Brescia Favre adds:

Master Francisco arrived here (in Parma) the very day I left for Brescia. He was undecided whether to follow me or not but his companions and the ambassador would not have it, which was all for the best. May the Lord grant that if we are to meet no more in this life we may rejoice together at our reunion in the next and rejoice, too, over these partings, made solely for Christ's sake.[10]

About ten days later Peter Favre fell ill with the first of recurrent fevers that laid him low for the best part of three months. Two families in Parma took turns at lodging and nursing him during that summer and for the rest of his life he remembered them in his prayers. Lainez, Domenech and other priests who joined them coped with the numbers who returned to the practice of religion and gave the Exercises to those who wished to do them. All in all it was a happy summer for the Parmesans. Pier Luigi Farnese and his cavalry had ridden south to Perugia, 'to quell a rebellion', then east to deal with corsairs who were raiding the Adriatic coast in the vicinity of Ancona and Loreto.

By the end of July Master Favre was back in his confessional again, but not for long. In August the Pope ordered him to accompany Dr Ortiz to Spain. Ortiz, the denouncer of Ignatius and his followers in Paris, was now so pro-Jesuit that he was setting off, with Pope Paul's blessing, to help establish the Society of Jesus in its founder's *patria*. The news of Peter's imminent departure caused consternation in Parma. One noble lady asked another, a relative of the Pope, to use her influence to have Favre left where he was doing so much good. The city fathers sent two ambassadors to Rome with the same request. Peter was embarrassed over this and wrote to Ignatius:

Five or six days ago Signora Jacoba, learning of my departure for Spain, ran weeping to the lady Laura, one of the most important persons in this city and a relative of the Pope, imploring her with tears to prevent me from leaving and to write to Cardinal Santi

Fiora to obtain from His Holiness to have me left in Parma. She did this without my knowledge. Also, I believe that the city has made similar representations in writing to His Holiness. I assure you that whatever comes of this I had no part in it.[11]

Despite all the appeals to Rome the original order held. In a farewell letter to his 'dearest children and brothers in Christ', Master Favre recommended frequent reception of the sacraments, daily prayer and examination of conscience, and constant care to observe a Christian's obligations to God, to his neighbour, and to his own soul.

Ortiz was sixty leagues north of Rome on his way to Piacenza, where Favre was to join him, when a messenger overtook him with counter orders. He was to proceed to Germany instead of Spain and he was to go not as a papal counsellor and theologian but as the representative of Charles-Quint at the forthcoming discussions to be held at Worms between Catholic and Protestant divines. Master Peter Favre, the Paris theologian, was to accompany him.

Pedro Ortiz, with whom Favre was to be closely associated during his remaining years, was a Spaniard of Jewish ancestry. Born near Toledo, he had studied philosophy at Alcalá before proceeding to Paris where he won renown as a theologian and scripture scholar. He became a professor in the Sorbonne but lodged in that abode of high thinking and meagre diet, the Montaigu, where the Rector, Noel Beda, shared his rigorist opinions and dislike of Erasmus. It will be recalled that in the summer of 1529 Ortiz denounced Ignatius Loyola to the Paris Inquisitor as a 'Spanish *extravagante*' who was fomenting disorder and seducing the scholars.* The following autumn, on hearing of his father's death, Dr Ortiz returned to Spain where he occupied the Chair of Scripture in Salamanca University.

Then this 'inquisitor out on grass' found in the bosom of his own family the tendencies he so strongly opposed. His Franciscan brother, a famous preacher, was thrown into the prisons of the Inquisition, following a scandal provoked by his public defence in the pulpit of a *beata* . . . suspected of illuminism. . . . Pedro availed of the occasion and of the close but confused links between Erasmism

*See pages 30–32 *supra*.

and illuminism to deliver a long and important denunciation of Erasmus and his works.[12]

The following year he left Salamanca for Rome, Charles V having commissioned him to defend his aunt, Catherine of Aragon, when that unfortunate queen was repudiated by Henry VIII. Ortiz acquired great authority at the papal court, acting as secretary to Clement VII and as counsellor and theologian to Paul III. When Favre and Lainez first presented themselves to the Pontiff Ignatius wisely stayed away from an interview at which his former accuser was sure to be present, but Ortiz surprised the delegation and Ignatius by showing himself most favourable and acting as their advocate with the Pope. His change of attitude may be attributed to the misfortunes of his brother, condemned to life imprisonment in a convent of his Order, to the lessening of opposition to the humanists since the advent of Paul III, to the attestations of orthodoxy sought and obtained by Ignatius and his companions, and above all to Ortiz' own conviction that reform was very necessary and could not be attained without the aid of men dedicated to self-reformation and resolved to work for the reform of the entire Church.[13]

Once Pedro Ortiz met Ignatius Loyola he realized how unfounded his suspicions had been and, as earnest of his good will, volunteered to do the Exercises. Not a man to do anything by halves, he left the papal court for the whole of Lent 1538 and went to the Benedictines at Monte Cassino to secure the silence and solitude he deemed necessary for attending to God and the affairs of his soul. Ignatius, despite his halt, travelled eighty miles to see how he was faring. He found Ortiz depressed, a week's concentrated reflection on death, judgment and hell having proved too much for him.

The Doctor admitted that he was beginning to feel the strain, whereupon Father Ignatius danced one of the Basque dances to cheer him up and rouse him from his stupor. This revived the retreatant's drooping spirits to such an extent that he was then able to resume his meditations with renewed enthusiasm and to carry them through to the end.[14]

When he emerged from the retreat, Ortiz, a new man, asked to be allowed to join the Jesuits but Ignatius tactfully dissuaded him, 'saying that his portly figure and delicate constitution would never stand up to the life' and that he was too old. Ortiz could have retaliated that he was eight years younger than Ignatius, but when Ignatius told him that God had placed him in a position where he could do much for His glory and the good of all Christian people the Toledan seems to have been satisfied to remain 'in the world' *ad majorem Dei gloriam.*

This was the man with whom Peter Favre rode towards Germany. Two more opposite temperaments it would be difficult to imagine: Favre the introvert, diffident, self-effacing, gentle, fearful of hurting anyone's feelings; Ortiz the extrovert, self-confident, flamboyant, fond of the limelight, easily roused to fury, not caring whose corns he trod on, plebian or imperial, Lutheran or Catholic. They are not many weeks in Germany before Favre is writing to Ignatius:

The Doctor (Ortiz) is preaching before the Emperor, without as much as one rehearsal or any practice in the neighbourhood or to any congregation less than Caesar's court. Each day, indeed, he increases not in wisdom and age but in vehemence and volume. His hearers shake in their shoes. Praised be to God for all his gifts and mercies.[15]

and a fortnight later:

The doctor continues to preach, giving several sermons each week . . . He is now so eager for the pulpit that he is not at all pleased with those who listen to him only once a day. His sermons bear such fruit that all marvel. I do not preach for fear of losing what reputation I have as a confessor and director . . . I made threats to many people that if no other preacher (except Ortiz) could be found I myself would mount the pulpit and preach. They soon arranged for three to preach before His Majesty, Dr Ortiz, Fray Alonso and another Augustinian.[16]

Not all the Catholics were pleased when Ortiz was nominated by the Emperor as his representative at Worms. Cardinal

Contarini, an ardent promotor of reform, was apprehensive.* The Cardinal, scrupulously fair and of such integrity that he was nick-named 'the peerless', was anxious that the Lutherans be approached in a conciliatory spirit and feared that Pedro Ortiz would prove unyielding on unimportant issues. Cardinal Aleandro wrote to a friend:

Doctor Ortiz has been named because he has experience of how they conduct discussions in Paris, and because he is well versed in Scripture. Also . . . because he is of Caesar's party. He is a bit too long-winded in debate and far too ready to regard the slightest error as a major heresy. On that account Cardinal Contarini is none too happy about him. But Cardinal Ghinucci and I are well satisfied; he is learned and has a very keen intellect. Besides, it is good that more and more Christians everywhere should know not only that our camp bears the name Caesar, but also that there are men of learning in it.[17]

Ortiz, unlike Favre, was not a person to accommodate himself to others or consider their feelings. Each was to influence the other in the year ahead. The Savoyard was to catch something of the passion for orthodoxy that possessed his companion, to share his distrust of anything bordering on illuminism. The Spaniard was to absorb some of Peter Favre's serenity of spirit, to calm himself, to adopt less violent, more pacific means of achieving apostolic aims. The Jesuit tactfully helped Caesar's theologian to be a more effective preacher; the Emperor's man sent hundreds to Favre for confession and the Exercises.

Although in his writings Favre mentions incidents that

---

*Contarini, like other Cardinals of his time, was a layman. Born into a noble Venetian family he was a man of the highest ideals and culture. 'His many-sided learning, his gentleness and open-mindedness, his exemplary life, won him the respect and affection of all.' He was a man of peace, easy to approach, always inclined to take the optimistic view, a friend of the humanists. He had a most attractive manner and was uncommonly handsome. Although a layman, he was an outstanding theologian. When news of his elevation to the Cardinalate reached Venice he, the youngest and humblest member of the City Council, was sitting in the lowest place in the Council chamber. The entire Council rose and gave him a standing ovation. Contarini was a close friend of Ignatius and one of the first prelates to do the spiritual Exercises. (Von Pastor: *History of the Popes*, Vol. XI: pp. 144 ff.).

happened on other journeys he is silent about his journey to Worms. Still inclined to scruples, he would have found it difficult to reconcile the, for him, luxurious mode of travel with his vow of poverty. His previous journeys and many subsequent ones, all of them longer than that from Piacenza to Worms, were made on foot. Ortiz and his retinue travelled on muleback and in the style befitting the Emperor's representatives on their way to an international meeting. They took three weeks to cover the route which wound through Hapsburg dominions and imperial cities.

Contemporary travellers refer to the bandits who infested the roads, to the wild beasts so plentiful that in some villages heads of foxes, wolves, bears and wild boar were to be seen nailed above the doorways. Most southerners who crossed the Dolomites made a point of stopping at Augsburg, the showpiece of southern Germany. In the mansion of the Fugger family, the bankers of Europe, the best rooms were always held in readiness for the Emperor. These bankers, unlike their modern counterparts, built a street of fifty-three houses 'for needy merchants and other unfortunates, all of whom might stay there for a year or two, or even three, without paying one florin until such time as their finances were again stable.' One hopes that Ortiz halted in Augsburg if only that Peter Favre, the best Greek scholar in the Ste-Barbe, might visit the library in the college of St Anne. A priceless collection of Greek books and manuscripts was housed in this library, one of the finest in Europe.[18]

At Spires travellers usually took passage up the Rhine to towns further north. We do not know what Favre's company did. They arrived at Worms on 24 October, feast of St Raphael the archangel. On the outskirts of the city was the Liebfrauenkirch, standing then as now in the midst of the famous Liebfraumilch vineyards. It was vintage time, but the grape-pickers hardly raised a cheer for the Emperor's party. A letter from a prelate reporting to Rome on the situation in Worms makes that clear:

This city is very infected (with Lutheranism). The people make many demonstrations in favour of the Protestants. They go out in crowds to meet them on their arrival, as though they were bosom friends, and accommodate them with good lodgings and similar gestures.[19]

Favre's first letters to Rome never reached their destination, a not unusual occurrence in those times. Two days after Christmas he writes to Ignatius expressing his joy that the Pope had given formal approval to the Society of Jesus. He continues:

Because of the feastdays I have been kept very busy hearing confessions and giving holy communion. I have acquired, without labour, several spiritual sons. (He lists some of them: the household of the imperial ambassador and many eminent churchmen).

Tomorrow I begin to give the Spiritual Exercises to a deacon of this city who has been Vicar General of Worms for a long time ... Now he does not wish to be Vicar any longer. He does not see how he can possibly continue to shepherd a flock so enamoured of the wolves ... In the church of St Dominic, Lutheran doctrine is being preached openly, notwithstanding the fact that there are Catholic theologians here. Just think of it, an imperial city where the Emperor's lieutenant is present and also so many and such eminent Catholic theologians, and where the Bishop is a Catholic, at least in name, and little hope of converting one Lutheran. How are the other matters of the universal faith going to go? So I go to my deacon, about whom no more just now, only beseeching you to pray to God our Lord for him.

As regards the talks, they have not even begun yet ... I am certain that not one of all the Lutherans of Worms and those here from other parts has been converted of a single error by those who have come here to convert them. I can see no results, no Lutheran converted. In fact it is they who gain ground, even among those who came here Catholics.[20]

At Worms Peter Favre, an intelligent observer, missed little of what went on. In his letters to Ignatius he sizes up the various parties congregated in the Rhineland town and the motives, in many cases more political than religious, that brought them there. He characterizes as futile the hopes, so firmly held by many Catholic theologians, of winning the Lutherans by argument. He saw more clearly than most the weaknesses of the Catholic position.

Granvelle, Chancellor to Charles V, headed the imperial party. His master's main reason for supporting the colloquies in Worms and elsewhere was to establish peace in Germany and throughout the empire. Peace was essential before he could turn his attention to his strangely-allied enemies, the Most Christian King and Islam's leader, the Grand Turk. Caesar's order was 'Peace at all costs', so Granvelle made this his chief aim. The German princes who came riding to Worms also wanted peace, but for a different reason. They had had experience of the religious wars that had torn Germany when extremist groups splintered from the Lutheran tree. They feared that further multiplication of sects would bring about new and bloody conflicts and weaken their position while strengthening the Emperor's. The Pope had been rather chary of sending representatives, but he did not wish it to be thought that he was thwarting the efforts of Charles V to unite Germany and the empire in face of the Moslem menace, or that he was yielding to the Lutheran demand that papal delegates be excluded from the talks.

The points the Lutherans had made at Schmalkalden three years before they reiterated at Worms: Justification by faith alone; rejection of the Mass, purgatory, pilgrimages, relics, indulgences and invocation of the saints; abolition of monasteries and convents, and denial that the papacy was of divine institution.

Favre, reared in the strong faith of Savoy, trained from childhood to practise good works, intensely devoted to the Mass, our Lady, the angels and saints, a fervent pilgrim, an inveterate if not very critical venerator and collector of relics, a friend of Carthusians and a staunch upholder of the papacy, makes no comment on these declarations, though they must have shocked him. What really baffled and distressed him was the attitude of the Catholics. He writes of 'the tendency to compromise, found only on our side'. He notes that of the eight Catholic theologians chosen to dispute with eight Lutheran divines three have already imbibed some of Luther's doctrine while the others 'do not agree among themselves and vacillate, even before the battle.'

Leading for the Lutherans were Melanchthon and Bucer.

Melanchthon, the pre-eminent theologian who had systema-tized Luther's teachings, was then forty-three. He was known to be in favour of conciliation and of the General Reform Council mooted since the beginning of Pope Paul's reign. Bucer, a former Dominican, was fifty; more attracted to Calvinism than Lutheranism, Bucer opposed Melanchthon on many points of doctrine but he agreed with him that uni-formity between the various sects was desirable and he thought that it should be possible for Catholics and Protestants to come to some agreement.

Favre might well write of the vacillation of the Catholics. When it was announced that Melanchthon would lead the Lutherans in the disputation, the Catholics became quite disheartened. Who, it was asked, could their side put up against such a formidable debater? Not even the valiant Johann Eck was considered adequate. Then someone proposed that the 'Paris theologian', Peter Favre, be asked not to enter the lists but to meet Philip Melanchthon and have a talk with him. Peter reports to Rome:

Many of the theologians are very anxious for me to have a talk with Melanchthon. They say that it would be fitter for me to meet him than others who are more punctilious . . . Indeed, I have felt many holy desires arise in my soul to do this; yet I do not wish to oppose the judgment of those who are in charge of the Colloquy. They do not want anyone to converse with the Lutherans, in case that the business which brought us here be impeded. For the same reason Dr Ortiz has held me back (from meeting Melanchthon) although he himself would like to meet the Lutherans. He knows that with God's help I would not approach them in the spirit of contradiction, nor would I exasperate anyone, or in any way obstruct the business that has brought us here.

I have not conversed with Melanchthon or any other Lutheran. I have quite enough to do to live up to my vocation among the Catholics.[21]

Through his penitents, especially the priest penitents to whom he gave more and more of his time, Favre was able to form a true picture of the religious situation in Worms. Easily depressed, his heart sank when things were not going well, and he pleaded as an excuse for not writing a detailed letter to Ignatius that things were not 'prospering'. He continued:

Here in Worms Lutheran doctrine continues to be preached openly in the Dominican church. I wanted to teach some children through an interpreter, but Monsenor Granvelle thought I had better not ... the Protestants are prompt to excite seditions and if I began teaching they might rush out, infuriated, to teach their doctrine ... However, he recommended two Turks to me, to teach and evangelize. Certainly they seem well disposed ...

The Lutherans say that their sole aim is to reform the Church; they assert this so convincingly that—because of our sins—the unlearned and ordinary people believe them, even when they see them overthrowing images and altars. They will only allow one altar in each church; they blaspheme all who hear private Masses or pray to the saints, and all this in the name of reformation. The blindness that has befallen this nation is a sight to make one fear Christ our Lord ...

... Would to God that there were in each town of this land two or three priests not living openly with women or guilty of other notorious sins. If there were I feel sure that, with God's help, the ordinary people would turn back. I speak of towns and cities from which Church rule has not as yet been totally expelled. Their citizens were deceived not so much by the seeming good and preaching of the Lutherans as by the bad example of their own pastors.[22]

On New Year's Day, 1541, Favre preached in French in the church used by the imperial party. Granvelle and all his household were by then among Peter's regular penitents, as were Cardinal Morone, Papal Nuncio to Germany, the Portuguese Ambassador, the fiery pamphleteer, Cochlaeus, and other famous men.

While Favre concerned himself with the reform of individuals the Catholic cause was suffering from petty differences between the leaders. The most trivial incidents gave rise to offence and friction, possibly because those in key positions were living at high tension. Granvelle 'did not uncover for the Pope, but swept off his hat each time Caesar's name was mentioned'. Cardinal Campeggio, one of the Papal Legates, made a point of speaking to everyone and anyone; he spoke too much and showed a lamentable ignorance of the true state of affairs in Germany. The Provost of Lubeck remarked, 'The Legate seems to be under the impression that everything can be set right by pleasant manners and soft talk.' Campeggio sent rosy reports to Rome. The Nuncio followed up these despatches with gloomy but more factual reports. Morone had been five years in Germany but when he tried to enlighten Campeggio and explain to him the harsh realities the result was that the two men became estranged. This quarrel and other disputes among the Catholics increased in acrimony until finally Granvelle advised the Emperor to dissolve the assembly.

Before Caesar had time to reply the conference opened, seventy-seven days behind schedule. Melanchthon spoke for the Lutherans, Eck for the Catholics. After four days of heated debate on the doctrine of original sin, a formula of agreement on this doctrine was drawn up and accepted, with some demurrings, by both sides. Next day, an imperial order came adjourning the meeting to Ratisbon (Regensburg). There the Emperor would be present in person and would do his utmost to restore religious peace in Germany. It was felt that a highly important turning point had been reached and Peter Favre, always an optimist when things were going well, rejoiced. He set off at once for Ratisbon with Dr Ortiz and the imperial embassy.

I left behind me, very desolate, my good deacon (the Vicar-General of Worms). There wasn't a sadder man in Worms. He has finished the Exercises in the first week, except his general confession. He will make that to the blind doctor (Archbishop Wauchop of Armagh)* . . . The doctor . . . like the rest of the papal party, remained in Worms.[23]

Ortiz and his party rode south, stopping for fifteen days in Spires. There Peter Favre found himself in much demand in

---

*Cromer, Archbishop of Armagh, and his successor, George Dowdall, having gone over to Henry VIII, the Pope appointed Robert Wauchop, a Scottish scholar and controversialist who later played an active part at the Council of Trent, to the See of St Patrick. Appointed in 1539 Wauchop could never enter Ireland, much less take possession of his ancient, primatial See. He was instrumental in having the Jesuits, Salmeron and Broet, sent to Ireland as papal nuncios in 1542 on a mission partly diplomatic, partly exploratory, and partly 'a gesture of sympathy . . . to a people faithful, but beleagured.'

high places. The bishop invited him to a dinner at which his fellow guests included the Duke of Bavaria, the Archbishop of Treves and the Bishop of Worms. He was plied with questions about the Society of Jesus; 'to which I replied at length, telling them about us and our way of life.' As in Worms prelates and priests came to him for confession. At Spires he also met two Dominicans from Salamanca; one of them had been in Salamanca when Ignatius had fallen foul of the Inquisition there. This Dominican, in 1541 Caesar's confessor, 'spoke very highly of Iñigo'.

In Spires also was a man Peter Favre had last seen in La Roche almost twenty years before when the scholars left their books to cheer him and his lady—Charles III of Savoy. By 1541 Charles the Unfortunate was a Duke without a duchy, his nephew the French king having taken the western half while his brother-in-law the Emperor appropriated the Italian half of his mountain realm. The unhappy Duke had lost more than his little country. One by one, eight of his nine children died in infancy. In 1538 the plague had claimed his duchess, the haughty Beatrix who had been the cause of his downfall but whom he had devotedly loved. One of his chroniclers describes him as he was when Peter Favre met him in the first weeks of 1541: 'Overwhelmed by so many and such great calamities, insulted and despoiled by his relatives and friends as well as by his enemies, he found life a weary burden. Besides, he suffered continually from the slow fevers that were to finally bring about his death.' Peter Favre reported promptly to Ignatius on his meeting, the first of many, with 'my prince':

Two days ago (23 January) I went with Dr Ortiz to salute the Duke of Savoy, prince of my native land. I told him about our Company and he asked me many things about it. He wanted to know did I travel about preaching, for he wished to help me financially should I go to Savoy. I replied, in the hearing of the many who were present, that I had no need of temporal goods but that I would be pleased to work for the good of souls. On hearing this he again offered to help me all he could.

I make no mention of the kindly way in which he received me, or of his affability, so that you may not attribute that either to his fall from greatness or to my own love for my prince . . .

We thought we could leave sooner but the Emperor's gout is holding us up, so we will be here for another five days. When I heard of the delay I began straightaway to give the Exercises to the Vicar General here, a man of sound judgment, a man of letters. The Bishop of Spires is also beginning them and will continue them in Ratisbon . . . Yesterday the son of the Duke of Medinaceli became my son in God and we talked for a long time about spiritual matters.[24]

The imperial gout delayed them nine days instead of five, and Favre did not waste the extra time. Finally they left for Ratisbon on 5 February.

Here, as in Worms, I leave spiritual sons who are grieved at my departure. Our Lord knows that if I were free to come and go at will, how tempted I am to remain in these places, seeing so many doors open for our way (the Exercises).[25]

Dr Ortiz, as usual, acted as Favre's publicity agent, rounding up Spanish and Portuguese noblemen, chaplains and captains —among them Peralta, last met with disappearing from the Montaigu in Paris to follow Iñigo de Loyola—to meet him. Peter's gentleness, sincerity and obvious holiness won them all. They came to talk and stayed for confession. Within a day or two they were back again, asking to be given the Exercises. Soldiers, statesmen, courtiers, clerics, all felt the attraction of holiness. Those who rode out with Ortiz when he left for Ratisbon were glad to see Peter Favre riding with them. But Peter did not speak much on the way. In his private journal he recorded that ride:

In the month of January 1541 we left for Ratisbon where the imperial diet was to be held. O my soul, what great graces of prayer and contemplation you received on that journey! All along the way you were shown new methods of praying and new subjects for prayer. Thus, in arriving at a place, in seeing new places or hearing what others said of them, you learned to ask our Lord for the grace that the Archangel of those domains and the guardian angels of the inhabitants might be propitious to us. Better still, you were moved to ask that Jesus Christ, true shepherd and guardian dwelling in the churches we passed, might aid us, granting us especially that which we needed most or would profit us most, and that he would take special care of dying sinners, the souls of the dead, and those who were in desolation or suffering or enduring some trial.

I also prayed for the prosperity of those we met, or begged pardon for their sins, or thanked God for all he had granted them, if, spiritually speaking, they were unenlightened and did not recognize that worldly goods are a blessing, and that they should remember the hand that gave them. I commended my petitions to the patron saints of these parts, and asked them to accomplish whatever the inhabitants neglect through ignorance, begging them to implore pardon for the people, to thank God in their stead and to obtain for them all that they need.

That same year at Ratisbon, I received other graces. In the first place our Lord allowed me to accomplish great things in his service, particularly in confessing many gentlemen in the Emperor's court or at the court of my prince, the Duke of Savoy, who chose me as his confessor.[26]

Lost in prayer, he hardly noticed when they entered Ratisbon, 'the treasure chest of the Empire', on 23 February. Ahead of them was the Duke of Bavaria with 400 horsemen. The emperor with all his court had already come. Over the hangman's bridge, across the bridge where the salt tax was paid, and the bridge where a toll of sausages was demanded clattered other parties: the Duke of Saxony; landgraves and princes and princelings come from all parts on Caesar's invitation, some hoping that their presence would bring them future wealth or power, others fearing to remain away lest their absence be noted and counted against them. If he had not been so absorbed praying for all and sundry Peter Favre might have noticed something vaguely familiar when they came within sight of Ratisbon. South of the city was a monastery built on the traditional Carthusian plan, its surroundings, cloister and roofs reminiscent of Reposoir and Vauvert. Its religious needed no reform, the sons of St Bruno having kept their original fervour intact through five centuries. Out of hearing of the noise and bustle, the arguments and dissensions that increased hourly within the three-mile wall that enclosed Ratisbon, the white monks prayed in solitude, silence and peace.

Soon after their arrival Lent began and Dr Ortiz, having discovered his own eloquence, could not be kept out of the pulpit. Disdaining to give a trial sermon to any humbler congregation the good doctor harangued Caesar and his entire court twice daily, 'making them quake.' Peter, who had a poor opinion of his own efforts at preaching, was happy to find his time completely occupied in 'hearing confessions, giving the Exercises, and holding spiritual conversations.' He tried to give an hour and a half to each, though how he found time to eat or sleep, considering the numbers who came to him for counsel, remains a mystery.

Letters between Germany and Rome frequently vanished in transit. Ignatius wished to be kept informed on the progress of the Diet so, to ensure that letters reached him, Favre had to make a few copies of each and entrust them to different messengers. This duplication took time already eaten up by the throngs of penitents and meant that Peter had to write at top speed and with a fine disregard for punctuation. He sprinkled letters written in not very good Spanish with Latin words and phrases, a habit Ignatius found most disconcerting. When called to order Favre replied:

I remember how you reproved me recently because I fling Latin around in my letters. I needed your correction. However, it is not so easy for me to amend my ways. I have to write so fast that words and sentences of the Romance languages elude me, so all my letters are ambiguous, badly put, and full of Latin phrases and words. If you can put up with this failing of mine, forgive me. If you find it intolerable I will try to marshal my thoughts better beforehand and write so as not to confuse the reader. I will also try to be more careful about punctuation in the more important letters.[27]

We do not know why Favre wrote these letters in Spanish, probably out of courtesy to Ignatius and the many Spaniards in their house in Rome. The language he wrote best was French, but only one sample of his French style remains—a letter to his Carthusian uncle, the Prior of Reposoir. Georges Guitton sees in its rhythmic, graceful French an affinity with the style of that other Savoyard, St Francis de Sales. Peter had a better command of Latin than of Spanish or Italian and used it throughout his *Memorial*, the private record of his own spiritual odyssey which he certainly would have destroyed had not death come upon him unexpectedly. He spoke Spanish and Portuguese fluently, thanks to his years in the Ste-Barbe where Spaniards and Portuguese students predominated. At Ratisbon the long queues of grandees, soldiers and statesmen from south of the Pyrenees at his confessional proved that he understood his Iberian penitents perfectly, and they him.

Those who suggested that Peter Favre meet and speak with Philip Melanchthon at Worms did not repeat the suggestion at Ratisbon. The Wittenberg theologian was there representing his master, the Elector John Frederick of Saxony, 'the stoutest man in Europe'. Although other Protestant princes had accepted Caesar's invitation to the Ratisbon Diet, John Frederick, Luther's protector and staunch supporter for over twenty years, refused to attend a meeting where 'the idolatrous and murderous Catholics' were to be present. Knowing that Philip had shown conciliatory tendencies in previous talks the Elector ordered his theologian to be absolutely inflexible at the 1541 meeting.

The talks were doomed from the start. The Venetian Ambassador, a shrewd observer, was one of the first to see how the political winds were blowing. He wrote to Venice: 'The German princes favour Lutheranism, not because they are zealous for that creed but because the religious issue serves to draw to their side others who dread the two Hapsburg brothers (Charles V and King Ferdinand). The position is that almost all the German princes oppose the House of Austria.' What Venice realized from the start was not clear to Rome until later. Cardinal Contarini, always ready to see the best side of men and things, did not appreciate the part politics was playing in the Diet until some months had passed. Then he reported to Rome that 'Caesar's enemies in Germany and elsewhere are so afraid that he may unite Germany and become still more powerful that they are sowing tares among the theologians; the Elector of Saxony and the French King find means to block agreement on every article.' The Duke of Bavaria and other Catholic princes found fault with the Emperor for not declaring war on the Lutherans. Their appeals to Caesar to bring his powerful armies to their aid and 'eradicate the Lutherans with the sword' were, in most cases, aimed at continuing or re-opening old feuds. His Imperial Majesty replied that he had no wish to set Christian against Christian; as he saw things, his duty was to fight the Grand Turk, edging daily nearer to Vienna. 'Besides,' he added, 'it is useless to make war on the Lutherans; even if they were defeated they would not change their opinions.'

For Peter Favre the six months spent in Ratisbon were months of unceasing work, his concern being the reform of individual Catholics. If he had ten Jesuits, he tells Ignatius, that would not be enough to cope with all who wanted to do the Exercises. Ortiz affirmed this but thought that a hundred, not ten, would be more like the number needed. Ortiz and blind Archbishop Wauchop also helped to give the Exercises. Cochlaeus made them himself and then gave them to several Germans whose language Favre did not speak. At Easter two Hebrews and two Moors were baptized. One of the latter was Juan of Granada, a son of Boabdil, the last Moorish king of Granada who had surrendered his city exactly fifty years before to Ferdinand and Isabella. In the early stages of Prince Juan's instruction Ortiz, who knew Arabic, helped. The Moorish prince, after his Baptism, became one of Favre's *hijos mios* and greatly edified his father-in-God by his extraordinary fervour and his desire for frequent Communion.

Easter Sunday fell on 17 April, and during Holy Week droves of Spaniards came to make their Easter duty. Many of them asked to be allowed to do the Exercises. 'It is Holy Week but every week is a holy week for me,' wrote Favre to Ignatius. He followed the advice Ignatius had given about adapting the Exercises to the circumstances, the free time, the gifts and limitations of each Exercitant. Not many of those who came to him in Worms, Ratisbon or other German cities could spare thirty days; a few like the Duke of Savoy and Juan of Granada spent several days in retreat; most had to be content with one day or two or three. Peter usually took his retreatants individually; as his time was completely taken up with these callers it was only in the few minutes' conversation before and after the spiritual sessions that he learned from them how things were going at the meetings.

When the inter-faith negotiations began Master Favre was highly optimistic. He writes to Rome, listing the disputants chosen by the Emperor to debate the religious questions: Melanchthon and Bucer—both humanists and thought to be in favour of conciliation—with Pistorius for the Lutherans; for the Catholics two humanists, Gropper and Pflug, also Johann Eck, rigorous, forceful and impetuous, whom Contarini was already imploring to be 'less contentious'. A few weeks later Favre discloses, in a report on the marathon sermons Ortiz is preaching, that things are not going well.

The doctor preached twice yesterday and today gave an oration on death at the funeral of a Spanish *caballero*. He seems bent on getting his revenge for not winning over any unbelievers by fervently exhorting the Catholics to live up to the teachings of our faith.[28]

By May Favre's optimism is noticeably waning. In a letter to some Jesuit students whom Ignatius has sent to the Ste-Barbe Peter says some wise words on higher studies and the spiritual life. He adds:

Remember that learning of itself will not convert anyone. The world is now come to such a pass that the only arguments needed are sweat and blood (bodily austerities). Unless we intercede in this way errors will simply continue to increase. Words and reasons are no longer sufficient to convince heretics, in Ratisbon or anywhere else. Remember me to Caceres, Miona, your Rector de Gouvea, and other old friends in Ste-Barbe.[29]

In June Favre names for Ignatius some of the Spaniards and Portuguese who visit him regularly for confession or direction. He mentions an abbot so well and truly converted that he has renounced the 12,000 ducats a year income his benefices bring him. He also mentions one of the Duke of Najera's family who had soldiered with Ignatius and who demanded full particulars of his old comrade's conversation and subsequent career. Despite the prevailing gloom at Ratisbon Peter was happy to report 'Not one of all my spiritual sons has turned back or lost fervour.'

Midsummer saw hopes of agreement vanishing. What some

prelates who had never approved of the meetings at Worms and Ratisbon foresaw was happening: defections from the Catholic to the Lutheran camp, but none in the opposite direction. The defections were attributed to the massing of so many able Protestant divines in one city. But it had to be admitted also that the Lutheran leaders were far ahead of the Catholics as propagandists and publicists. Too late, the Catholic theologians who wrote treatises in Latin for perusal by theologians on the other side realized what the Lutherans had known all along—the importance of simply-worded, direct, forceful pamphlets, written in the vernacular and aimed not at the learned but at Everyman.

The Catholic theologians relied too little on scriptural argument and too much on the Fathers and ecclesiastical authors . . . They showed themselves credulous, notably on historical matters. Even the most critical of them utilised apocryphal documents of the first centuries, documents the authenticity of which the Protestants contested. They were too ready to believe every legend about Luther and to label him as a drunkard, a liar and a demoniac. Many Catholic theologians expressed doubts about their opponents' good faith, criticized their private lives and adopted a violent, often a haughty tone. To them the innovators appeared as guilty men, traitors who should be punished. They doubted, not without reason perhaps, the usefulness of the Catholic-Lutheran meetings. It must not be forgotten, however, that the Protestants proved themselves intransigent, to say the least of it. And, following Luther's lead, they excelled in invective and insult.[30]

John Calvin, for some time exiled from Geneva, came to the fore at Ratisbon where he, with Bucer, represented Strasbourg. During the half year he spent in the imperial city he became close friends with Melanchthon and helped to widen the religious split by writing and circulating a broadsheet warning the Germans of 'the bloodthirsty Roman tyranny and the empurpled, godless company.' Another writer referred to two of the Catholic spokesmen as 'the cunning Pflug and that besotted quibbler, the bellowing Eck'. Cardinal Contarini, who had come to Ratisbon with hopes as high as Peter Favre's, was sadly reporting to Rome in June, 'My soul is in anguish at seeing things moving fast on the road to ruin.' A few weeks later the Diet collapsed completely on questions concerning the sacraments, Transubstantiation and the authority of the Pope.

On 30 July news came that the Grand Turk had taken Buda, defeating Caesar's brother, King Ferdinand. For a century and a half to come the Hungarian capital was to remain under the rule of the Crescent. 'In Rome the news aroused such alarm that it seemed to many as if the infidel were already at the gates of the city; not less was the consternation in the territories of the Hapsburgs. In Vienna the thought of a second siege filled men with terror.'[31] The Emperor prepared to leave Ratisbon for Lucca where he was to confer with the Pope. From thence he intended to go to the Mediterranean where he hoped, by attacking the Ottoman ports in Africa, to divert Suliman from the Danube and to repeat the great naval victory he had won at Tunis six years before.

While the Emperor was riding south John Calvin was travelling north, having been invited by Geneva to return and restore order among the Reform churches there. He was to remain in that city for the remainder of his life. Peter Favre had left Ratisbon at the end of July with Ortiz who, when the Ratisbon meeting broke down, was free to resume the journey to Spain, postponed because of the order to proceed to the meetings with the Lutherans. In Peter's wallet was a little book of devotions ascribed to St Gertrude he had bought in Ratisbon, also a copy of his solemn vows which he had pronounced on the feast of the Visitation 1541.

Following the Upper Danube, then the Aar, the ambassador and his suite rode through Bavaria and the Swiss cantons. Finally they came to Savoy. Leaving the main party to rest in Annecy or some nearby town, Ortiz, Favre and a Spanish priest named Diego Caballar, set out on foot for the Grand-Bornand, Peter Favre's native valley.

5   Beyond the Pyrenees

THE road to the Grand-Bornand winds from the northern
shore of Lake Annecy through the mountains and along the
Fier valley to the waterfall of Morette.* On an August morning
in 1541 Marius d'Arenthon, *seigneur* of Alex, was riding over
his estates when he met three strangers. Though barefoot, they
were obviously men of some distinction. One was richly dressed,
his two companions were priests—one undoubtedly a Savoyard.
The men of Savoy had physical traits that distinguished them
from the non-Celtic races surrounding them, traits they were
not ashamed to proclaim in the *patois* of their valleys:

> *Grous pis, grousses mans, grousses faces,*
> *N'sins Savoyards!*
> *Na vrita raça d'homme bin fottus!*

> *Big feet, big hands, big faces,*
> *Savoyards are we!*
> *A true race of well-built men!*[1]

d'Arenthon invited the strangers to his château where they
remained three nights. A daughter of the house, Guillelmine,
heard them conversing with her father. 'Peter Favre answered
many questions about the Company of Jesus and their way of
life and told my father of the persecutions in Germany.' Fifty-
five years later Guillelmine, amazed that no one was making
any move to recognize the sanctity 'of that man so great and
holy, the honour of our country, Peter Favre', insisted that

*Here 105 maquisards killed in action in World War II sleep in peace. They
fell holding back an entire German division supported by air and artillery fire.
Their cemetery with its rows of crosses is sited in a clearing near the river gorge.
Only the sound of rushing waters and the murmur of leaves break the silence. The
waterfall, flashing from a great height, salutes unceasingly those who died in this
modern Thermopylae.

her priest son interrogate Favre's relatives and others who remembered meeting him. She herself gave evidence, evidence confirmed eleven years later before no less a person than the Bishop of Geneva, better known now as St Francis de Sales.

She had been present when Peter said Mass in the château. With others she had pried on him through a slit in a door and saw him so absorbed in prayer that he seemed kneeling on air, a foot above the ground. She recalled how little he ate and told of the groom who had been ill for more than a year but who recovered after Favre had prayed over him. She described Peter as 'wonderfully attractive, humble, grave, eloquent and very learned.' Others used the same adjective, 'attractive', adding that he was 'well built, blond haired, open, saintly looking, a very good man.'[2]

From Alex they proceeded to Villaret, rounding the bridge now utilised as a vantage point for spectators gathered to cheer the Tour de France cyclists. The young folk were on the high Alps tending the livestock. If Peter felt any emotion on hearing the choruses he himself had sung as a child, if his heart lifted when the roofs of Villaret, the Grand-Bornand plateau and the scenery familiar to his childhood came in sight, he kept it to himself. His sole reference to his last visit home is one line in the *Memorial*: 'We journeyed through my native land.' In 1596 and again in 1607 others came forward to record their memories of Peter's stay in Villaret.

He visited all his relatives, 'including his Aunt Jeanne, who lived in the house farthest up on Chenaillon. She had been a complete invalid for eight months and the Father was filled with compassion for her as she was the mother of a numerous and very young family. He offered Mass for her, prayed over her, and a few days afterwards she was cured. He preached in the church where he had been baptized, St-Jean-de-Sixt, and in the church of Grand-Bornand which was larger. He was very devoted to our Lady and exhorted us to say the rosary, teaching us to meditate on the mysteries. He encouraged us to wear our rosary beads on our belts as a way of professing our Catholic faith openly. All the people around considered Peter of Villaret a saint. When he was going to preach, the news would spread like wildfire and everyone would stop work at once and hurry to the church to hear him. He had a great devotion to the holy angels and would greet not only people he met but also their guardian angels.'[3]

Among the relatives to be visited were his first cousin, Dom Claude Périssin, and other members of the Carthusian community at Reposoir. His uncle, Prior Mamert Favre, had long since gone to his reward. Since Favre's last visit home in 1534, the year of his ordination, the Order had given hostages to heaven in the persons of the monks of the London Charterhouse who could not, 'for reasons of conscience, not out of malice', acknowledge Henry VIII as Supreme Head of the Church in England. The first to withstand, unwaveringly and as a united group, the royal will, they were punished barbarously as an example of what awaited others who might follow their lead. Four were hung, drawn and quartered at Tyburn; the others, less fortunate, were immobilized, starved and left literally to rot alive.* Ortiz, one of the defence for Catherine of Aragon when Henry's demand for a divorce was being pleaded at Rome, was in constant correspondence with London at the time of the Carthusians' death and would have a harrowing tale to tell their brethren in Reposoir.

Two witnesses at the 1596 enquiry stated that Favre's brother, *petit*-Louis, complained of his poverty when Peter visited him in 1541. It was natural that this small farmer, forever engaged in a struggle with the mountains and the snows, should feel envious of his brother, a brother who was educated, cultured, travelled, accustomed to feeling at ease in the company of men like Ortiz, the Spanish *hidalgo* whose fine clothes were the talk of the Grand-Bornand and whose walk and bearing proclaimed him as a man of rank and substance. According to the first witness Favre's reply was: 'You long for wealth and cannot find it. I long for poverty and the incon-

---

*Ten who remained obdurate were sent to Newgate where, as one of Henry's clerics said, they were 'despatched by the hand of God.': that is to say, they were tied to posts, like the others in the Tower . . . standing bolt upright, tied with iron collars fast by the necks to the posts of the prison and great fetters fast rived on their legs with heavy iron bolts; so straitly tied that they could neither lie nor sit, nor otherwise ease themselves, but stand upright, and they were never loosed for any natural necessity. Chambers, R. W. *Thomas More*. (London 1935 and 1963) pp. 313, 316, 1963 ed.

veniences it brings and I cannot find it.' The second witness quotes the reply differently: 'I have never sought anything but poverty and so far I have not found it; perhaps if you do not seek wealth you may find it.' The only son of *petit*-Louis, another Peter Favre, became the local notary. This Peter never married and in his old age was reduced to great poverty, so much so that the Jesuits in Rome wrote to him several times inviting him to spend the rest of his days in one of their Piedmont colleges. Piedmont was the Savoy territory on the Italian side of the Alps and by that time Savoy was once more a sovereign state.[4]

Savoyards, then as still, were very legal-minded and Peter, whose father had died since his previous visit, would no doubt as the eldest son and heir be asked to renounce his claim on the little farm in favour of *petit*-Louis, next in line to inherit. The document drawn up to meet the situation would have been detailed, unambiguous, and all contingencies would have been foreseen and provided for. In the archives of Chambery and Annecy many wills of that time may be read.*

Ortiz insisted that his companions call him *Frère*. This puzzled the Grand-Bornand people who concluded that the Spaniard was either a layman awaiting admission to the

---

*One Pierre Grosjean, a farmer of Cusy, 'sick, but well in spirit,' declares 'I do not wish to risk my eternal salvation by dying intestate, so I remit my soul to God my Creator and rule that my body is to be interred honourably in the graveyard of my parish church. Thirteen priests are to officiate at my obsequies, each to receive twelve *deniers,* and all of them, also seven extra clerics, are to be dined well afterwards. I leave a small legacy of wheat to Cusy church, and some money to my neighbour, Mme. ——, a sick woman. For seven years after my death an anniversary Mass (with ceremonial he describes minutely) is to be offered for my soul's repose.

My wife, Jeanette, is to live with my three children. (Foreseeing the day when a daughter-in-law will come in he makes alternative arrangements for his wife. If Jeanette wishes to live elsewhere she is to have so much wheat, so much wine, the milk of whichever cow she chooses, lodging and firewood; also a patch of land to let or till as she wishes).

I consider my eldest son, Jacquemet, a man unfit to succeed me as owner of the farm. He has run up debts which I paid. He abandoned learning for a village smithy, I paying all the costs, but which costs my heirs are not to claim from him. Jacquement is to have two fields, some meadows, the two cows and furniture I have already given him; because of this legacy he is to be content and hold his tongue about being disinherited.

The remainder of the will consists of detailed instructions as to how the other two sons, the 'universal heirs', are to have the property divided between them and the right of succession should one or both die childless.[5]

Society of Jesus or a man who had entered late in life and was doing his novitiate on the journey from Germany to Spain. However, they could not reconcile either hypothesis with his rich clothing; neither could they reconcile his rich clothing with his bare feet. For long after his departure he remained— an enigma—in their memory. After a six-day stay in Villaret the trio resumed their journey, the local people accompanying them as far as Thônes. There Peter saw the little school where he had first begun to satisfy his desire for learning. He preached in the parish church. Though pressed to remain he did not delay; when the priests and people assembled to bid the travellers God-speed knelt and asked his blessing, Peter of Villaret complied, made his farewells, and left for Spain.

One would have expected them to turn south but instead they went north-west, possibly to see the magnificent new church at Brou with its stained glass, carved stalls, rood-screen and the tombs of princes and princesses of the Houses of Austria and Savoy. It was an unfortunate detour for they fell into the hands of the French garrison at Nantua. Ortiz, fond of the sound of his own voice but forgetful of his Spanish appearance and accent, was a natural suspect. All three were thrown into prison where they remained for a week. Recounting the adventure in his *Memorial* Peter thanks God who caused them to be freed without having to pay ransom and who gave them the grace to become friends with their captors and help them spiritually. Even the officer in charge went to confession, to Favre himself.

On their release they proceeded down the Rhône, then west through Nîmes, Montpelier, Béziers and Narbonne. Finally they crossed the Spanish frontier and made their way to Montserrat near Barcelona, the shrine at which Iñigo de Loyola had finally relinquished his dreams of worldly fame, laid his sword and insignia at our Lady's feet, and emerged a nameless pilgrim ready to wander the world seeking God. Favre wrote a lengthy letter to Ignatius from Montserrat describing their adventures on the way. Like so many other letters it got lost in transit. To his diary he confided the emotions he felt on entering Spain, then the richest and most powerful country in the known world.

As I entered Spain I felt great devotion towards the Principalities, the Archangels, the Guardian angels and saints of that country and was inspired to pray to them. Some saints attracted me more than others—St Narcissus at Gerona, St Eulalia at Barcelona, Our Lady at her shrines in Montserrat and Pilar (Saragossa), St James, St Isidore, St Ildefonse, the martyrs Justus and Pastor, our Lady of Guadalupe and St Engracia of Saragossa. I asked them to prosper my journey in Spain and by their prayers make me bear good fruit there.[6]

From Montserrat they rode by slow stages, via Saragossa, Medinaceli and Alcalá, to Madrid, and all along the way Peter Favre, the man who sought poverty, found himself welcomed as the friend of Ortiz, the friend of Ignatius, in the castles of the great:

I truly believe that the persecutions Iñigo suffered in these places have merited for us the goodness and bounty we receive. Where he laboured hardest, there we find the most rest.[7]

At Alcalá Peter met Beatrix Ramirez, 'now quite down and out. She is too dispirited to persevere in her works of charity, looking after prostitutes etc.; she has gone into the hospital of St John, not to serve the poor but to have some ease and be attended for her own infirmities.' Beatrix was the *beata* who gave evidence for Ignatius when he fell foul of the Inquisition at Alcalá in 1527. Another witness on that occasion, the garrulous widow Benavente, had remarried. All wished to be remembered to Ignatius.

On the road outside Alcalá the party met the churchman who later became famous as Cardinal de Quiroga of Toledo. He insisted that they turn back to Alcalá and lodge with him that night; he talked with Peter Favre asking him about the Society; 'on parting from me he said that he wished I could spend some days with him, that he was ready to go with me to prison or to death.'[8]

At the various halting places Favre was surprised to meet not only men who had been his fellow students in Paris but also nobles and captains who had become 'my spiritual sons' in Worms and other imperial towns the previous winter and spring. In a letter to Ignatius he regrets that Ortiz would not allow him to visit the father of Lainez whose home was less than twenty miles from Medinaceli: 'And I longed very much to visit him, more so than to visit my own countryside'.

Ortiz had his own reasons for hurrying Peter along. Like so many clerics of that time he, though a doctor of theology, was not an ordained priest. Nevertheless he enjoyed the revenues of a benefice some leagues north west of Madrid. More conscientious than other absentee pastors he paid 'an honourable vicar, a licentiate in arts and theology', to look after the spiritual needs of the people of his parish—Galapagar. Since his retreat under the guidance of Ignatius at Monte Cassino and subsequent 'conversion of life' Ortiz had become more aware of his pastoral obligations; so it was to be expected that on his return to Spain he would make up leeway in this regard. He fetched Favre to this *pueblo* in the foothills of the Sierra Guadarrama, confident of good results. The doctor, having given three of his famous sermons in two days, departed for Madrid, leaving his friend to spend November and December in Galapagar.

Peter's letters to Rome during November followed the usual pattern:

We must return from here to Madrid and from there go on to visit the Doctor's brother, Fray Francisco at Torrelaguna. (This was the Franciscan friar convicted by the Inquisition of having publicly defended a *beata* suspected of illuminism. He was sentenced to life confinement in the Torrelaguna friary of his Order.) We are also invited to visit the Count of Cifuentes, who is in charge of the Infantas. After that we have to go to Toledo and perhaps to Salamanca, not knowing how long we will be in any of these places. So our peregrinations, begun on July 27 last in Ratisbon, are long drawn out. We may be more than two months more here. At least it cannot be said henceforth that the Society and its aims will be unknown in Spain. With all this, I must admit that I am as far away as ever from winning fame as a preacher; so, in spite of the favour I enjoy in God's sight and in that of our betters and of all conscientious Catholics, there is no danger as yet of my rising in my own estimation.[9]

Every afternoon Peter rang the bell in the parish church, rousing the Galapagar people from their *siesta*. A hundred youngsters would hurry to his catechism class to learn the commandments; on feast days double that number came. The children's enthusiasm for the catechist was infectious and their elders began to attend the classes; for them he expanded and explained more fully points of doctrine. Local priests joined the throng and soon found themselves doing the Exercises. Peter was asked to preach in neighbouring parishes. He agreed to do so, 'knowing that no priest will lose the esteem of his people because of my preaching.'

Meanwhile Ortiz was doing the rounds of his Castilian friends. He had become the precursor of Favre, going before his friend to prepare the way:

Favre was attached to the household of Ortiz, not a very accommodating man and probably a man not easy to live with. Nevertheless he never dreamt of questioning his decisions. 'Ortiz came to tell me that I should remain at Galapagar for thirty or forty days.' So Favre stays. It is through Ortiz he will receive in 1545 an order from Ignatius summoning him to the Council of Trent. His writing on the meetings and colloquies in Germany, his distrust of mystical illusions, his scrupulous orthodoxy, bear the mark of the fiery Spaniard. On the other hand, he was the one who spurred his companion onward in the spiritual life: he helped him to improve as a preacher, he defined his spiritual values, he pacified the other's rich nature, giving it greater depth. And Ortiz, the young cock of yesteryear, the one time power-seeker, becoming docile, alters his position, turning towards men to preach the word of salvation—in his own way, of course, 'making his hearers quake'. He became the propagator of the Exercises, introducing the Jesuit everywhere among the wide circle of his friends and acquaintances. He is the first visitor, sometimes making a noisy entrance. Favre is the second visitor, entering into the hearts his friend has unlocked for him. It was a curious association, that of this corpulent, generous Spaniard and the sensitive, refined Savoyard. The one with a passion for violence, the other all for persuasion. On their journeys they call one another *Brother* and that they are—a living symbol of all the friendships that spring from a shared zeal in the same apostolate.[10]

Peter Favre, working for God in Galapagar during the

winter of 1541–1542 did not forget the outside world. On the feast of St Elizabeth of Hungary, 19 November, his thoughts went to those in whose hands lay the destinies of many:

The Pope, the Emperor, the King of France, the King of England, Luther, the Grand Turk, Bucer and Philip Melanchthon are eight persons for whom I mean to pray much, regardless of their failings. My soul is saddened thinking how harshly these men are so often judged and the Holy Spirit moved me to compassion for them.[11]

If the Grand Turk could have heard of this resolution he would surely have laughed in his beard. Some weeks previously he captured, by a combination of cunning and force, the Hungarian capital; it was to fly the Crescent flag for the next 145 years. All Hungary, Hapsburg territory, was now in Suliman's hands. Rome was in a tumult, anticipating the arrival of infidel armies to besiege the city. Vienna, the Austrian imperial capital, was terrified. A sigh of relief went up from both cities when the Sultan returned to Constantinople on hearing that the Emperor was about to attack Algiers. But the imperial expedition ended in utter disaster; a tempest of wind and rain favoured Islam and foiled the besiegers who were routed with heavy losses of men, galleys, artillery, tents and provisions. Caesar disembarked in Spain on 3 December, refusing to listen to Hernán Cortés, the conqueror of Mexico, who wanted to turn back, the storm having abated, and resume the siege.

Paul III, first on Favre's list of men to be prayed for, was at this time making tentative arrangements for a General Council. It was no easy task to prevent powerful rulers from interfering and posing as 'protectors' of the assembly. Draft plans for convoking the Council were prepared by Contarini, dates and venues were suggested and a reform programme outlined. The Pope nominated Cardinal Morone as Nuncio to Germany with a special mandate to reform the Catholic Church in that country; the Nuncio's assistants were also appointed: Archbishop Wauchop of Armagh and three Jesuits, Favre, Bobadilla and Jay. Other matters also claimed the Pontiff's attention; during 1541 his 'nephew', the ferocious Pier Luigi Farnese, had broken the power of the Colonnas and ended the brief but bloody Salt War. The punitive measures adopted by Paul III against the Colonnas, his former vassals, after their defeat were so harsh that the Emperor pleaded for leniency. His plea went unheard.

The King of England, another on Favre's list, had just turned fifty and was on the look out for yet another wife. In the preceding five years England had had five queens. Catherine of Aragon had died in 1536; her supplanter Anne Boleyn went to the scaffold a few months later; Jane Seymour died in childbirth; Anne of Cleves, 'the Flanders mare', was repudiated, and Catherine Howard suffered the same fate as Anne Boleyn. Henry VIII would never allow anyone to accuse him of heresy; he clung fast to his title *Defender of the Faith*; he also claimed to be the Supreme and only head of the Church in England. In defence of these claims he made martyrs, burning at the stake Protestants who denied the Real Presence, and hanging, drawing and quartering Catholics who refused to recognize him as their spiritual head. A foreign visitor to London exclaimed, 'Merciful God! In this city they do extraordinary things. Papists are hung on one side of the street while on the opposite side anti-papists are burned!'

Francis I, three years Henry's junior, had his own matrimonial troubles which he solved in a more adroit and civilized manner. A royal mistress could be rewarded and raised to high station in France without casting off or executing one's queen. Francis was also more subtle than Henry in the political arena, managing his nobles, his ministers, his parliament, his churchmen, his heretics with wariness and skill. He excelled at playing off his adversaries against one another, and made wars, truces, alliances now with Caesar, now with the Pope, now with the Sultan, trimming his sails to the prevailing political winds. In the last weeks of 1541, when Peter Favre was resolving to pray for him, Francis heard of the rout of the Emperor's army and fleet at Algiers. The news gave him an excuse to hold the truce he and Charles had signed in 1537 as null and void and to renew his former alliance with the Grand Turk.

Luther, Bucer and Melanchthon, also included in Favre's prayers, had cause to bless the Turk, since the Ottoman menace diverted the attention of the Church and the Emperor at a time of crisis in the Reformers' camp. During the 1530's Protestantism had expanded and as it expanded, splinter groups began to break away. Leaders and princes saw a better future for themselves in a disunited Christendom and led their peoples in the 'stampede from orthodoxy.' Luther, who had initiated the Reform, saw moral reform further away in 1541 than in 1521 and angrily castigated his followers, the women as 'profligate sows', the students as a worthless lot, the peasants and merchants as a 'pack of drunkards, addicted to every known vice', the town of Wittenberg as a 'Sodom and Gomorrah' deserving of heaven's direst punishments. The spectacle of the rapidly multiplying sects dismayed him. 'How many different leaders will men have a century hence?' he asked Melanchthon, 'What will the confusion be like then? Will anyone be found to submit to government by the ideas or authority of another? Every man will then want to be his own Rabbi'.

A papal letter ordering Favre 'under holy obedience' to leave Spain at once and accompany Morone to Germany was received by him in January 1542. He had previously received instructions from Ortiz to leave Galapagar for Ocaña to visit the Infantas. The letter caught up with him there.[12]

Since the death of his beloved wife, Isabella of Portugal, in 1539 the Emperor, though often absent from Spain for long periods, issued strict instructions as to how his children were to be brought up. The dead Empress's friend, Doña Leonor Mascarhenas, had been the royal governess and, following Isabella's death superintended the education of the Infantas, Maria and Juana of Austria, at Ocaña. The future Philip II resided in a separate establishment at Madrid, 'being separated from the Infantas by the Emperor's orders, not because the prince showed any dislike or coldness towards his sisters, but to conform with Spanish court custom and etiquette, and the impossibility of accommodating the households of all three in one palace, and also for reasons of morality, as His Imperial Highness did not wish his daughters to grow up in the company of court gallants or his son among court ladies and maids in waiting.'[13]

When Favre first met the Infantas Maria was thirteen and
Juana six. Maria suffered from a recurring skin ailment,
described by the doctors as 'a humour of the blood which
begins with a multitude of pimples and ends with the skin
peeling to such an extent that it resembles the rind of roast
pork'. Juana, destined to become the only female Jesuit and an
embarrassment to Ignatius in his later years, was healthy.
Favre remained three days in Ocaña. His visit could have
coincided with the Emperor's, for after his return from Algiers
Charles had collected his son in Madrid and brought him with
him to celebrate Christmas in Ocaña.

The Count of Cifuentes, Major-domo to the Infantas, and
the great ladies of the household listened to the Jesuit preacher
who had such a poor opinion of his own pulpit efforts; the
Infanta Maria was in bed ill, but young Juana was present.
Afterwards Cifuentes and others went to Confession. Doña
Leonor Mascarhenas, who had befriended Iñigo in 1527 and
again in 1535, had long talks with Peter about their mutual
friend. Favre was asked to leave some written notes on the
spiritual counsels he had given in his sermon. The Infanta
Maria sent him a letter regretting that she was unable to see
him and requesting him to offer three Masses for her mother's
soul. He would have remembered that the dead Empress was
sister to the Duchess of Savoy, the high and mighty Beatrix
who died in 1538.

When Peter Favre left Ocaña the Infantas sent their two
chaplains, Juan of Aragon and Alvaro Alfonso, to accompany
him as far as Toledo. Pedro Ortiz was at Toledo and there the
two said farewell, 'not without a *grandissimo* sorrow in our
hearts'. The impetuous Ortiz sent a letter to Rome at once,
protesting at Favre's recall, just when he was beginning to
reap such a spiritual harvest in Spain, and when there were
hopes of establishing a Jesuit house there.

The Papal Nuncio to Spain, following instructions from
Rome, sent a mule to Peter and told him to proceed to
Barcelona and from there to Spires where Morone would
assign his duties. This time, Ortiz not being on hand to forbid
him, Peter made the detour to visit the parents and sisters of
Diego Lainez. At a town further north he was overtaken by

8

the two chaplains from Ocaña. They had been so taken by Favre that while he visited Ortiz and the Lainez family they had returned to the Infantas and asked and obtained permission to leave the court and follow him.

Although surrounded by distractions and constantly on the move Favre did not lose his spirit of prayer and interior recollection:

About that time (early 1542) I adopted a devotion which our Lord suggested to me to help me to recite my Office. It consists of the recitation of this aspiration taken from the Gospels, *Heavenly Father, give me the good spirit,* between every two psalms. I offer it asking to be renewed in spirit and I find that by saying this short prayer often and in different needs one experiences very good effects.

Another devotion suggested to me I use as a prelude to each of the seven hours of the breviary to help me to concentrate on intentions we should specially pray for. I say *Jesus, Mary,* ten times at the beginning of each hour of the breviary. That reminds me of the following ten intentions: 1. The honour of God our Lord. 2. The glory of the saints. 3. That men of good will may make progress on the good road they have taken. 4. That those in mortal sin may get the grace, through the Office I recite, to cease from sin and return to God. 5. The increase of the Catholic faith. 6. Universal peace between Christian kings and princes. 7. All who are now suffering bodily pain or illness. 8. All who are now suffering distress and sorrow of mind. 9. All who are now at the point of death. 10. All who suffer in Purgatory that they may obtain, through the Office I recite, some ease and relief.[14]

The chaplains brought letters from Ocaña. One, from the Count of Cifuentes, asked that a Jesuit foundation be made in Spain and expressed the hope that Favre would come back as its superior. The other, from Doña Leonor, ended:

How readily I would follow you and Iñigo on the road of perfection you have chosen, were I a man. But I am only a woman, a sinful one who makes no progress in virtue, so I may not join you in meditating and speaking on holy things, much less on matters concerning the Society of Jesus.[15]

At Barcelona the three priests were hospitably received by the Viceroy of Catalonia, the Marques of Lombay, and his wife. As a widower the Marques would become a Jesuit; he is known to posterity as St Francis Borgia. Like so many others this nobleman was immediately attracted to Favre and 'opened his heart and soul' to him. Isabel Roser, a widow, and others who had been friends of Ignatius in the difficult year following his conversion, came to meet and greet Peter Favre. Fourteen years had passed since Iñigo had bidden them farewell before leaving for Paris. They had known him since his conversion, almost twenty years before, and their alms, prayers and encouragement had followed him ever since then. Of all these benefactors Isabel Roser was the most generous. Isabel told Favre that she and her friend, Isabel José, were planning to go to Rome and live as religious under Iñigo's direction. Isabel José was a blue-stocking; 'a Latin scholar and well versed in the philosophy of Scotus Erigena, she had once been invited to preach in Barcelona cathedral.' Later, in Rome, this learned lady was to lecture in the presence of the Pope and Cardinals.[16] One senses some uneasiness in Peter's next letter to Ignatius:

In a conversation with the lady Isabel Roser she told me that she and other ladies would have a sum of money collected by Easter for the rebuilding of Pietro Codazzos's church.* . . . She said she was awaiting an answer from Master Iñigo, to be brought her by a Father coming here, to know his decision about her future way of life. She says that she is ready, if Master Iñigo agrees, to go to Rome, there to serve God better, and without any hindrance. She says she will bring with her 1800 ducats, to be used according to directions. Doña Isabel José is also in a state of great agitation, wanting to leave Barcelona and go to Rome. I do not know what will come of this matter.[17]

Peter might well wonder. What did happen was very embarrassing for the Jesuit community in Rome. Though repeated letters from the good lady they called their sister-in-God elicited no encouragement or invitation from Ignatius, Isabel Roser and her maid and the other Isabel set off, arriving in Rome towards the end of 1543. Their arrival on the doorstep

---

*Pietro Codazzo, a Roman priest, impressed by the charity and goodness of the early Jesuits, paid their rent and eventually placed his church, Our Lady of the Wayside, at their disposal. Later he entered the Society.

of the Jesuit house seems to have stunned Ignatius who threw up his hands and cried, 'God bless me, Isabel Roser. You here! Who brought you?' 'God and you, Father' was the reply. A difficult time followed for the Founder. Finding him disinclined to regard them as a female branch of the Society, or to take on their spiritual direction, the ladies went over his head to the Pope and obtained a rescript permitting them to make solemn vows under obedience to the Jesuit General and making him responsible for their spiritual guidance.

At first they were amenable and helped on his good works, especially those charities the management of which is best left to women. Then they began to make impossible demands on their director's time and patience. The sorely tried man confided to a friend, 'These ladies and their souls give me more trouble than the entire Society'. Isabel Roser, accustomed all her life to wealth and independence, was getting on in years. Highly strung and more used to ordering than obeying, her ideas of the religious vows were not those of Ignatius. Finally the Founder asked Paul III to dispense him from the office of spiritual director of the group, now four in number. The Pope granted the dispensation but when Ignatius wrote to tell Isabel of the 'eminently prudent judgment, decision and wish of His Holiness' he brought a storm of wrath upon himself.

Soon Rome was ringing with reports of an impending lawsuit in which the defendants were the recently founded Jesuits, and the plaintiff the woman to whom they owed so much. Isabel's nephew, who had followed her from Barcelona in the hopes of marrying a Roman heiress, was her spokesman when the case was heard. 'The Jesuit Fathers are a dishonest lot. Iñigo, a hypocrite and a thief, wished to steal all my aunt's fortune,' he said. Fashionable Rome packed the court to hear the tearful Isabel tell her tale and list the clothes, some of them second-hand, and altar linen she had given her erstwhile friends. But the Fathers proved that they had had to expend far more money on Doña Roser since her arrival in Rome than she spent on them and the case collapsed. Later she retracted publicly all her accusations and departed for Barcelona, leaving the Fathers older and wiser men. By that time, 1547, Peter Favre was no more, he having arrived in Rome to die just when the Roser affair was approaching its climax. It is pleasant to record that Doña Roser deeply regretted her hastiness and temper and did what she could to make amends. She and Ignatius parted good friends. If anyone grieved more than Isabel over the sorry business it was Iñigo, for he was a warm hearted man and could never forget his benefactors, especially those who helped him in the first years after his conversion and in the anxious early days of the Society. Of these Isabel Roser was one of the most generous. Some eighteen months before his death he wrote to one of the Fathers, 'We have just had word of the death of Doña Roser and we have said the Office for her with affectionate remembrance. *Requiescat in Pace*.'[18]

Leaving Barcelona in early March Peter and his companions were escorted by a Spanish officer to the French frontier. At Perpignan was one Master Lawrence, a Spaniard who had tried his vocation with the Jesuits in Rome but whom Ignatius had advised to leave. Restless, moody, inclined to melancholy, Lawrence had gone to Paris, taken out a doctorate and was now in Perpignan. Peter and Lainez had been his closest friends in Rome and, hearing that the man was in Perpignan, Favre sent him word that he would like to meet him:

He came to the inn where we were and entered, widly excited and with tears in his eyes; then he threw himself on his knees before me begging pardon and refusing to rise until I begged him to do so. I had some trouble getting away from him for he followed us for four leagues, telling, amid sobs, of his life since he left Rome and of his ardent desires to be one of the Society. He besought me to write to you in his name, begging your pardon and asking to be *taken back even as one of your hired servants*. I do believe that before long he will set out for Rome.[19]

In his *Memorial* he thanks God for preserving himself and his companions from the perils that threatened: 'from the brigands in Catalonia, from those who imprisoned us in France, from the soldiers we met on our entry to Switzerland and our passage through Savoy, from the heretics in Germany, from the sicknesses into which those of us who were not feeling well might have fallen. And, most important of all, I thank him for preserving us from temptations that could divide us—from the spirit of disunion.'

What sentiments of love and hope God gave me on that journey towards all heretics . . . He gave me in particular a devotion which I mean to practise to my dying day with faith, hope and charity: i.e. the salvation of the following seven cities: Wittenberg in Saxony; the capital of Sarmatia*, although I do not know the name of that city; Geneva in the Duchy of Savoy; Constantinople in Greece; Antioch, also in Greece; Jerusalem; and Alexandria in Africa. I resolve always to keep them in mind and hope that I or some other Jesuit may one day be enabled to say Mass in each one of these cities.[20]

Peter knew just where the Church was menaced most: Wittenberg, the Lutheran capital; Moscow or Kiev, capital of the new orthodox empire; Geneva, the Calvinist capital; the lost capital of Byzantium, now—with the ancient Christian patriarchates, Jerusalem, Antioch and Alexandria—under Moslem rule.

The geography of Favre's prayer is the geography of the Church's spiritual conflict; it refers directly to the frontiers of the faith. His thought is more with the Near East than with the Far East . . . Perhaps that is because of the contacts between Savoy and the Near East.† But Favre had lived in Paris where the Moslem problem was then all the vogue; in the list of geographical works published in French at that time more than two thirds dealt with the Holy Land and the Turkish empire. Peter had been educated at the Ste-Barbe, a college where there was a passion for geography. Finally, he was the friend of William Postel who, unlike the other group who followed Ignatius, succeeded in reaching the Near East in 1535.[21]

In Dauphiny, near the town of Valence, a French courier with an escort stopped them, emptied their satchels and saddle-bags and asked to see all their documents; he took the letters for inspection by his superior officers, promising that they would be left to be collected at Lyons. While waiting for

*An ancient name for Russia and Poland.
†After the marriage of one of its medieval Dukes, Louis, to Anne of Lusignan, princess of a famous crusading family who ruled Cyprus, Savoy became a link between the West and the Near East through the many Cypriots who visited the Duchess in her new home.

his documents Peter wrote to Ignatius, telling him how things were going. The only place where he had preached on the journey was Serrières, near Tournon. From Lyons they turned towards his native Alps again and passed through Savoy. Although they passed within eighteen miles of Villaret he did not go there.

On my way from Lyons to Spires I preached once, in Savoy, and in a locality where sermons were badly needed. I was very consoled there. (I did not dare go on to my native place, although we were only six or seven leagues from there). We stayed at Soleure on Holy Thursday and Good Friday (6–7 April) I had two long conversations with Mgr. Beauregard, the French Ambassador . . . We spent Easter in a locality still in the mountains where we said Mass, taking the place of the clergy no longer there. I even sang a High Mass. I could find only one person there whose language was not German; I heard his confession.

Thank God for his mercies towards us on this long journey, and for saving us from many and great dangers: dangers from robbers, dangers from the conflicts of kingdoms at war; dangers from heretics, dangers from the soldiery, dangers from the pest, now raging in the cities; through all these we have come safe and sound, praise be to our Saviour, and are arrived in high Germany.

It is a frightening and sorrowful sight to see so many places, places neither small nor insignificant, where the people have no priest to say Mass for them. There are other localities served by one priest, localities where many and good priests are needed.[22]

He goes on to lament the neglected condition of the churches, particularly the altars, altar linens and sacred vessels, and says that if zealous workers for religion came to Germany and saw what he saw 'they might be moved to still greater distress at the state of those spiritual altars, the souls of men where God should have his dwelling place. Indeed, they would witness such sights here that nothing else in Germany would surprise them save the fact that there are not more Lutherans.'[23]

One wonders what the French officers made of the papers they took for inspection. Francis I and the Emperor were again at war and all travellers were suspect, particularly Spaniards like the two chaplains accompanying Peter Favre. Favre's baggage was neither heavy nor incriminating. He travelled light, carrying only his breviary, letters for Ignatius, Lainez and others, writing materials, a few spiritual notes and a change of linen. He arrived in Spires after nightfall on the Friday of Easter Week. The previous day, 14 April 1542, was his thirty-sixth birthday.

6 Return to a Church in Crisis

MORONE, the Nuncio to whom Favre had been appointed assistant, was an outstanding prelate. Born in Milan, he was three years Peter's junior, irreproachable in his manner of life, conscientious, prudent and far-seeing. He began his diplomatic career in his twentieth year when Clement VII sent him on an important mission to France. Paul III appointed him to the thorny post of Nuncio to Germany in 1536.

A keen observer and cool-headed judge of men, he sent concise and clear reports of the dangerous situation to Rome, even at times when he had good reason to fear that what he had to say would be unpalatable to the Sovereign Pontiff. The despatches of this nuncio, not yet thirty, whose personality is modestly kept in the background, while they fascinate by reason of their contents and the agreeable style in which they are written, often astonish the reader by their accurate grasp of events and the maturity of their judgments. Paul III understood the value of such a diplomatic talent and in July 1539 Morone had to return to Germany as Nuncio.[1]

When Morone and six others were nominated Cardinals in early 1542 'the Roman nobility and merchants complained loudly because no rich and important men of rank were raised to the Cardinalate.' At Worms in 1540 this great man had knelt at Favre's feet and numbered himself among Peter's 'spiritual sons'. But when Peter Favre and his two companions arrived at Spires they found that Morone, Wauchop, Bobadilla and Jay had all left the town. Bobadilla had been sent to Vienna 'where the Lutheran preachers were very active, the clergy in need of improvement and the soldiers of chaplains'. Dr Wauchop and Jay were in Ratisbon, incurring much opposition and being threatened with a ducking in the

Danube.* The Nuncio was visiting other German towns preparatory to returning to Rome to receive the Red Hat.

Peter was rather upset to find that the Nuncio had expected him sooner and had waited in Spires for some days, hoping that he might arrive. His next letters to Ignatius have undertones of self-accusation, as though he had scruples for delaying in Spain to visit Ortiz and the Lainez family, and at Lyons to await the return of the documents the French officer had confiscated at Valence. The Cardinal-elect left a letter telling him that he could either follow Bobadilla to King Ferdinand's court at Vienna or visit the Archbishopric of Mainz 'to see what fruit could be gathered there'. Then, remembering Peter's occupation at Worms and Ratisbon during the winter of 1540–41, he added a postscript, saying that Peter was to consider himself free to do whatever God inspired him to do, until further orders from Ignatius, the Pope or the Nuncio himself.

Uneasy, Favre wrote to Ignatius asking advice: 'For well you know the difference there is between actions prompted by self-will and those done under holy obedience . . . Monsignor (Morone) has left me too much freedom of choice.'[2] Advised to stay in Spires for the time being, he was grateful when a Cathedral Canon he had met in Ratisbon took him to the presbytery and insisted on his remaining there as a guest. Kindness was welcome, and in scarce supply, in Spires. Rumours had been spread that the new-comers were papal spies, sent to report on the morals and orthodoxy of the priests and people of the Rhineland, and the Jesuit, known to be the Nuncio's assistant, was treated with coldness and hostility. At the same time he suffered intense depression over the religious 'state of the nation'. 'Only God knows what I endured in Spires and the despair that overwhelmed me, despair for Germany's spiritual welfare'.[3]

Morone, knowing Favre of old, guessed what he would do if left free to choose his work. The citizens of Spires soon realized that here was no spy but a man of God, disinterested, selfless, wholly intent on serving God and helping others to do

---

*'We told them,' reported Jay, 'that it is as easy to reach heaven by water as by dry land.'

the same. His gentle, attractive nature wore down the barriers of suspicion and within a month many people, especially priests, were coming to him for confession and the Exercises. The two Spanish chaplains also completed the Exercises and had become Jesuit novices, doing their novitiate under Favre's guidance. Ignatius wished novices to be tested in various ways; one test of a candidate was to send him alone and penniless on a distant and arduous pilgrimage. Favre sent Juan of Aragon to visit the shrine of the Three Kings at Cologne and Alvaro Alfonso to Trier to venerate the Holy Shroud.

Juan carried neither scrip nor staff nor bread for his journey and he saluted no man by the way, being totally ignorant of German. Seeing people boarding a Rhine barge, he followed them and found himself seated beside a Lutheran who, noticing his rosary and breviary, began to heckle him in Latin. The novice gave a good account of himself, *ad majorem Dei gloriam*. When the passengers disembarked the boat-owner, a woman, demanded the fare. 'Mosén Juan could not pay,' Favre reports to Ignatius, 'whereupon the boat-woman abused him roundly and insisted on taking his cape in lieu of the money, the Lutheran and the other spectators laughing loudly at his discomfiture. But he spoke to the Lutheran in Latin, explaining that he was penniless and asking him to please beg some alms for him, for love of our Lord. And the poor Lutheran—though half ashamed—had the goodness to interpret the pilgrim's words, collect the alms and give them to the boat-woman. She, hitherto so importunate, was overcome with a holy confusion, would not take one *dinero* and humbly begged Juan's pardon, asking him to pray to God for her. Although he did his best nothing would induce her to accept anything. This completely astounded the Lutheran and the others; they said it was a miracle, for that woman had never been known to refuse money.'[4]

Pilgrims and pilgrimages had fallen into disrepute at this period, and the Reformers ridiculed pilgrimages as they ridiculed other pious practices and good works. It was typical of Ignatius to devise a test that would stress a point of doctrine assailed by the Lutherans and at the same time afford him an opportunity of assessing the courage, faith, humility, resourcefulness and powers of endurance of a candidate serving his apprenticeship to the Society of Jesus. As a psychologist the Founder was centuries ahead of his time. 'The Ignatian pilgrimage was not merely a penitential and devotional journey to some famous shrine . . . It was an apostolic journey . . . a journey which the traveller did on foot, visiting sanctuaries, begging his sustenance, and lodging in hospitals where he served the sick. The pilgrim was an itinerant apostle, a traveller for God.'[5]

When Mosén Juan returned he was sent to the kitchen of the Canons' residence where 'he gave general satisfaction and much edification to those of the household and to people outside'. The other chaplain was then sent on pilgrimage to Trier and Cologne, 'with a safe conduct from St Louis the Confessor, King of France,' not in the shape of a formal document but under the protection of the saint on whose feast, 25 August, he set out. He returned at the end of September and Peter, writing in Italian this time, reported to Ignatius:

M. Alvaro Alfonso, our pilgrim, is back from Trier and Cologne; I cannot describe his experiences to you, so many and varied were they, nor the corporal and spiritual trials that befell him. I will only mention perils from robbers, from wild and fierce forest animals, and from incurring the punishments meted out to spies; dangers from hunger, from thirst, from infected beds, from having to sleep in the open . . . Blessed be the Lord of all, who mortifies and vivifies.[6]

Before they left Spires and during their absence Favre prayed for his two pilgrims. On 19 July and on another date he remembered Juan of Aragon and he thanked God joyfully when 'after Compline on 9 August, the eve of St Lawrence' he saw Juan return. He duly noted the return in the *Memorial* and begged God to reward all who had helped Mosén Juan: 'for the kindness they showed him, in word and deed; for their sympathy with him; for some who were good enough to give him alms; for those who directed him along the way; for others who gave him all the needful information; for those who celebrated his happy return to us . . . and I prayed just as much for people who were harsh or rude to him.'[7] Neither we may be sure was the Lutheran forgotten nor the boat-woman on the Rhine barge. Alvaro, too, was remembered daily by the man who sent him on his hazardous pilgrimage.

With the exception of ten days spent in Mainz, Peter remained at Spires until October. He had the happiness of seeing many people return to the practice of their religion, and the numbers of those approaching the sacraments soared. As usual, he makes no reference, in his letters or his diary, to his surroundings.

Spires, or Speyer, was the seat of the imperial High Courts of Justice, and many of the fine buildings Peter Favre saw may still be seen, the city having escaped the bombs of World War II. The visitor can sit on the stone steps of an immense stone holy water font which, in pre-Renaissance times, marked the limit of the right of sanctuary. A fugitive from imperial or civic justice had only to run past it to be on cathedral ground where he could claim Church protection. Large portions of the city walls and the underground *Judenbad* or Jewish baths still remain, relics of earlier times, and the main street with the tower-gates at one end and the massive Romanesque cathedral at the other has not changed much since Favre's time.

That summer in Spires Peter began to write the spiritual journal entitled *Memorial*. He began it to remind himself of the favours he had received during life and for which he owed God thanks. Its opening pages are strewn with the phrases, *Recall, O my soul,* and *O my soul, remember.* Further on, the journal serves a different purpose. After prayer and meditation Favre would jot down the thoughts that came to him and analyse the effects these thoughts had had upon him, whether they brought consolation, enlightenment and peace of mind or caused him discouragement, sadness and loss of tranquility. Then he applied the Ignatian rules for discerning the source of these thoughts and judged whether they were temptations, autosuggestion, or the promptings of the Holy Spirit. Thus the *Memorial* became for him an instrument for discovering the will of God in his regard, a help to decide—in the light of that discovery—what to undertake and what to relinquish. The entries, made almost daily for over a year, later became intermittent; they map his spiritual ascent. Favre's early and unexpected death revealed what was obviously intended for no eyes but his own. Indeed, it is difficult to read this simple log-book of a heavenly pilgrimage without feeling that one is eavesdropping on the author's dialogue with his own soul, a dialogue too intimate and sacred to admit of any listener but God.

In September the Nuncio, Morone, instructed Peter to visit Mainz where the Cardinal-Archbishop, Albert of Brandenburg,* was concerned about the low spiritual and moral state of his clergy. The Cardinal was then fifty-one. Twenty-five years previously he had accumulated three bishoprics, not without bribery, and in consequence found himself heavy in debt to the Fugger Bank at Augsburg. To clear his debt he invited the Dominican, Tetzel, to preach an indulgence for the souls of the dead, an indulgence that could be gained by monetary contributions. It was this scandalous 'traffic in indulgences' and the sermons given to publicize it that provoked Luther's wrath and precipitated the Reformation. Albert had wavered in his allegiance during the early years of the Reformation and had sent Luther and his bride, Catherine de Bora, a wedding gift of twenty gold pieces, but by 1540 he was insistent in his appeals to Rome for a General Council. He had met Peter Favre at Ratisbon and now wanted 'the Paris theologian' to censor some writings of doubtful orthodoxy.

Before Peter left Spires for Mainz and its Cardinal, another Cardinal, dear to Ignatius, Favre and the early Jesuits, died. Contarini, still busy preparing draft plans for the Council, contracted pneumonia and died at Bologna. His last days were spent under a cloud, his fellow theologians in the Curia having taken strong exception to a pronouncement he made on justification. 'In Rome they regard me as a Lutheran', he wrote to a friend. 'That the peculiar theory of justification which he supported at Ratisbon was not in entire accordance with Catholic teaching was a notion of which he had no

---

*Often confused, even by reputable historians, with his cousin of the same name, the Grand Master of the Teutonic Knights who founded the Hohenzollern dynasty and the Duchy of Prussia. The Grand Master went over to the Lutherans in 1525.

conception. On the contrary he held his view to be perfectly sound and truly Catholic.'[8]

The news of Cardinal Contarini's death was a blow to all working for reform in the Church, but a much worse blow was to come. Two days after the noble Venetian's death Bernardino Ochino, Father General of the Capuchin Order, left the Church and fled first to Calvin and Geneva, then to England and Henry VIII.

Since the days of Savonarola no preacher enjoyed such a reputation. Cities and princes made the most strenuous efforts to secure his services . . . It often happened that he was bidden to different places at one time; then the Pope himself had to take the matter in hand and settle which town was to have the good fortune to receive him within its walls.[9]

Ascetic in appearance, his extraordinary eloquence 'would draw tears from the stones'. He frequently preached before the Cardinals and numbered among his personal friends Paul III, Contarini and the famous Vittoria Colonna. In mid-August on his way to Rome to answer charges of teaching heretical doctrine, Ochino called to Bologna and found Contarini on his death-bed. Proceeding to Florence he met there the Vicar General of the Augustinians. Like Ochino, the Augustinian had been airing views far from orthodox and had been summoned before ecclesiastical authority. The two decided not to obey the summonses and turned their faces towards the north.

The news caused the greatest surprise and the most painful impression; it was a scandal without parallel . . . but their defection, however painful in itself . . . cleared the air. A crisis had come . . . the period of transition, during which elements fundamentally opposed were able to work together, disappeared and with it many momentous obscurities. It became clear that the question no longer turned round particular theological opinions and errors, but centred on the basic principle of obedience to the highest ecclesiastical authority.[10]

Favre remained in Mainz from 15 to 28 September. On his departure the Cardinal offered him a precious vase as a gift; Peter excused himself saying that he was not 'of those who collected silver *objets d'art*, but of those who carried with them good will to all: in that way I escaped having to accept the gift.' But the prelate waylaid him later 'with violence not only of manner and word but also of hand' and stuffed a hundred gold *valerians* into a pouch he wore. Favre sent sixty florins to Jerome Domenech and other Jesuit students who had been expelled from Paris on the outbreak of war and were in Louvain. The remaining forty coins he spent 'on the poor and other good works.'

The impression he made on Albert of Brandenburg was such that, within a few weeks of his return to Spires, he received an order to transfer, with his two novices, the Infantas' chaplains, to Mainz. During his last weeks in Spires his prayer became more intense; when others dishonoured and threw away statues and relics, ridiculed simple devotions like the Sign of the Cross, the Holy Name and the use of holy water, forgot the saints and their feasts, Peter Favre dwelt on these things. His journal for those weeks shows the trend of his thoughts:

29 September (1542)
Feast of St Michael the archangel . . .
In saying the office I desired greatly that the angels might praise the Lord each time we recite these words, words which they understand and experience so much better than we do. I wished, too, that all the saints might do the same, not only the saints whose names we repeat in the prayers and hymns but all the saints.

At the Offertory I wished that the Mass I was celebrating might add to the glory of St Michael and all his heavenly army. If the angels had our bodies how perfectly they would imitate Christ; on the other hand . . . if we had the power and the knowledge of the angels we could praise Christ as we ought. I was glad to think that here below I can work and suffer in the angels' stead, while they can act for me, presenting to the divine Majesty the praises I owe him whom *a thousand thousands serve, while ten thousand times ten thousand stand before him.*

But then I realized that for me it was enough to know, serve, honour, and imitate Christ in as far as in me lies. I reflected on how he lived here below, satisfied with so little, leaving behind him his vicars and representatives—*He who hears you, hears me; and he who despises you, despises me*—leaving to us also his poor, the poor of whom he said: *What you do to one of these, you do unto me.*[11]

On St Jerome's day, 30 September, Peter prayed to St Jerome's angel guardian and decided to pray to the guardian angel of every saint mentioned in the Roman and other calendars. On that day, too, he recalled the great crucifix he had venerated in the church of the Holy Cross in Mainz. The more his enemies and executioners ill-treated Christ, the more freely he shed his blood for them. The more Peter Favre offended his Lord, the more Christ forgave him and poured graces upon him. The more men blasphemed against Christ, his saints and the Church, the more the divine bounty treated men with love and goodness and patience. On the vigil of St Francis, 3 October, Peter prayed not only for all his deceased relatives and friends but for all deceased relatives and friends of his Jesuit brethren. On the feast of St Francis he asked the saint of Assisi 'and every saint in heaven' to remember him, now that they had entered into their kingdom. He took his soul to task on the subject of good works, works done to himself, to his neighbour and to God. Works of penitence to self, works of charity to the neighbour, works of piety to God.

Again and again during those weeks he recalls the great crucifix of Mainz. Its memory roused in him a greater devotion to the Sign of the Cross; he reflects on the power of that Sign against the demons, on holy water and the other sacramentals, 'all sanctified by the word of God, the blessing of the Church and the Sign of the Cross'. He thinks of relics and on the unique atmosphere of holy places, which he himself experienced, always after leaving those places. He repeats, with Jacob, *This place was holy, and I knew it not.* He meditates on the Holy Name and on the name of Mary, 'that very real person, the Virgin Mother of God.'[12]

Only once does a classical allusion find its way into the pages of the *Memorial.* Favre is meditating on the passion and exclaims:

Yours the labour, O my Lord, so that men might find rest; yours the sadness, so that they might have joy; yours the death, which you longed for so that they might have a resurrection. How truly the poet said,

> *Sic vos, non vobis, vellera fertis, oves;*
> *Sic vos, non vobis, mellificatus, apes;*
> *Sic vos, non vobis, nidificatis, aves.*[13]

9

He omitted the second line, *Sic vos, non nobis, fertis aratra, boves,* of a verse attributed to Virgil in which the poet reminds the sheep, the bees, the birds and the oxen that their labours benefit not them but others. Favre had not forgotten the lessons of Peter Velliard, his teacher at La Roche, 'who taught the classics in such a way as to make them seem like the Gospels.'[14]

When leaving for Mainz in November 1542 Peter Favre wrote to a friend, 'It is with a sorrowful heart that we leave Spires; but in spirit we remain there always.' Already he had left Savoy, Paris, Parma, Worms, Ratisbon and several Spanish cities and towns in the path of the past. From Mainz he would visit neighbouring towns and go on to Cologne, Bonn, Antwerp and Louvain, back again to Cologne and Antwerp before sailing for Portugal. A two year itinerary in Portugal and Spain would precede the final journey to Rome. At every stopping place he made friends only to part from them again when the order came to move on. At every departure he felt the same heartbreak. 'The nostalgia he had for Spires extended to every city he visited; the places he left remained in his memory as he continued his way and formed new friendships.'[15]

One of the last entries in his journal mentions the particular temptations for the priest traveller who had to lodge in inns or the houses of seculars:

In these places one may encounter all kinds of men and women. A good remedy against the temptations often met with is to say *Peace to this house* the moment you enter and meet whoever is there. Show that you profess piety and the truth; do this to edify. If questioned, begin to speak of edifying topics. Thus, you at once close the door on impurity. Some religious yield to the diabolic temptation of hiding their calling; people take advantage of this and become all the more daring in making, by word and deed, impure advances. Behave so that none will dare to reveal, either to you or in your presence, the evil Satan may suggest to him.[16]

A Spanish diplomat, describing the German inns of that period, says:

In all the inns there are three or four pretty young chambermaids.

The hostess, her daughters and servants, although—unlike their French counterparts—they do not permit guests to embrace them, nevertheless shake hands courteously and allow themselves to be given a friendly squeeze. They often invite themselves to drink with people who come to the inn; then their manners and language are very free.[17]

Dangers to health were other hazards faced by Favre and his contemporaries on their journeys. Epidemics of pneumonia claimed many victims but the real pest was a form of bubonic plague, transmitted from rats and other rodents to fleas and from them to humans. It was particularly prevalent in Germany and summer was its season. The only effectual antidote was flight from the infected district. A slogan for survival was 'Quick, far, and late', which meant, 'Get out quick; go as far away as possible; put off return until late.' But only the rich and powerful could escape in this way; others tried all kinds of remedies, mostly useless. The habit of throwing sanitary cordons around infected towns and villages spread from Italy to other countries and quarantine was introduced. Peter Favre, though he travelled through many plague-stricken areas, seems to have escaped. The other scourge of Europe in that century, war, he met more than once. It was the age of mercenaries and the passage of an army across a countryside meant loss of crops, looting and burning of homes, and outrage and death for unfortunates unable to escape to the woods or mountains. Though Peter was held up by soldiers at least three times he came to no harm; when imprisoned for a week he calmly continued his apostolate of the confessional, confessing his captors.

The Council of Trent was to open early in 1543 and the Pope sent invitations to prelates far and near; he also wrote to the warring monarchs, Charles V and Francis I, begging them to make peace. The war suited the Lutheran princes, to whom it gave many opportunities of harassing the Emperor. It frightened bishops, many of whom were aged and dreaded having to travel through territory where fighting was in progress. The Most Christian King refused to attend or to allow any French Prelate attend a Council in Trent, a city on the Italian side of the Brenner Pass, an imperial city peopled with German-speaking subjects of Caesar.

Albert of Brandenburg had intended sending one of his suffragan bishops with Peter Favre to Trent that winter, but no one was surprised when news came that the Papal Legates sent from Rome had to postpone the Council, hardly any bishops having arrived at the chosen venue. Favre and his two priest novices began to hear confessions and give the Exercises to the clergy of Mainz. Juan of Aragon gave them to a priest who had been 'living with a girl of seventeen or eighteen, to the great scandal of his parishioners and others.' Mosén Juan got this pastor to amend his ways. The lady was sent away and soon won much sympathy in Mainz. Favre reports to Ignatius:

There has been much murmuring against us. The girl herself, meeting him (the converted priest) one day and complaining because he had sent her away, said: 'Poor you! See how these new friars who have come to Mainz fooled none of our priests, save you alone. Have the others sent their concubines away?'[18]

The Cardinal-Archbishop arranged for Peter to lecture on the Psalms to the theological faculty of Mainz University. The lectures were popular, attracting three times the usual audience. Later he was told to preach on the same theme to the general public. These sermons, in accordance with the custom, were delivered in Latin, a language once the *lingua franca* of Europe, but no longer generally understood. Indeed the rapid success of the Lutheran and Calvinist preachers was attributable, in some measure, to their use of the vernacular and their ability to translate with eloquence and verve the language of scholars and theologians into the everyday speech of sixteenth century man.

During the Christmas vacation the University lectures were suspended and Peter was invited to visit the Cardinal in his palace at Aschaffenburg, two and a half days' journey from Mainz. The great man had a noted collection of relics, which he showed to his guest. Peter, a devout and, it must be confessed, uncritical venerator of relics, was duly impressed. He was also asked to examine some ideas the cardinal had committed to paper on a certain plan of reform:

It is not as edifying as I would wish; the style, for one thing, seems to me to weaken the teaching on approved customs; also, the expected profit all depends on how the thing is carried out. I certainly would not like to put myself in a similar difficult position. But I dare not be the only one to oppose the Cardinal in this business of reform, so desired by all German Catholics . . . especially when we recall that all the German prelates save those of Mainz Archdiocese have more or less gone over to the Protestants . . . as will be seen clearly when the Council commences.[19]

On his return to Mainz in January 1543 Favre resumed where he had left off before Christmas—preaching, lecturing, confessing and giving the Exercises. He induced the Cardinal to open a hospice for pilgrims and needy travellers.   He begged alms for the sick poor, brought them to a house of charity where he visited, tended and consoled them. His reputation as a man of God spread down the Rhine as far as Cologne, a city then threatened with the secession from the Church of its Archbishop, the Prince Elector, Hermann von Wied.

Hermann, who had never mastered Latin or theology, was fonder of riding to the hunt than ministering to the flock of God in Cologne. The Emperor's terse description of him, 'Neither Protestant nor Catholic. So lacking in Latin that he flounders even in the *Confiteor*. Said Mass hardly three times in his whole life,' may have been biassed, since von Wied was a key political figure in the 1540's. An Imperial Elector, if he turned Lutheran the Reformers would have a majority vote whenever the question of Caesar's successor came up. In the early years of the Reformation von Wied was a persecutor of Lutherans but later he became friendly with leading Reformers. By Easter 1543 he had gone so far on his new friends' road that the Pope wrote to him lamenting the course he was taking and imploring him to remember his responsibility before God as pastor of the archdiocese of Cologne. Although the University, the clergy, the Burgomaster and city councillors stood their ground staunchly Cologne seemed destined to go the way of Cleves, Brunswick, Hesse and Saxony.

Meanwhile, Alvaro Alfonso, sent by Favre to study at Cologne University, met there a young Fleming named Peter Canisius. Already a Master of Arts, Canisius was doing the last of a three-year theology course. He was friendly with the Carthusians of Cologne and might have entered that monastery if he had not heard rumours of a 'new Order of priests', rumours that Alvaro confirmed. Canisius heard about Master Favre, a priest of the new Order to whom Alvaro owed his vocation; he heard about the Order of which Alvaro, though already an ordained priest, was a novice. So eager was the young Fleming to meet Favre that he decided to visit Mainz. His friend, Dom Gerard, Prior of the Carthusians, had also heard of Peter Favre; he encouraged Peter Canisius to set off for Mainz and gave him a letter inviting Favre to Cologne.

That Easter Favre rented a small house in a not very reputable quarter of Mainz. His first care was to kneel in every room, every nook and corner of the house and say the prayer that concludes Compline: *Visit, O Lord, we beseech you, this dwelling and banish from it all snares of the enemy. May your holy Angels dwell therein and may they keep us in peace; and let your blessing always remain with us, through Christ our Lord.*

Having said this prayer I invoked the guardian angels of all those living near, which I felt was the right thing to do when one changes one's living quarters. I prayed for all who would stay with me in that house, that they and I might not fall into sin through the temptations of evil spirits, especially the spirit of fornication, for I had been told that prostitution, adultery and debauchery flourish in this district.

I also prayed to St Odile, to St Jodoque, and to St Lucy whose chapel is next door to this house. My soul was sad to see this ruined chapel and the filthy state to which drunken revellers have reduced it. How I wish that I could rebuild it and restore the cult of God and his saints, saints whose feasts are no longer celebrated in their chapel and who are neglected and forgotten in the very place where once people prayed to them and had confidence in their protection.[20]

One of the first who came to stay in the newly rented house was Peter Canisius. His letter of introduction from the Cologne Carthusians was a certain passport to the heart of Favre, so attached to the sons of St Bruno. Soon Canisius was doing the Exercises. On 12 April his director, replying to Dom Gerard in Cologne, wrote:

Just now I have the pleasure of Master Peter's (Canisius) company. Words fail me to say what a pleasure that is. Blessed be God who planted such a tree in his vineyard, and may they who tended and nurtured it be for ever blessed. Well I know that Your Paternity is one of these and that you have helped to make this young man what he is, a youth very different from other youths of his generation. My love for Cologne, a city that knew how to cherish and preserve so pure a soul, has been greatly increased. [21]

On 8 May, his twenty-second birthday, Peter Canisius became a Jesuit novice. He, too, wrote to Cologne:

Favourable, in every sense of the word, was the wind that brought me to Mainz. I found, to my great profit, the man I sought—if he *is* a man and not an angel of God. I have never met a more learned or profound theologian, or a man of such lofty and unique sanctity. His only desire is to cooperate with Christ in the salvation of souls. In public or private conversation, and at table, his every word breathes of God and devotion to God, and that without irking or boring those present. He is so highly esteemed here that a number of religious, bishops and theologians have taken him as their spiritual director . . . Thanks to him and no one else several priests and ecclesiastics have sent away their concubines, renounced worldly ways, broken with vice and are now living holy lives. As for me, I cannot say how completely those Exercises have changed my soul and my opinions, enlightened my mind . . . and revigorated my will. Even my body has benefited, the divine graces received overflowing on to it, so that I feel myself strengthened, transformed, as it were, to a different man. [22]

This first Flemish follower of Ignatius was sent back to Cologne to complete his studies. The enthusiastic account he gave of Favre to the Cologne Carthusians impelled the Prior, Dom Gerard, to write to the Prior of the Trier Chartreuse:

. . . God has not deserted his Church in these dreadful times, but has given her some new apostles, men filled with the Holy Spirit and heavenly virtue . . . Our holy Father, Paul III, has given them approval and sent them to various countries. Their founder is named Ignatius and they are now working in God's vineyards in Rome, Italy, Spain, France and Portugal. One of their theologians (Jay) is in Ingoldstadt, another is in Mainz with the Cardinal.

This last, Master Peter Favre, is a man of great holiness. He gives certain wonderful Exercises to men of good will who come to him for guidance. After a few days spent doing these Exercises they come to a true knowledge of themselves and their sins and obtain the grace of sorrow and complete conversion of heart; turning from created things to God they make progress in virtue, attaining to intimate friendship and union with God. Oh, would that I had some excuse for going to Mainz! Surely it would be worth any man's while to go even to the Indies seeking such a treasure. God grant that before I die I may see this man, His special friend, so that he may direct me to reform my spirit in union with the will of God, this being the goal of our calling.[23]

On 28 May Favre wrote to his Carthusian cousin in Savoy, the Prior of Reposoir. His previous letters to Dom Claude Périssin had not arrived so this one was sent to the Grande Chartreuse in the Dauphiny Alps in the hopes that the monks there would forward it. He mentions that he has made the acquaintance of the Carthusians of Mainz and sometimes retires from his work in the city to spend a few quiet days with them:

All of them are eager to advance in holiness and do me the compliment of listening to me as willingly as their brothers in Reposoir . . . Some days ago the Prior of the Cologne Chartreuse wrote urging me in strong and affectionate terms to visit that city, three days' journey from here. His letter states that Cologne is in dire straits, so I mean to go there provided that the Cardinal of Mainz, expected back soon, agrees.

Already I find in this land of Germany many who are returning to their former faith, to the example and teaching of their fathers. They are beginning to realize that the heresies of today have no other origin than lack of devotion, patience, chastity and charity. So it is up to us to exercise ourselves in these virtues.[24]

He goes on to recommend ways of avoiding distractions during Mass and Office and gives advice on various spiritual matters. He has no news for his cousin 'neither of the Emperor nor the Council, which seems to be further postponed; in any case Carthusians, having chosen the better part, will not be anxious and troubled about such things'. He enquires for the Carthusian nuns of Melan, hopes that they are faithful to their strict rule and that they find joy and contentment in their vocation.

One must renounce, declare war on and vanquish self, a nothing compared to the promised reward and the magnificent exchange received in return. For, in leaving ourselves we gain Almighty God, Father, Son and Holy Spirit. In forsaking this world we gain the kingdom of heaven.[25]

Further letters from Dom Gerard and Peter Canisius urging Peter to come to Cologne were followed by the arrival in Mainz of a special messenger from the resistance leaders—the clergy, university and civic dignitaries who were determined that the Archbishop would not hand his diocese over to the Reformers. The messenger prevailed on Favre to leave Mainz for Cologne.

From the day Peter left for Cologne no entry appears in the *Memorial* for a long while. On his arrival he found himself immediately thrust into the front line of the Cologne resistance, being sent as messenger to the Emperor. Caesar was just then marching at the head of 35,000 men to subdue the Duke of Cleves who was planning, with French help, to annex Guelders. On 17 August Favre went to Bonn where the imperial army was encamped. He presented a letter from the University of Cologne, met and spoke with the minister and confessor of Charles V, both of whom had been his friends at Worms and Ratisbon.

Though no Latinist, the Prince-Bishop of Cologne was an opportunist. Hearing that a complaint had been sent to the Emperor about his introduction of Protestant preachers and forms of worship into his diocese he hastened to Bonn and paid his respects to Caesar. On the following Sunday he celebrated High Mass with full ceremonial in the presence of Charles and his retinue. Peter Favre, a born optimist, was delighted and believed that von Wied had turned over a new leaf. Others had their doubts. So had the Emperor; he asked the Archbishop to dismiss the Lutheran preachers and theologians, to cease publishing his own ideas on reform, and to make no innovations in the liturgy unless instructed by Rome. Von Wied readily promised to do as requested.

Back in Cologne, Favre gave the Exercises and preached in the religious houses of the city. Of the sixty nuns in Saint-Maximin some, unlike their bishop, were good Latin scholars. More and more priests and laymen made their way to Peter's house for confession and guidance. One evening towards the end of September a Jesuit student from Louvain arrived there. He was a sorry sight, having been set upon by bandits, stripped to his doublet, robbed of his food and, because he had nothing else of value, badly beaten up. The young man had come with an order from Ignatius. Master Peter Favre was to take ship for Lisbon.

When news of his impending departure got around, his Cologne friends pressed parting gifts on Peter. It must have been common knowledge that the only gifts he would accept were relics, because the Carthusians, the nuns of Saint-Maximin's and other convents, and the city clergy—all of whom had large collections of relics—presented him with some of their treasures. Alas, few of these relics were authentic, and like the collections in Aschaffenburg drew ridicule instead of reverence from Luther. But Favre was uncritical and was delighted to find himself the possesser of 'seven heads belonging to seven of St Ursula's eleven thousand virgins, and many other relics . . . relics of the Four Crowned Martyrs, of St Catherine and St Suzanne.'[26]

The cult of relics was as flourishing then as in medieval times and Cologne, mainly because of the St Ursula legend, had a superabundance of them. The story of St Ursula's vocation, of her parents' opposition, of her setting off down the Rhine with eleven thousand maidens of Cologne determined to follow her example and dedicate their lives to God, of their ambush and massacre by savage tribes, had its origin in the martyrdom of an Ursula of the fourth century who, with a few companions, had been on their way to found a convent when they were killed by the arrows of bowmen. In 1155 a great number of human skeletons was found near Cologne; immediately the cry went up that the remains of St Ursula and her companions had been discovered. Some king-sized bones and skulls that could not possibly be explained as those of young girl martyrs were accredited to 'King Papunus of Ireland' and other monarchs. No one pointed out that Ireland was still pagan in the fourth century. The business instincts of two monks present when the find was made, and the art of Memling and others who painted St Ursula and her army of virgin martyrs, resulted in the veneration of these relics in Cologne. Later and more critical investigation proved that the discovery was that of a burial place of earlier centuries. Peter Favre, however, lived in an unscientific age, so he went away very happily with his seven heads. As likely as not the relics were those of good Christians who died friends of God and deserved to have their remains venerated.

Within a few days Favre went on to Louvain, not without noting sadly that the Archbishop showed signs of going back on his promises. He made no delay in Louvain, staying but one night with the students and pressing on to Antwerp, from which he was to sail for Portugal. But at Antwerp the port commander told him that he had better return to Louvain and wait until advised of the next sailing, which would not be until after Christmas. Returning to Louvain on St Luke's Day (18 October) Peter immediately fell ill with fevers that kept him in bed until the beginning of December. The students were anxious about him, none more than the priests Jerome Domenech, last met with in Parma, and Emilian Loyola, a nephew of Ignatius.

The Jesuit students were living as guests of a priest who had joined the Society some time before, Cornelius Wischaven. A native of Malines, Wischaven was an exemplary and holy priest, but eccentric. His greatest asset was his fine singing voice, his greatest worry some debts accumulated before he became a follower of Ignatius—and his sister Catherine, his housekeeper, who was anything but pleased at the turn her brother's life had taken. Favre had heard of Cornelius and met him on the night he stayed in Louvain on his way to Antwerp. Disappointed because Peter would not stay longer than one night, Wischaven warned him that he would pray that something, even illness, might keep him in Louvain. When Favre returned and was laid low with fever Cornelius, somewhat conscience stricken, did all he could for his guest. The patient was bled, 'three dishes of very good blood being taken,' but the illness dragged on until Favre summoned his host and told him 'since he had prayed for him to be ill, to now pray for his recovery.' Cornelius prayed and Favre recovered.

Though ill, Peter continued his apostolate; people came to his room for confession and the Exercises; he prepared sermons that a young and eloquent Jesuit, Francis La Strada, delivered; he tested the novices, especially the older novice, Cornelius Wischaven. Well known in Louvain for his virtue and his fine voice Cornelius was in great demand as a preacher and a choir soloist. Favre sent him to sit, an hour-glass in his hand, on the steps of La Strada's pulpit, where all the congregation could see him. Catherine Wischaven was furious. When her brother told her that, in consideration of his vow of poverty and because of the advice of his novice-master, Peter Favre, he intended to resign his parish and sell his goods to pay his debts, the poor woman was reduced to tears, 'saying that it was impossible to have patience with these Spaniards, who were destroying her brother and reducing him to beggary and breaking up the tranquil life she and Cornelius had enjoyed together.' Some merchants came to dinner one evening and one of them asked why it was that the householder, Wischaven, was not seated with the guests but serving at table with some junior novices. Favre replied with the quotation from St Luke's Gospel: *Let the greatest be as the youngest and the master as he who serves.*[27] Impetuous and not very prudent, Cornelius was generous-hearted enough to submit, despite Catherine's protests, to Favre's training programme. His enthusiasm once channelled in the right direction he became a pillar of the Society.

To Peter's illness was added the worry of an order that conflicted with obedience to Ignatius. The papal nuncio to the imperial court, Cardinal Poggio, sent him instructions to return to Germany and continue his apostolate there. Favre wrote to Ignatius explaining his perplexity, 'having received your command before my illness and a contrary one from His Holiness since.' He asked for an immediate decision, which was given, Ignatius bowing to the higher authority. Favre was to return to Cologne for the time being with two novices; Mosén Juan and two others were to take a group of students from Louvain University who were seeking admission to the Society and leave for Lisbon. Father Wischaven, now adept at giving the Exercises, was to remain in Louvain.

The students leaving for Lisbon were given a parting address by Master Favre and a letter for their new superior, none other than Simon Rodriguez, his old companion of the Ste-Barbe and one of the original band of *iniguistas*. He recommended the raw recruits to Master Simon's loving care but pointed out that the eight who had just entered from the University were untried and that their religious formation would need time and attention; above all, they would have to do the Exercises.

They left on 8 January, 1544 and Peter Favre returned to Cologne. Things were going badly there. The Archbishop had changed direction again and invited Bucer, Malanchthon and other Lutheran preachers to the city pulpits. Peter Canisius was at home in Nijmegen, settling up his father's affairs and helping his step-mother, 'than whom no one was ever less a step-mother'. His father, the Burgo-master of Nijmegen, had left considerable property and two young sisters of Peter's and the eight children of the second marriage were comfortably provided for, as was Vrouw Kanis herself and Peter. But when Peter announced that he intended to take his inheritance back to Cologne for the support of his religious brethren and other needy people the widow took a very poor view of his plan. When he returned to Cologne she wrote him a letter, abusing 'that vagabond foreigner, Peter Favre' who had fooled him into parting with what his father had left him. Favre wrote to her:

Very dear and honoured lady in Christ our Lord,

You bewail that Master Peter Canisius, hitherto the most loving of sons to you, is now utterly changed; and this change is due, in your opinion, to no one but myself. I, on the contrary, seeing this fine, this best of youths, joined with me in closest bonds of spiritual love and endeavour . . . cannot but wish him from my heart every kind of good. And so, I feel greatly indebted to all his kindred, not only those dear to him in the faith but those united to him by friendship and ties of blood. Therefore I pray a great deal for the souls of his dead parents, for your consolation and that of your children.

Why then, you will ask me, have you taken Master Peter away
from us, when you must know what a help, what a consolation, what
a counsellor he was to us? O Christian lady, I ask you what would
you do if you saw on one side Christ Jesus taking delight in Peter's
spiritual and intellectual progress, and on the other Peter's family
and friends wanting nothing but the joy of his presence among the
fleeting, uncertain glories of this world? . . . How few care for
Peter's soul, and how many complain because he gives away what
is his by right of inheritance . . . I solemnly assure you that I have
not benefited by one penny of his money . . . As a matter of fact I
do not know what property he has . . . What you say has been
taken from him has, I know, been given by him to charity; and
what is that but restoring to God, the giver of all good gifts, what
is His?

Regarding the reports about myself, too silly to be taken note of
by people like you who fear God and do not speak evil of others:
I plead guilty to the charge that I am an unknown foreigner. That
is true indeed. I and all my companions of our Society are foreigners
and strangers on earth, not only in Germany and Flanders but
everywhere. And a stranger I shall be to the end of my days wherever
God may place me, for my only hope is to be made a servant in the
house of my God and a fellow-citizen of His saints.[28]

Peter Canisius knew that his old friend, Cornelius Wischaven,
had not yet cleared his debts, so portion of the inheritance
went to Cornelius. The remainder went to assist poor students
at the University and to rent a small house where he, with
Favre and other followers of Ignatius, might live and work.
Five in number, they soon became known as men of charity,
zeal and learning. During early 1544 Peter Favre seems to
have concentrated on the University students and city clergy.
A letter written by Peter Canisius at that time reports that
Favre and Bucer met in disputations several times, 'Master
Favre being able to prove to Bucer and other heretics the truth
of the faith he himself professed.' Hermann von Wied was not
at all pleased with the news that the 'new Order' from Rome
was becoming well known in Cologne; reports of the numbers
of clergy and students seen visiting the little house reached
him, as did the rumour that his friend Bucer had been routed
in argument. Something would have to be done.

7 Words No Longer Suffice—

TOWARDS the end of January 1544 Favre received a letter from Cornelius Wischaven, the priest-novice left behind in Louvain. Cornelius was in trouble with the canons of St Peter's church. Since he resigned his benefice he no longer chanted the Mass and offices in St Peter's and the canons plotted ways of getting their golden-voiced cantor back. First they invited him to spend an evening with them; they praised their guest's singing but laid on the flattery so blatantly that Cornelius was not deceived. Then they appealed to him to leave his new friends and return to St Peter's where he was sorely missed. Finally they said that if Master Peter Favre were in Louvain he would surely accede to their request and order Cornelius to resume his chanting. Wischaven retorted, 'Why did you not ask him when he *was* here? However, write now and ask him. I will be glad to abide by his decision.' The canons wrote to Favre, then in Cologne.

Their letter to Peter drew from that usually mild man a sharp reply. He fears that if he refuses their Reverences he will be in their black books, but if he grants their request he will be acting against the Pauline injunction: *Be zealous for the higher gifts*. He admits that Cornelius, by chanting, is rendering service to God, but he is certain that still more service is rendered to God by his present occupation—hearing confessions and giving spiritual counsel. The canons may be right in holding that in all Louvain no one chants so delightfully, as 'our Cornelius', but it would be more difficult to find in all Louvain anyone who gave himself to pastoral work more devotedly and more disinterestedly than the same Cornelius:

I grieve—not because the best singers are sought for the worship of God and because divine worship, thus adorned, will attract the lukewarm to the practice of religion—but it grieves me to the heart to see that what is more important and of most value to souls is not appreciated and cherished by leading churchmen . . . I grieve that our leaders busy themselves with trivialities, that highly gifted men are preoccupied with paltry nothings, that eminently distinguished men are taken up with what is of no consequence. The first and foremost duty of the ministers of the Church is to feed the flock of Christ. Yet no one seems to want to assume this charge except for the advantages it brings. Church positions are evaluated not by the scope they afford for doing good but because of the riches and honours they bring.

. . . The Louvain persons I have in mind could very well find a better singer than our Cornelius if they looked a bit harder and paid a higher fee. I myself know many in Louvain who could work harder than Cornelius for the good of souls. But all can see how those who are the best paid for their pastoral work show the least interest in that office. So, let a man who works for nothing be free to busy himself about higher things. That is my opinion and my answer to your letter about our Cornelius.[1]

These were strong words, extraordinarily strong for Favre. A few days later Cornelius was in further trouble. An aged professor met him in the University and threatened to throw him down the stairs if he entered that seat of learning again; his anger arose from the fact that some of his best students had deserted him and were on the high seas heading for Portugal, lured away, he believed, by Master Cornelius. This time Peter wrote advising Wischaven to simmer down and to turn aside the old man's wrath with mild words: 'Visit him on my behalf. Give him my greetings and best wishes. And oh, my Cornelius, take care, take care never to shut your heart against anyone.'

While Favre was writing these letters the Emperor was at Spires where yet another meeting of Catholic and Protestant leaders was in progress. On his way to Spires he had halted at Cologne and remonstrated with van Wied who had not kept the promises made at Bonn. To show his orthodoxy the Archbishop accompanied Charles to Spires. Despite Peter Favre's labours in that city the Venetian ambassador reported in January 1544:

Spires is wholly Lutheran. Mass is no longer said. There are not many churches in the city and in these few not a painting is to be seen, not even one of our Lord Jesus Christ. The church walls are white-washed and in the centre stands a pulpit from which the Gospel is preached daily and everyone in the town comes to hear. The preacher is paid as if he were an official. He dresses in ordinary clothes and is married. He consecrates the bread and wine and often gives Holy Communion under both species. These preachers, when speaking of Papists—their nickname for Catholics—use very insulting expressions.[2]

When the Emperor came riding in* from the north Spires turned the Catholic side of her coat. Church bells rang out the *Salve Regina* and the Diet opened with High Mass, only one Elector, the Elector of Saxony, daring to absent himself. The discussions, however, were concerned with politics rather than religion, Pope and Church being hardly mentioned. Now that Charles was again at war with France he needed to win the German princes to his side. The papal legate took offence over a point of protocol and relations between Caesar and himself were so cool that Luther could write in March, 'The latest is that the Pope, the French king and the Turk are allied against the Emperor.' A few weeks later the German princes denounced Francis I as 'the common foe of Christendom and the German nation' and promised to prove themselves his enemies 'by word and deed.' The legend that the Most Christian King had sworn to water his horse on the Rhine spread far and wide and ancient Germanic antipathy towards Gaul revived. To keep his German subjects on his side the Emperor made concessions that amazed the Lutherans themselves and caused dismay among the Catholics.

Peter Favre had by this time lost his earlier hopes in Diets

---

*The Emperor travelled with an impressive retinue. His personal bodyguard comprised a hundred German and a hundred Spanish archers. A private chapel, with chaplains, choir and musicians, went everywhere that Caesar went. Doctors and apothecaries with remedies for the gout were always at hand as were horses and Irish wolfhounds for the chase. His kitchens, cook and 'taster' also travelled, although the doctors held that his Flemish appetite for salted and highly seasoned food and fine wines aggravated his gout. His minister, Bishop Granvelle of Arras, spoke six languages, while his trusty Adrian, the great man's valet and private messenger, could neither read nor write.

10

and Colloquies. 'I hear they are to meet again in Ratisbon,' he wrote to his Carthusian friend in 1546, 'but the remedy is not in colloquies, as has been proved more than once.'[3] He had seen how little the dissertations of the Catholic theologians achieved. He had proved the truth of the adage, *Win an argument, lose a convert*, in his own debate with Bucer and had seen it proved again and again in the disputations of Eck, Gropper and others with leading Reformers. He had noted how the Diets and Colloquies gave the Lutherans splendid opportunities for spreading their doctrines by sermon and pamphlet, in the vernacular and in racy language intelligible to all. 'Words no longer suffice. We need to labour and shed our blood,' he wrote to his novices. In 1544 he was fully convinced that moral reform preceded rather than followed the recovery of a faith not dead but sleeping, that reform began with the clergy rather than with the people and with the individual rather than the community. In Favre's opinion what the Church needed most was saints.

Meanwhile, Archbishop von Wied, determined to run the new comers out of Cologne, discovered a loophole in the civic laws. The city had over ninety convents and monasteries all of which were exempt from municipal taxes. To prevent further exemptions a statute had been enacted some years previously prohibiting the foundation of new religious communities. Neither Peter Favre, a stranger, nor Peter Canisius, whose money paid the rent, knew of this regulation until the Cologne authorities, prompted by von Wied, called them to account. Favre was summoned before the city fathers and questioned about himself and his companions, their religious and canonical status. The hearing was adjourned until July 28 by which time Peter had left Cologne and the other Peter, Canisius, appeared in his stead. The Archbishop declared that these 'pests and disciples of Satan' should be hounded out of Cologne. A campaign of defamation followed, the little group being hooted at in the streets and called the 'Black Chestnuts' and 'the Jesuits'. Although the title *Jesuati* was not unknown in Italy the members of the Society of Jesus were first called Jesuits—to ridicule and belittle them—in Cologne. An expulsion order was being prepared when news came that the

Emperor was marching north at the head of 50,000 men. The Duke of Cleves was dealt a crushing blow and Luxemburg recaptured. Then Charles rested before preparing to march on Paris. Von Wied deemed it wiser to expel no Catholic clergy while Caesar was near, so the persecution of Canisius and his friends died down, for the time being.

Favre, carefully carrying the seven heads and other relics, left for Portugal on 12 July. John III had asked the Pope and Ignatius to send Master Peter Favre, so highly spoken of by Simon Rodriguez, to Lisbon. 'Our Cornelius' and his sister Catherine saw the voyager off. A few years later Catherine would become a Carmelite while her brother would go first to Bruges, then to Messina and Rome. Discretion was a virtue Cornelius never acquired. During the ballot for General that followed the death of Ignatius in 1556 he prophesied the election of Nadal, causing considerable embarrassment not only to Nadal himself but to Lainez, the new General. For fear people might suspect a rigged election Lainez held a veritable inquisition among the brethren in Rome, an ordeal for which the holy Cornelius was to blame.[4]

Although his voyage to Lisbon was Favre's first experience of sea travel he is silent about it. Portugal, then immensely wealthy and a premier trading power, had ships constantly plying between her own ports and the principal seaports of all known countries. The merchantman on which Peter sailed must have stopped at several ports between Flanders and Lisbon for the voyage lasted six weeks. Contemporary travellers advised those sailing in European waters to carry lemons, oranges and rose-petals in summer, cloves, rosemary and angelica in winter, to offset the smells aboard ship. There were dangers from pirates, dangers from thieves and thugs in ports of call, dangers from sea-sickness, storms and shipwreck. There were also the delays encountered in discharging or taking on cargo, the hours lost waiting for tides to turn, the days and weeks wasted for want of a favourable wind.

Jesuits had been in Portugal since 1540, Simon Rodriguez having been sent there when King John requested missionaries for his colonies in the east. Francis Xavier followed Rodriguez and the two should have left together for Goa in 1552 but the

king had grown so attached to Simon that he kept him to
educate the royal children. Thus it happened that Xavier set
out alone on the ten-year odyssey that was to end on the lonely
island at the gates of China where death awaited him. King
John approved of Master Simon's dream of building a Jesuit
college at Coimbra; novices could study at the University and
then go on to evangelize Portuguese colonies in India and
places further east. Ignatius sanctioned the project and
students from Rome and Louvain, some of them Favre's
novices, were sent to Coimbra.

Peter made no delay in Lisbon but proceeded to Evora
where the king and Simon Rodriguez awaited him. Extrovert,
sure of himself, an abhorrer of heretics, Simon was the very
antithesis of the retiring, diffident and gentle Peter. They had
been firm friends since their University days in Paris, but the
able and charming Simon was indiscreet, obstinate and somewhat irresponsible and was yet to cause Ignatius and the
brethren serious embarrassments and trials. Peter remained
three months at the court and was seemingly in very indifferent
health during that time. In a letter to Ignatius he laments that
he is 'in a neutral state between action and suffering, having
done nothing worth mentioning nor suffered anything worth
being deemed even a fragment of a cross.' He was also suffering
from an access of timidity and feelings of inadequacy but
whether these arose from his poor health or from forebodings
regarding Master Simon, who seemed more at home at court
than it behoved a follower of Ignatius to be, it is difficult to
know.*

On 3 December he wrote to William Postel, another old
friend of the Ste-Barbe days, an eccentric and brilliant professor of mathematics and oriental languages. Postel longed for
a Utopia, dabbled in mysticism, was on visiting terms with the
rulers of Persia and other faraway lands and managed—when
Ignatius and all his companions failed—to visit the Holy Land
in 1535. He 'would have joined the Carthusians only that their

*It will be remembered that Simon Rodriguez was the nephew of de Gouvea,
principal of the Ste-Barbe. Yet, when King John first asked de Gouvea about
missionaries for his eastern dominions de Gouvea recommended, not his nephew,
but Favre, as 'the principal, with Ignatius, of the Companions'.

rule forbade preaching, and the Minims, only that my wretched indigestion could not stomach their fish diet.' In 1543 Postel walked to Rome, took his vows as a Jesuit novice, the Society appealing to him as 'the providential instrument of a universal religion'. He had been ordained a priest before coming to Rome and he greatly edified Ignatius and the community, all of whom marvelled to see so erudite and travelled a man humbly submitting to the tests for novices. Father Brodrick, who remarks that they should have known better, writes of William Postel:

His trouble was Hamlet's, too much speculation. Marguerite de Valois called him the *merveille du monde*, and that, coming from so unbalanced a lady, ought to have been a warning to the Jesuits. They accepted him into their noviceship in Rome and there, worn out by long travels in the east searching for ancient manuscripts, he began to have grandiose visions, one being of a universal monarchy for the rightful heir of the ages, the King of France, lineal descendant of Japhet, son of Noah. He found no sympathy for his dream among the puzzled fathers, who were mostly Spanish anyhow, so he retired disappointed, but remained on the friendliest terms with them to the day of his death.[5]

Peter Favre could not know that while he was writing to Postel three Fathers in Rome were passing judgment on the edifying William's latest prophecies. They condemned them as 'manifest illusions of the demon, purely human fantasy without the slightest foundation, writings likely to deceive the curious, who are many, and to cause damnation and grave scandal in the Church of God our Lord.'[6] Favre wrote to his old classmate in the bantering tone educated men, old and young, use to the genius whose daft ideas and mannerisms endear him to them. He jokes about Bembisina and Bembitaro, two Arab scholars Postel was forever quoting—Abou-Ibn-Sina the philosopher and physician, and Ben-Beithar the botanist. He quotes Clenard, the Hellenist, another Ste-Barbe man who taught Greek to the Portuguese Infantes until his death in 1539. He presumes that William, now going through the mill of the novitiate, is really learning arithmetic and what it means to be a mere cipher, but he encourages him to go ahead courageously on the Ignatian road.[7] As a matter of fact poor William was told to take another road the following year.

In December Peter went to Coimbra where he got a warm welcome, particularly from those who had left Flanders the previous February. Rodriguez had admitted twenty-three Portuguese with little regard for their suitability and, because of his absences at court, these were receiving inadequate training. Master Simon left all the Coimbra students in charge of Martin Santa Cruz, a young priest who was himself a student and a novice and felt quite unequal to the responsibilities he was commanded to shoulder. He had written to Ignatius drawing attention to irregularities: young men were admitted to profession after a noviceship of only two or three weeks; the Coimbra community numbered sixty, which was in excess of that permitted by the papal Bull, and no dispensation had been obtained for the Portuguese province of the Society to exceed that number.[8]

Favre seems to have sensed that all was not well. In a heart to heart talk Santa Cruz 'disclosed many things, some sinister, some good', so Peter reports to Ignatius; the young man is in a difficult position; when he needs a direction from his superior, Master Simon is several leagues away and cannot be contacted. As far as Favre can judge all is well with the novices, 'but all that seems gold in my eyes, is lead in the eyes of others.'

In January at Coimbra he resumed his journal entries. After a Saturday spent hearing the young Jesuits' confessions he reflects on the duty a confessor has not only to instruct, reprimand, correct and perfect, but also to console and encourage. When hearing confessions one must remember always to be 'a good and faithful servant'. During that first month of 1545 he meditated much on the infancy and boyhood of Christ and the example of obedience he gave in his home in Nazareth. The fruit of these meditations was given to the novices in a talk on obedience. 'The man who withdraws himself from obedience to those God has placed over him also withdraws from and forfeits the grace God was holding out to him through his superiors.'

Melchior Nunes, the first Coimbra student to join the

Society, had a brother Juan, a priest in Braga diocese, who was so strongly drawn to prayer that he spent six hours daily in contemplation. The novice, Melchior, returning from a pilgrimage to the not too distant shrine of Santiago Compostella, visited his brother and tried to persuade him to join the Jesuits. 'But Juan, being enamoured of the peace and calm of contemplation, excused himself on the plea that he was not suited to that kind of active life, though it was indeed an excellent way for those who could follow it.' When the novice returned to Coimbra Juan remained in his quiet retreat. 'Not many nights after, he dreamt that he was serving a Mass celebrated by a strange priest. When he went to the right-hand side, as was customary, to give the *Pax*, the priest made a sign to him to go to the other side. Juan, obstinate, stood his ground; waking up suddenly he realized that for him the *Pax* or peace was not to be found on the right-hand, the contemplative, side but on the left-hand, in that active life where he imagined peace could never be found. The very next day he set out for Coimbra and the moment he met Father Favre he recognized him as the priest of his dream, the celebrant of the Mass.' He told Favre of his dream and was received by him into the Society.

Peter Favre's work was not confined to the Jesuit novices. The students and professors of Coimbra University came to him for confession and the Exercises and he gained for Ignatius and the Society more than twenty future members, some already eminent in their fields of study, some at the start of brilliant careers. Many of these were to work for God in Goa, in the East Indies and in Japan.

Heavy rain storms swept northern Portugal during the second half of January. In Coimbra granaries and wine cellars were flooded and their contents carried away or ruined; dwellings and churches were under water and their foundations damaged. Favre does not dwell on these disasters but they coincide with meditations he was making on the end of the world and the signs that are to precede it. Having prayed that all sorts and conditions of men, his contemporaries and those of future ages, might 'watch and pray and foster in their souls a filial fear of God' he continues:

When the fury of war increases in a city, how the hearts of the citizens throb with fear. When a disastrous famine spreads, bringing desolation to an entire people, how souls are distressed and troubled. Likewise, when earthquakes and epidemics occur, how scared and terror-stricken people become. But men will be still more filled with fear when they see the floods that are to overwhelm the uinverse, when they experience this anguish of mankind, when they hear the roaring of the waves as the oceans rise in tumult, when they see those terrifying phenomena in the heavens.[9]

On 20 January he makes one reference to the floods. 'When thinking of the fine weather, so greatly desired and anxiously prayed for during several days past I prayed the Lord to spare all these unfortunates who have lost their homes and all their belongings in this flood.'

He left Coimbra with two companions towards the end of January and, arriving at Sardoal before midnight on 23 January, wrote at once to Martin Santa Cruz:

We arrived at Sardoal tonight after eleven, each of us with sore feet from causes other than the weather . . . Yesterday we could not hire mules so we travelled with one mule between the three of us; each got his third of the mule by day and by night. Blessed be the Lord who is no respecter of persons . . .

Day is dawning; this is the day of the conversion of St Paul, 24 January 1545.

Your brother in the Lord, Pedro Fabro.[10]

Nine days later he writes to this *carissimo* brother in Christ, telling him that he is in Evora and has given Master Simon a precious relic for Coimbra, 'the head of one of the eleven thousand virgins. I brought it from Cologne.' It is to be treated with the honour due to the remains of the saints and the history of St Ursula and her companions is to be read at table for at least three days.

Court life did not agree as well with Favre as with Rodriguez. On 21 February, the Saturday following Ash Wednesday, he retired after dinner 'to recollect myself and to pray'.

As I finished I suddenly recalled the trials of a certain person who had opened his heart to me. As I reflected on the reverses and trials of all kinds endured by most men for material good, I was stricken to the heart and moved to tears seeing how I myself have never met any opposition during my life. Others, it seemed to me, all meet here below with many difficulties; as for me, I never experience any hostility . . .

That same day, in the evening when leaving the king's palace, I ran into a great assembly of cavaliers, all mounted, ready to receive a general. That grand and magnificent spectacle drew a great crowd of onlookers. Avoiding the crowd and all the hubbub, I slipped into a nearby church. There, a little curiosity tempted me to go out again to see what I had just evaded. When I lifted my eyes and looked at the crucifix the temptation left me . . . I realized that there was the truly comforting and fortifying spectacle: to recall how Almighty God willed to become man and suffer his soul to be separated from his body in the presence of all the people, as he hung between two thieves.

He parted with two more of the treasured heads on 'the day of St Matthias, 24 February', giving one to King John and one to Queen Catalina, the Emperor's sister. The crown prince also received a relic and their Highnesses had Peter place these gifts in a reliquary in the queen's oratory. Favre had received orders to proceed to Spain but had some difficulty in obtaining permission from John III to leave Portugal. Finally he and the Spanish Jesuit, Father Araoz, were allowed to take their departure. Before leaving Evora he sent a farewell note to the novices at Coimbra. After telling them how much he regrets being unable to visit them to say his farewells in person he continues:

And so, my dearest brothers, I write the farewells I would have wished to say. Will this parting be for long? I cannot say . . . but live happily in Christ and serve the Lord with joy. Never separate yourselves from him who is all our strength. Attach yourselves to no one but Jesus who can never be taken away from you . . . Only one thing matters: to fix our hearts on him whom God wishes us to follow, Jesus Christ, the mediator between God and man, he who is all in all.[11]

Letters from Peter Canisius followed Favre to the Peninsula. One told of how Canisius and another Jesuit were visited by members of the Cologne city Council and given eight days to fix up their affairs and depart. 'At every festivity and gathering we are tried and condemned and the most popular songs in Cologne just now are ballads and parodies holding us up to ridicule.' Another mentioned the offers being made to Peter if he would leave 'an institute that cannot last.' He was asked to accept a chair in the University or a canon's stall in the cathedral of St Gereon's. In December 1544 Canisius wrote to tell Favre that a brother novice, Master Lambert, had died and that the others, all but Peter and one companion, had been summoned to Rome by Ignatius.

One who would have defended the young Jesuits in Cologne was absent. Dom Gerard, Prior of the Carthusians, had gone to the Grande Chartreuse for a General Chapter of his Order. He told his fellow-Carthusians about the Society of Jesus, its work and its co-founder, Peter Favre. Other Priors from Italy, Spain and Paris were able to supply further information on Ignatius, Favre and the reform work they had undertaken. The Chapter voted that the Carthusians become co-operators of the Jesuits in their apostolic work by offering for them their Masses, prayers, fasts and other exercises of devotion and that their ancient Order and the Society of Jesus share the merits of the good works of both, 'in this life and the next'. This news must have pleased Favre whose life had been 'sign-posted with Carthusian friendships'.

. . . The two Carthusians, his father's brother and his mother's nephew, were the men who introduced him to the spiritual life, who encouraged his studies and who without doubt, when he left for Paris, put him in touch with the Chartreuse of Vauvert. In the valley of the Grand-Bornand the Priory of Reposoir was both a religious centre and a family home. People went to Reposoir to visit uncles, brothers, cousins who had entered there and to hear them speak of God . . . Their library, burned in 1793, seems to have possessed the contemporary spiritual classics . . . and the good Fathers encouraged their guests to avail of this collection. Was not the 'great desire for purity' voiced by the young Peter, the child who knew the monks in his early years, the echo of their life, a life totally consecrated to *virginity of mind and purity of heart?* The language his Carthusian relatives spoke to the little shepherd boy evoked secret resonances within his soul . . .[12]

In the course of his life Favre reinforced again and again, the links forged in childhood with the monks of the Chartreuse hidden away in the folds of his native Alps. In Paris, Italy, the Rhineland, Spain, some spiritual instinct seemed to draw him towards the ancient Order that never needed reforming. One wonders would he have become a Carthusian had he never met Ignatius—another who was greatly attached to the white monks. Certainly the spirit of contemplation and zeal for the active apostolate seem equally developed in him. The most contemplative of the early Jesuits could have passed for an itinerant Carthusian.

Favre, with Araoz, arrived in Salamanca on 12 March 1545. He was welcomed by two old friends of Paris days, now risen to eminence as university professors, Alfonso de Castro and the Dominican, Francisco de Vitoria. Peter should have made the journey from Evora to Spain the previous autumn, had not illness delayed his departure from Flanders for several months. He was to have accompanied the Infanta Maria of Portugal and her suite from her parents' court to Salamanca and Valladolid for her marriage to Philip of Spain. It was hoped that Maria, daughter of a king so partial to the Society of Jesus, would pave the way for a Jesuit foundation in her bridegroom's country. The young couple could hardly have helped the project financially as Caesar's wars involved huge expenditure and the heir apparent and his sisters were almost destitute. The Infantas and their Major-domo whom Peter had met at Ocaña in 1543 were continually writing begging letters to the Emperor: 'Their Highnesses will go to Madrid if they have enough money to pay for a room and a carriage; also we cannot leave here without paying the servants, already much in arrears . . . We have not a *dinero* and the cost of food and paying our poor servants is considerable; the chambermaid has not received a single *maravedi* this year.' To buy outfits to enable them to attend their brother's wedding the young sisters were about to sell their jewels when the minister Cobos intervened, seeking and obtaining authority to 'raise funds by other means'.[13]

The travellers delayed on the plain of Castile at Medina del Campo, so dear to Isabella the Catholic, the town where that great queen breathed her last. They arrived in Valladolid on 24 March, the eve of the feast of the Annunciation, and Favre made a long entry in his journal. He cheered his soul with several 'annunciations': with the good news of salvation; with the thought of the Father giving the Son to become an instrument of propitiation for man. He reflected at length on the value of correction, especially correction received from superiors. He considers how he ought to correct others; the self-satisfied are resilient enough to benefit by reprimands. 'Act then with the melancholic and phlegmatic in a different manner from that you would use with the choleric and the sanguine. And you yourself, be neither choleric nor sanguine, nor phlegmatic nor melancholic; as has been said, *The wise man is master of his fate.*'

Though he quotes a stoic maxim Favre's reference to a man's stars reflects the contemporary vogue for astrology. All the rulers of the time, even the Pope, had their astrologers to advise on the propitious hour for entering on any transaction of importance, consistories, audiences, journeys and so on.[14]

Prince Philip, heir to all the Spains, and his wife, Maria of Portugal, received Favre and Araoz hospitably and gave them a lodging next the church of Nuestra Señora la Antigua. In his next letters to Ignatius Peter mentions that Pedro Ortiz had paved the way for them; he also appeals for some letters from Ignatius. 'Since last July not a word have I received from Your Reverence . . . We saw the letter you sent to Doctor Ortiz and got a copy of one you sent to the Fathers now in Valencia.' Among those he met at Valladolid was a niece of Ignatius, Catherine de Loyola, who was married to a court secretary. He was very pleased to meet again Poggio, Papal Nuncio to Spain, whom he had known in Germany and the Netherlands. Poggio was one of a group of learned and eminent men who gathered often in the house of Hernán Cortés, the discoverer and conqueror of Mexico, 'now old, ill and disappointed,' trailing his person and household in the train of an itinerant court. They formed an informal academy and discussed the mysteries of nature and religion. One member acted as secretary and recorded these discussions in the form of dialogues.[15] A year before Peter Favre arrived at the court the discussion one evening was on the life of a courtier. One of the academicians, possibly the founder, Cortés himself, said:

At court we eat by weight, drink by measure, sleep without rest, and live with so much leisure, that every dot of time is ticked off by a dot of the clock; yet, though our time is so well measured, our life is so empty that we mistake death for life unlike you (the rustic) whose life is death. At twelve I go to bed and at eight I rise; I transact business till eleven; from eleven to twelve I dine; from twelve to one I pass the time with fools and gossips, or in fruitless talk; from one to three I have my siesta; from three to six I transact business; from six to eight I haunt the court or go walking round the valleys; and from eight to ten I dine and rest; from ten to twelve I am idle and hold conversations, and from twelve on I sleep, as I said, accompanied rather by ambition and greed, or by fear and mischief than by quietness and contentment.[16]

Favre would not have enjoyed this kind of life any more than Cortés. But, as happened in other places, the courtiers came to confession to him. One penitent was Prince Philip's secretary, Gonzalo Pérez, a priest. Some years before this cleric had fathered a son who was to be known to history as Antonio Pérez and to figure with the one-eyed Princess of Eboli and other flamboyant contemporaries in plays, novels and films of later centuries. Perhaps it was after his confession to Peter Favre that Gonzalo removed his son, whom the Emperor had legitimized, from his foster parents and tutored him himself before sending him first to Alcalá University, then to Louvain, Venice, Padua and Salamanca.*

Father Araoz, like Doctor Ortiz, had a good opinion of his own preaching powers. In a letter to Rome he records that on the day before he left Portugal, 'they paid me the compliment of getting me to give five sermons', and he lists for Ignatius all the sermons he gives in Valladolid and the important persons who attend. Favre was content to leave the

---

*Gonzalo, like other clerics in similar case, passed the boy off at court as his nephew. The secretary himself seems to have been a man with a chip on his shoulder who believed himself poorly rewarded for his services. He 'distilled into Antonio's soul his own grudges against the powerful' and could write 'I have a nephew ready for them who will know how to revenge all the snares that have been laid for me.'

preaching and the letter-writing to his companion, who seems to have preached in Spanish, his native tongue. The Nuncio was another penitent of Peter's; he insisted on paying the two Jesuits an allowance of a ducat a week.

Though Favre did not write long letters from Valladolid he made several notes in his journal. The very day they arrived, the eve of the Annunciation, a sermon was being preached in the royal chapel and Peter went to hear it. The porter, not knowing him, refused him admission.

I stood there for a while by the door, reflecting on the many times I had allowed blameworthy suggestions and thoughts to enter my soul. I had left Jesus to stand at the gate and knock, with his words and his Holy Spirit. I meditated on how poorly Christ was received everywhere by this world. And I prayed that we, the porter and myself, would not have too long to wait in the place of purification before the gates of heaven were opened to us. Many other thoughts came to me while I waited and my heart warmed to that porter, the cause of the devotion I experienced.[17]

As he waited there he prayed also for all future Jesuits, 'that any of them who might meet similar or greater refusals would not allow the affront to harm their souls by yielding to pride or impatience'. While Araoz was writing long letters to Rome, full of important names and such items as 'the Prince, Don Philip, ate neither eggs nor fish nor conserves during Holy Week', Peter was noting in his journal his struggles against depression and temptations:

On the Parasceve (Good Friday) I was hearing the confessions of some young people and all the children of one of my spiritual sons when certain proud thoughts troubled me and this question arose within my soul: 'Is this what you came here for, to busy yourself with the young? Would it not be better to be where adults come to you for confession?' But when I resolved, if such were God's will, to devote my life to that kind of pastoral work, which had just been represented to me as contemptible and trivial, I felt an increase of humility. I saw too, clearer than ever before, the value of all done with a right intention, for little children as for all whom the world despises and disdains.[18]

That same day, assisting at the Good Friday liturgy and hearing the choir sing, *Popule meus; quid fecit tibi?* as the congregation went to kiss the crucifix, Peter was overwhelmed: 'I was touched and penetrated on hearing these plaints of Christ: his vine yields him only vinegar and gall: his people reject him and prefer Barrabas . . . and I heard these reproaches as addressed specifically to me.' On Easter Sunday he reflects on Christ's saying, *Because wickedness is multiplied the charity of many will grow cold,* and on the passage from Corinthians, *Charity is patient, charity is kind:*

How few will voluntarily undertake the spiritual works of mercy . . . Even those who direct works of charity do not know how to be kind and patient, how to gain people's confidence and raise their spirits. They cannot bear any inconvenience or suffer with joy the imperfections of others. So too, in church and civil administration, the suppression of abuses is often carried out with irritation born of the wrong kind of zeal, irritation that springs from an icy and bitter zeal for justice, not from the ardour which inspires the zeal that proceeds from charity.[19]

He recalls his own annoyance when a young man who had twice made an appointment for confession failed to turn up on both occasions though Favre waited six hours:

Our Lord, for whose honour I waited for the young man, comforted me thus: You often have to wait hours at the doors of princes and great men, for the service of God; you wait without annoyance; you know well how you will be rewarded. Why then take it ill if someone else, one of My little ones, makes you wait? Will God give you a lesser reward for one rather than the other? And you, how often have you left Me wait at your gate? Yet . . . you do not wish Me to hold it against you . . .[20]

On 16 April Peter presented one of the relics, the heads brought from Cologne, to 'Don Philip, son of Charles, Emperor and King of all the Spains'. He regrets being unable to spare one for Doña Maria, but he has further to go and other friends to remember. On 30 April, feast of St Catherine of Siena, that great lover of the Church, he prayed with all his heart for the success of the Council of Trent. The Nuncio Poggio kept him informed on what was happening north of the Pyrenees. That spring at the Diet of Worms Luther had circulated another pamphlet, the most scurrilous of all his fulminations against the Pope and the projected Council. Calvin, not to be outdone, produced an equally violent anti-papal pamphlet. A peace treaty between the Emperor and the King of France had been signed the previous September but in 1545 Caesar was girding himself for a war with the troublesome German princes. So Peter Favre, awaiting notice to set out for Trent, went on his knees in Valladolid and prayed for all the needs of the Church, 'especially for those sinners who would be easily converted if the men who administer the sacraments and the Word of God were themselves reformed.'

Prayers were needed if ever the Council were to get started. A papal legate travelling incognito through southern Germany that year found Ulm cathedral, 'as white as a mosque inside and as empty as a barber's basin'. In a bookshop he found only Protestant books and ventured to wonder aloud if it were wise 'to leave the old secure path at the bidding of a private individual guided by his own passions'. To which the bookseller retorted that no man needed any guide only Holy Writ and therefore the Council being called by 'Antichrist in Rome' was quite unnecessary.

Peter Canisius wrote from Cologne giving word of the brethren and lamenting on not having received any letter from 'your fatherly hand'. He tells of the wonders 'our Cornelius' is working, exorcising the possessed. Cornelius had written to Canisius from Bruges describing his visit to a matron who had been a demoniac for ten years:

The demon treated her so horribly that no priest or secular doctor, even though implored, dared approach her. He mangled and burned her, often dragging her from her bed and flinging her naked into the fire where he held her for two or three hours. Those present were unable, though they tried their best, to pull her out. With my own eyes I saw her stuff her mouth with the burning coals all around her and chew them. I saw her thrown in the air . . . and taken out of the house by the demon. I saw her swallow a pile of gold rings and more than two thousand bits of twigs . . . also a large iron nail, a glass siphon, a ploughshare . . . a pair of spurs, coins, missiles, a quarter-pound of lead, a dagger and a ten-inch knife . . . I never in my life saw the like. Sometimes she had lucid intervals when she was a model of patience and would go to communion piously—I observed her. Another thing: that demon used to hang her up by the neck; but as he has no power against human life he was unable to strangle her. She used to throw glass objects against a wall without smashing them and once after she lay with her face in the fire she emerged without a burn; neither were her clothes nor her hair singed.[21]

Canisius, reporting to Master Favre, added that though other priests' exorcisms had had no effect Cornelius had cast eight demons out of the woman. Peter wrote to Cologne at once:

Regarding Master Cornelius and his exorcisms: I do not at all approve of this, for I have known many frauds and deceptions in such cases. Let him attend to the ordinary work of a priest, i.e. banishing the devil from men's souls, and let him leave exorcising to the exorcists. Has he not himself experienced the illusions of the demon and that more than once? He has indeed, and not without incurring danger.[22]

While Favre was in Coimbra with Martin Santa Cruz and the student novices, Magdalena de la Cruz was the talk of Spain and Portugal. A Poor Clare of Córdoba, she had passed as a *beata* for thirty years, foretelling the battle of Pavia, Caesar's capture of the French king and other events, and working signs and wonders. So great was her reputation for sanctity that no hands but hers were allowed to sew the christening robes of the Spanish Infantes and Infantas. The Inquisitor General himself visited her to beg her prayers. Then in 1544 she caused a tremendous sensation and scandal when she publicly declared that in 1514 she had made a pact with Satan and that her prophecies, ecstasies and miracles had a most unholy origin. Martin Santa Cruz, the young Rector of Coimbra, had made a detour to visit this supposed *beata* when on his way from Toledo to Italy to join the Society in 1541. One evening in Rome he held the community spellbound with

11

his accounts of the nun of Córdoba. Ignatius reprimanded him sharply, 'saying that no man of the Company should speak in that manner or judge by such exterior signs'. More than likely Favre heard about this from Martin when in Coimbra: hearing of how Ignatius disapproved of that young man's visit to Magdalena would have been an added reason for his order to Cornelius to desist from exorcising.

Everybody was inordinately preoccupied with the devil at that time. Even among Catholics belief in the devil, that very real adversary against whom Christ warned his followers, had assumed inflated and fantastic proportions. It was the age of Faust, of witchcraft and sorcery and spells, of astrologers and horoscopes, of alchemy and auguries, of werewolves and vampires, of griffins' eggs and the Philosopher's Stone. Favre, like his contemporaries, feared demons; he referred to the 'bad spirits in this neighbourhood', to the 'terrors of the night', to 'the contagions of the world the flesh and evil spirits'. But not many of his contemporaries had his unshakeable faith in the protection of *les bons anges*. He knew himself to be surrounded and protected by them; they were to him an invisible, an invulnerable rampart and not only to him but to all the faithful. When he crossed frontiers there marched with him, as surely as if he beheld them, bright legions of Dominions, Principalities and Powers. Meeting travellers on the roads he saluted them and then, in his soul, bowed low in more reverent salute to the guardian angels who accompanied them. This quiet man moved in two worlds, turbulent sixteenth-century Europe with its saints and sinners, and another celestial *milieu* peopled with beings dear to God and kind to men. He felt himself sustained by these unseen helpers in his active apostolate; he felt himself assisted even more by these heavenly adorers of God in his life of prayer. His belief in and devotion to the angels gave him an assurance of being always in the presence of him 'who is our companion on every road.'[23]

During 1545 Claude, Emperor of Ethiopia, sent an ambassador to the King of Portugal. He wanted to have his people 'converted and instructed in the customs and obedience of the Roman Church', and asked that a Patriarchate be set up in his realms and a zealous priest appointed Patriarch. King

John wrote to Ignatius, putting the request to him and pointing out that Peter Favre, 'whose person and virtue are known to me', was the ideal man for Abyssinia. The letter did not reach Rome until after the first day of August 1546, the day Favre's journeyings ended for ever, 'the Lord having called him to Himself.' Ignatius wrote to Portugal offering Father Broët for Ethiopia, but King John would not accept a priest not personally known to him. Ignatius wrote again, 'offering the king the entire Company so that he might choose whoever he thought most suitable for this mission, and adding that, if His Highness judged it necessary, he himself (Ignatius) would leave all and go in search of Prester John'. This letter suggests that Ignatius and his contemporaries believed in the existence of an oriental Christian kingdom governed by the legendary Prester John.

Araoz continued to send highly coloured bulletins to Rome. He reported that people were speaking about them in complimentary terms and that 'our' sermons were making an extremely good impression. Favre was hearing confessions day in day out and 'good Doctor Ortiz is never done telling people about the Society.' In May Favre went to Madrid; on the road he fell in with a *romero* or palmer, an old man who had spent his life making his way from shrine to shrine and from *fiesta* to *fiesta*. Peter instructed him as they walked along. Further on he met a woman who had many troubles and was glad to unload them on to this sympathetic wayfarer. In the inns he 'tried to leave some trace of good and holy conduct; for everywhere there is good to be done; in every place one can plant or reap some good. We are debtors to all men, in every circumstance and in every place.'

Since his arrival in Portugal the previous year poor health, depression, and a constant anxiety lest he waste time, plagued Peter Favre. In Madrid he received copies of letters his old room-mate Francis Xavier had sent from the East. Overjoyed at the missionary achievements of his friend, he felt himself to be doing nothing for God or men. As news trickled to him from all sides of his brethren's undertakings *ad majorem Dei gloriam*, and of the growth of that Society which had once been the dream Iñigo shared with Francis and Peter in the little room at the Ste-Barbe his heart sank within him. Everyone had done something for God. Only he, Peter Favre, was empty-handed, an unprofitable servant.

The Cardinal of Toledo, then in Madrid, invited him to visit the Infantas. Afterwards the great man accompanied him to Galapagar where they were lodged by Doctor Ortiz, then giving the good example of living in and looking after his parish. The Cardinal made them read for him 'every line of the letters from our dearly loved Master Francis Xavier, which pleased His Eminence very much.' At Pentecost Peter returned to Valladolid, saying a *Pater* and *Ave* for every town, *pueblo* and solitary dwelling passed on the way. There was great rejoicing throughout Spain and particularly in Valladolid when on 8 May a son was born to the Emperor's heir, but four days later joy turned to sorrow when Maria of Portugal died. Favre noted both events in his journal and immediately wrote a long letter of condolence to King John. The mourning period over, Don Philip moved, with the court, to Madrid, taking Favre and Araoz along also. By then negotiations to establish a foundation in Castile were well advanced. Some Flemish and Spanish Jesuits from Coimbra and others whom Favre had received in Spain, with some sent from Rome by Ignatius, were to form the nucleus of the new house. In November, when Araoz left for Barcelona, Peter is arranging for a Jesuit foundation at Alcalá with seven men, and sending three others to Valladolid, 'than which city as in no other, not even in Rome, Paris or Parma, have I found so many people so understanding of spiritual things.'[24]

All the time, wherever he is, whether sick or well, he continues his ceaseless and unobtrusive apostolate of the confessional. Again and again he reminds his younger brethren that often a decay in morals preceded the loss of faith and just as often moral rehabilitation led to recovery of faith. He wrote regularly to Canisius, then going through a particularly bad time in Cologne, to Martin Santa Cruz in Coimbra and to Rodriguez, still at King John's court. He thought a lot about Francis Xavier during the autumn of 1545. He does not mention Doctor Ortiz again though he must have met him when he paid a second visit to Toledo, where he remained for ten days, in November. While there he visited the family of

Santa Cruz, to the latter's great joy. When writing to thank Favre, Martin enclosed copies of further letters from Francis Xavier, letters written in Cochin and Malacca the previous January. These letters had such an effect on the Coimbra student-novices, then eighty in number, their Rector reported, that there would be no trouble in transplanting the entire college from Portugal to the East. One novice, son of Portuguese colonists in Goa, had actually spent six months with Xavier in India. The natives there called Francis *Balea Padre*, the Great Father, and revered him more even than their own holy men. He went about his missions on foot, wearing only one wretched *vestecilla* and an old cape far too small for him. The money given him by wealthy Portuguese and Indians went to the destitute and to the building of the forty-five churches he had erected on the coasts of southern India; he himself subsisted on meals as scanty as his wardrobe.

An improvement in Peter's health, and no doubt some propaganda work on the part of Doctor Ortiz, meant that Favre was kept busy giving the Exercises in Toledo where more exercitants flocked to him than in Madrid. In December he returned to the new capital. When the court was transferred there the previous September Doña Leonor Mascarhenas, governess and chief duenna to the Infantas, was appointed to take charge of the infant Don Carlos who was sent to be reared in the household of his young aunts, Maria and Juana. The unpaid servants must have then lost all hope, for their numbers were greatly augmented by 'damsels and servants of the late lamented Doña Maria of Portugal and many persons appointed to the service of the orphaned prince'. There was little hope of money from Caesar who was then preparing for the German campaign. He sent word that the new arrangements for his children displeased him; he feared that Don Philip, the young widower of eighteen, might get involved with one of the many ladies-in-waiting on his visits to the motherless Carlos.

Before the end of 1545 the entire household moved to Alcalá. Cifuentes, the major-domo of the Infantas, had died in the autumn, leaving Favre thirty ducats, a sum which came in useful as it defrayed the expenses of one of the students attending Alcalá University. Doña Leonor, young Maria of Austria and the Condesa Osorio offered to pay a similar sum for other students there. Peter went to Ocaña, to the bereaved family of Cifuentes, for Christmas. In January he went on to Hyepes to join the Nuncio, Poggio. There he received the news that the long hoped for Council had opened at Trent on 13 December 1545.

8   Death on the Way to the Council

PETER FAVRE, one of the theologians nominated by Paul III to the Council of Trent, did not receive his summons to that assembly until spring 1546. The first five sessions would have ended before he reached Rome, his halting place on the way to Trent, and neither he nor anyone else foresaw how the great Council would continue intermittently for all of eighteen years. But every day brought opportunities for the reform Peter strove to bring about, not only in his penitents and 'spiritual sons' but in himself. Early in 1546 he writes to the Coimbra community wishing them a happy New Year and asking their prayers for his own 'conversion':

For I remain this year the same as ever. I find myself as little prompt to suffer or obey or serve as if Christ had never been born. *Christus natus est parvulus mihi et omnibus, deditque sese totum mihi in filium.* But as for me, I do not know what true sonship or service is, nor do I realize that I was born the slave of all. I am aware of this when, as son, servant or slave, I receive a command. The order given me, I find myself questioning the power of authority of my superiors. This is because I am not yet completely re-born to God. Pray for me then, my very dear brothers, so that in time I may be able to give you the good news that *a child is born to us, and a son is given to us,* not only the Christ-child born at Christmas, but the Christ re-born in me.[1]

In another letter written that January he confesses how far he is from perfection and asks prayers that he may improve in his celebration of Mass, in his administration of the sacraments, in his sermons, in his recitation of office, in his own confessions, in recollection, in his conversations with Jesuits and others. 'May we not spend this year as we spent last year and the years previous to that . . . so that we may not see the winter of our lives pass in vain, as did our springtime, our summer and our autumn.'[2]

In mid-February a particularly bad bout of fever confined him to bed but illness did not put a stop to his work for souls. Araoz, arriving back from Valencia on 5 March, reports to Ignatius next day that Master Peter is beginning to get up and move about, 'during his fever he continued to do good, the principal men of the Spanish court visiting him often, for they all love him.'[3] Visitors, however, have to be entertained. Favre reports to Ignatius in a letter of 6 March that the Nuncio now gives fifteen *escudos* a week towards the maintenance of the five Jesuits in the Madrid house. 'If it were not for the constant comings and goings of visitors, and the invalids whom we have always with us, this sum would more than suffice . . . but we are deeply grateful to him.' He begs prayers for Germany, especially Cologne.[4]

In January 1546 a Portuguese novice, Gonçalvez da Câmara, spent some days in the Madrid house of the Society. He had met Favre in 1536 when he arrived in Paris to begin his university course and found the first Companions preparing to leave for Venice where Ignatius awaited them. Gonçalvez was then fifteen, a not unusual age for entrance to university in those days. In the Ste-Barbe he gained some repute as a Latin, Greek and Hebrew scholar; his degree obtained, he returned to Portugal and pursued further studies in Coimbra University. When Peter Favre visited that seat of learning in 1544 da Câmara was one of a group of students and professors who offered themselves as candidates for the Society. In Madrid Gonçalvez met Peter for the third time and recorded his impressions:

While in Madrid I made my confession to Father Favre and had some long conversations with him. He amazed me; I told myself that there could not possibly be found in the entire world a man more filled with God. So much so that, when I heard him speak afterwards of the pre-eminence of Father Ignatius above all the other Jesuits, I had to make an act of faith . . . But when I saw Father Ignatius in Rome and came to know him through talking to him . . .* Father Favre seemed to me only a little child in comparison with our Father . . . Father Favre held that there were three kinds of language: that of words, that of thoughts and that of deeds; he used to say that this last, the language spoken by the good example of our actions, was the most effective and the most easily understood of the three.[5]

Da Câmara also noted that Favre always referred to his old room-mates of the Ste-Barbe as Iñigo and Francis and told the Spanish Jesuits to address one another by their Christian names. This was also the practice of Ignatius who did not wish the brethren in Rome to be called *Father* or *Brother*. In letters and other documents, however, the appellations used were *Father*, *Brother* and *Master*, this latter being usually written *Misser* or *Messer*.

Ignatius wrote to Doctor Ortiz and to Prince Philip on 22 February 1546, requesting that Master Peter Favre be allowed to leave Spain at once and proceed to Trent for the Council. Four days before Ignatius signed those letters in Rome, Luther died at Eisleben, the town of his birth. The Reformer's last publication attacked not the Pope but the Jews whom the German princes were advised to chase from their realms. In his last moments he recited the Latin prayers of the Church

*Da Câmara was appointed minister or Bursar of the Rome house for 1555. His duties kept him constantly in the company of Ignatius, and he decided to play Boswell to the Founder's Johnson, faithfully recording his hero, warts and all. He described in detail the appropriate if sometimes drastic corrections Ignatius gave his men. Gonçalvez had a habit of rushing up to a person and gabbling his news so excitedly that he stammered unintelligibly. He was ordered to tie two tiny bells on his ears. Only a slow, decorous gait and a head held absolutely still could prevent the bells tinkling. A cure was effected in record time. As a trainer puts his most promising athletes through the stiffest tests, so Ignatius reserved his most severe corrections for Jesuits obviously destined to do great things *ad majorem Dei gloriam*. One Father Otello, revered as a saint in Rome and greatly loved by all, received a heavy penance for a pulpit 'bloomer'. He was proceeding to perform his penance, humbly and without complaint, when Ignatius remitted it *in toto*, satisfied that Otello was the very man for an onerous preaching assignment in Sicily. Da Câmara relates that a few days after Otello's departure from Rome Ignatius was saying Mass in a public church. When he came to *mea culpa* in the *Confiteor*, an old dame kneeling behind him shouted aloud, 'You may well say your *mea culpa*, you who have taken Father Otello away from us!' The Founder knew that these incidents were being recorded, but made no attempt to suppress them; indeed the diarist often adds, 'Our Father laughed aloud at this', or, 'Our Father had difficulty in hiding his amusement'.—Tandonnet, R., (ed.) *Mémorial 1555: Louis Gonçalvez da Câmara.* (Paris 1966) pp. 99—100.

of his earlier years and was helped, no doubt, by the prayers of a man unknown to him, a man who prayed for him daily, Peter Favre. Germany gave the dead reformer a magnificent funeral and cities and towns set his statue in their main street or square, usually on the site formerly occupied by a crucifix, a *pièta*, a statue of our Lady or the patron saint of the parish or diocese.

Meanwhile the Council was slowly gathering momentum. The Lutherans had always insisted that it be held at Trent, a city within the borders of the Empire, yet no Protestants attended and at the early sessions the Catholic delegates were indeed few. 'It was twenty years too late and Luther, at the end of his life, had come to reject the very idea of a Council.'[6] We who recall the more than two thousand prelates assembled in Rome on 11 October 1962 for the opening of the Second Vatican Council, not to mention the armies of theologians, authorities on canon law, liturgy and scripture, and the many observers of other faiths who graciously accepted Pope John's invitation to attend, are amazed at the pitifully small number of bishops, less than 8% of the total, who travelled to Trent and were present at the opening sessions of that Council.*

Upon receiving orders to set out for Trent Favre went to Galapagar to bid farewell to Doctor Ortiz. The ambassador who once harangued Caesar and his court so vehemently now spent almost all his time in his country parish looking after his parishioners. He and Peter Favre would not meet again. The fifth of the seven heads was presented to Doña Leonor Mascarhenas; we are not told what became of the remaining two but possibly one was intended for Rome and Ignatius, the other for Francis Xavier whose face was then turned towards

---

*There were then, in one country and another, round about seven hundred bishops. In the first session (of the Council) there were present fifty-one bishops, in the second fifty-eight, in the third fifty-nine and in the fourth sixty-two. And there was the staff of forty-eight theologians and canonists. It is indeed a small assembly . . . Even in general councils bishops will be human, and there *modus operandi* is itself but a natural thing. Certainly at Trent there was all the liberty anyone could desire, but only one real scene where, as the prelates streamed out after a stormy debate, the Bishop of Chioggia took the Bishop of La Cava violently by the beard, and they had to be parted. Next day there were solemn words from the president, and due apologies, and warm embraces between these two brothers from the deepest south the Church then knew.

Hughes, P. *A Popular History of the Reformation* (London 1957) p. 266.

sunrise and Cathay. When Peter left Madrid on 20 April Araoz accompanied him for some miles on the road towards Valencia; then, with sad hearts, they parted. For Favre, whose affectionate nature felt intensely each of the farewells with which his life was studded, it was yet another parting, yet another 'little death'. From Valencia he wrote to Araoz:

When we said farewell the other day and went our different ways I noted how you stood beside the flock of sheep we passed and waited there until I was out of sight. Even though I kept walking on I looked back again and again, very often indeed, until at last I was so distant that you could no longer see me.[7]

At the same time Araoz was writing to a fellow Jesuit:

If all knew as I know how holy our Father (Favre) was . . . they would kneel and thank God to have had the chance of conversing with him . . . No words of mine can describe what good God our Lord accomplished for the men of Madrid through Master Peter. What tears his spiritual sons in that city shed at his departure! Alas for me who must now carry on without him.[8]

The traveller reached Valencia on 29 April and on the following Sunday, Low Sunday, was in Gandia, some forty miles south of the city on the coast. There he was received by the Duke, Francis Borgia, whose Duchess had died some weeks previously. They had met before on Peter's first visit to Spain. The Duke was looking forward to this second meeting; having already made up his mind to leave his family, his country, his titles and estates to become a Jesuit he wanted Favre to tell Ignatius, with whom he had been corresponding, of his decision. In Gandia there was a Poor Clare convent that Peter made a point of visiting. Francis Xavier's eldest sister, once a lady-in-waiting to Queen Isabella, had been Abbess of that convent when Xavier was a student in Paris. She had interceded for him when his brothers, hearing unfavourable reports of Francis the undergraduate, wanted to withdraw him from the University. Thanks to her Francis was allowed to finish his course. She died before Francis left Paris but her holiness was still spoken of in 1546 when Favre visited the Collettines of Gandia.

On 4 May Master Favre blessed the site of a college the

Duke was having built for the Jesuits. It was the first of the
many educational establishments of the Society. Next day he
set out for Valencia where he was detained for some days. He
mentions meeting Juan de Castro, the confessor to whom, on
Iñigo's advice, he made his general confession in Paris sixteen
years previously. de Castro became a Carthusian soon after
leaving Paris and was Prior of the Val de Cristo monastery,
some thirty miles north of Valencia, in the 1540's. Peter does
not mention visiting this monastery but it was on his route to
Barcelona and considering his life-long affinity with the
Carthusians he more than likely broke his journey north to
visit the white monks.

Arriving at Barcelona on 20 May he fell ill again with a
tertian fever. This illness kept him three weeks in bed and by the
time he was fit for the sea voyage the galleys had sailed. In a
letter to Ignatius he explained the delay and stated that if no
galley was likely to leave in the following week, the fourth
week of June, he would embark on the first brigantine sailing
for any port near Rome. While waiting for a ship a letter from
Araoz caught up with him. In Madrid a cleric named Munoz,
evidently known to them both, was preaching sermons so
preposterous as to give scandal in the principal churches of the
city. 'Rumour says that Doña Maria de Mendoza got up and
walked out, and a Councillor asked me if the preacher was one
of ours. May God protect Munoz who has been the cause of
such mortification to us.'*

*Araoz, a prodigious and wordy letter-writer, gave a fuller report on Munoz to
Ignatius a few weeks later: 'We have here in Madrid a cleric who goes around
dressed in sacking and looking like an apostle. He captures the popular imagination
but he is giving great scandal. Wherever he preaches, his first sermon is his last
for he is not allowed into the pulpit a second time. Most of the *madrilenos* and even
some notable persons take him to be one of our Company and are greatly scandalized, asking why do we let him preach. Worse still, when they see him more
austerely dressed than ours some think that he is our Superior and are actually
saying, "That's Iñigo". At daybreak yesterday he went completely off his head,
racing through the streets shouting at the top of his voice and striking and buffeting
those with whom he collided. The rumour then spread "Iñigo is out of his mind.
He is running around the city *loco*". Others said he was an *iniguista*. Others still,
some very good friends of mine, hearing that the preaching Doctor (myself) had
gone mad, were deeply pained, though they could hardly credit it. However
they were relieved to find that they were mistaken and to learn that I am to
preach tomorrow (Trinity Sunday) where I preached at Pentecost, in the principal
church of Madrid. On that occasion there was an overflow congregation, all aisles
and doorways being packed.'—MHSI: *Epp. Mixtae*, (I) 291.

Three Jesuits were already in Trent, Jay from the opening session at which he represented the Cardinal-Archbishop of Augsburg, Lainez and Salmeron, nominated with Favre as papal theologians, since May. Lainez wrote to Favre asking for advice on 'how to deal with heretics'. The reply, written when Peter was ill, shows that the ecumenical spirit was not a twentieth century phenomenon. It deserves quoting in full:

Carissimo brother in Jesus Christ,

May the grace and peace of our Redeemer be always in our souls. Excuse me for not having replied sooner to the letters in which you asked me what line of conduct should be adopted by anyone wishing to help in the salvation and spiritual profit of heretics. I can only plead lack of time to consider the matter; also, there is little quiet in this house and little power in my hand, which makes it unsteady.† But my principal excuse is that I do not know if what I write will meet your query. However I shall say some things that occur to me regarding this matter:

1 If we would help the heretics of this age we must be careful to regard them with love, to love them in deed and in truth, and to banish from our own souls any thought that might lessen our love and esteem for them.

2 It is necessary to win their good will so that they will love us and readily confide in us. This can be done by speaking familiarly with them on subjects about which we agree and by avoiding points of discussion that may give rise to argument; for argument usually ends in one side lording it over the other. We must first seek to establish concord by dwelling on what unites us, rather than on matters which give rise to conflicting opinions.

3 Neither should we act towards the Lutherans . . . as though they were pagans, but rather address ourselves to their will, to their hearts, as a means of prudently approaching matters of faith. The opposite procedure we adopt with those who never heard of Christianity; they need to be taught the truths of faith and how to live by faith, that faith which comes by hearing; when they know the truth they can then be led through right teaching to good works—that is if they (pagans) accept the faith preached to them.

4 When we come across someone who is not only in bad faith but who is also leading a bad life we must first find some roundabout way to dissuade him from his vices before mentioning errors of

†Favre lost power in one hand after his illness in March 1546.

belief. Once I visited a man who wanted to draw me into a discussion on the celibacy of priests. I set myself to win his confidence. Then he told me that for many years he himself was living with a woman. Little by little I had the happiness of persuading him to abandon that life and return to his former celibacy. Meanwhile I refrained from disputing matters of faith. As soon as he gave up his sinful life his errors of faith vanished and he never even mentioned them again, they being nothing more than the result of the bad life he was leading.

5 Regarding the good works which the Lutherans say are not necessary, it is necessary to proceed from the works themselves to the faith itself and to speak of the things that will rouse them to the love of good works. If someone says to you that the Church cannot oblige anyone under pain of sin to recite the Office, assist at Mass, etc., one must first try to move his soul, so that he will get a liking for prayer, for good works, for the Mass. It is the loss of the love of prayer that causes many to lose the faith.

6 Take special note of this: many heretics' main objections are to the rules and regulations of the Church and the Fathers; they find themselves so weak to obey and to suffer that they think it is impossible to keep the Ten Commandments and the precepts of the Church. Because of this one needs to persuade them that the Commandments can be kept, that God gives us the grace to keep them as he does to bear the trials of life. This is one point where ardent exhortation is needed to help them to recover the hope and confidence they have lost. I dare to go so far as to say that if anyone were learned enough and zealous enough to be able to persuade Luther to abandon his position and place himself once more under obedience, resuming the habit he has cast off, he (Luther) would by that very act cease to be a heretic and there would be no need of further theological dispute. But, oh, what spiritual fortitude, what zeal would be needed to make him descend to the humility, the patience and all the other virtues a man would need to rise from such a fall, such a complete overturn as his! However, nothing is impossible if God lends a hand. Without his help it is difficult, nay impossible, to win back those who stray so far from him. The hour of their return is not something to build one's hopes on.

7 The man who can speak with heretics on the necessity for a well-regulated life, on the beauty of virtue, on the love of prayer, on death, judgment, hell and heaven—on all that leads to true amendment of life—will do them more good than those who would confound them by sheer weight of theological argument.

8   To sum up, these people need to be advised and encouraged to grow in the fear and love of God, to lead good lives, to do good works. This will help them in their spiritual weaknesses, in their lack of devotion, in their distractions, trials and other evils which do not have their origin in the understanding but in the senses and emotions.

Perhaps another time I may say more, but I fear I have exhausted my ideas on the subject . . .

Your brother in the Lord,

Pedro Fabro.[9]

Exactly one month later he wrote in the same strain to Dom Gerard, the Prior of the Cologne Carthusians. He also expressed his sorrow at the policy of force being adopted by Catholic rulers against those who professed beliefs different from theirs:

I grieve that those in power are planning, thinking of, trying no course of action but one—the extirpation of public heretics. How often have I not said to them that here we have a situation where both hands of the builders of the City of God are active in brandishing the sword in the face of the enemy. Good God! Why do we not leave at least one hand free for the tremendous work of reconstruction awaiting us? Why do we not see a finger being raised to bring about a real reformation—not in dogma or doctrine, for all is well there—but in the moral standards of our Christian people.[10]

The instructions Ignatius gave to the three Jesuits who went on to Trent without waiting for Favre were very definite. They were to be friendly to all, to listen quietly and try to understand every speaker's viewpoint. When speaking themselves they were to give reasons for and against 'so as not to appear prejudiced or give offence to others.'

The aim of our Fathers at Trent should be the greater glory of God. This you will achieve by preaching, hearing confessions, giving lectures, teaching children, visiting the poor and the sick in hospitals, and exhorting the neighbour according to your various gifts for moving people to prayer and fervour; then all will be able to implore God to pour out his Divine Spirit on those who are participating in this Council.

In preaching, avoid referring to the differences between Protestants and Catholics. Content yourselves with getting people to foster the virtues; stir them up so that they may come to a true knowledge of themselves and increase in the knowledge and love of God our Lord . . .

When hearing confessions you might make some reference to the Council, remarks that would be repeated afterwards by your penitents to others; and for a penance you might prescribe prayers for the Council.[11]

These words of Favre and Ignatius, written at the time of the Council of Trent more than four centuries ago, find echoes in the words of Pope John and Pope Paul spoken in our own time and in connection not with Trent but with Vatican II.

While waiting in Barcelona Peter became interested in children of an orphanage newly opened there by a lady, 'my daughter in confession'. He tells Ignatius that 'six of them have already been dressed in white (for First Communion), but twenty others have yet to be provided with white outfits.' He also refers to the reformation of some lax convents in Barcelona and north east Spain, especially the Benedictine convent of Santa Clara, a matter which moved Ignatius to write to Favre, Araoz and even Prince Philip. Favre does not think that anyone capable of coping with the situation can be found in Barcelona and suggests that the Pope, the Emperor and the Prince are the persons to approach.*

On 21 June he was still waiting for a passage. The famous

---

*This convent, formerly a Poor Clare foundation, had been taken over by the Benedictines. The rules were ignored and one nun, in constant correspondence with Ignatius in Rome, found her life endangered when she attempted to keep them. Ignatius' interest in the reform of convents in Catalonia began in 1524 when he, a poor pilgrim back from the Holy Land, converted a Barcelona community long a cause of public scandal. These nuns, nicknamed the Old Angels by the citizens, had thrown all restraint to the winds. Hearing of their far from angelic conduct Iñigo 'visited them day in, day out, neither rain nor heat keeping him away. He told them some home truths . . . and kept returning with prayers, penances and little sermons . . . until finally their visitors and suitors, cause of all the dishonour and scandal, were sent packing; with them went the vanities and frivolities that made the Old Angels a by-word in Barcelona.' But the Iñigo of 1524, burning in the first flush of that zeal that marks the newly converted, was not the Ignatius of 1546. And the Favre of 1546, or indeed of 1536 or 1526, never applied the military tactics of siege and attack to conversion; his method was to set himself out to win the good will, affection and trust of those alienated from God, to wait and pray until the hour of grace struck. Ignatius went to the sinner. The sinner came to Favre.

story of his friends begging him not to sail because of his impaired health, of Ignatius—after consultation with the Fathers in Rome—sending a peremptory order to come at once, and of Favre's alleged reply, 'It is not necessary to live, but it is necessary to obey', has not the slightest foundation. The legend probably arose from a desire on the part of Peter's early biographers to emphasize his obedience, quite unnecessary in the case of one whom the Jesuits of the first generation, all trained in true obedience based on interior submission to God, described as the perfect example of an obedient man. His journal has many reflections on obedience and it is interesting to note how he saw unworthy rulers in Church and state as the kind of ruler God reserved for those not prepared to obey the divine will as manifested through lawful authority.

To those who refused to obey unworthy, mediocre or blundering bishops or superiors, Favre opposed the need of interior reform and a more truly religious submission as the only means of 'meriting' better superiors. In this manner of envisaging the Reform he was one with Ignatius ... Reform does not come from without but from within—not through those who leave the Church (in fact or by their criticisms) but through those who submit themselves to her.[12]

In the scorching Barcelona mid-summer Favre could look back on seven years of incessant toil. It was natural that he, hearing of the achievements of Francis Xavier and other early Jesuits, should regard himself as an unprofitable servant. He had never been long enough in any one place to see notable results and in any case he had worked in the fields of individual souls where the harvest was known only to God. A year in Parma, eight months in Germany followed by five in Spain; back again to the Rhineland where he spent six or seven months in Spires, ten in Mainz and almost a year between Cologne and Flanders; finally there was almost half a year in Portugal and fourteen months in Spain. He would not have counted the long journeys, more than 12,000 miles on foot or muleback, or the two sea voyages as work, though even during these he won men for God. He made friends everywhere. He could not remain anywhere. Always there was the order to move on.

12

Peter Favre's apostolate was exercised during the first phase of the Reformation. It is debatable whether he was acquainted with the writings of leading Reformers. Lutheran books and pamphlets, though forbidden to the Paris students in his time at the Ste-Barbe, circulated widely in the French capital; German Catholics were also forbidden to read these works and Ignatius disapproved of his followers reading them. Though Peter admired Melanchthon and sent a copy of one of the Protestant theologian's letters to Ignatius from Worms in 1541,[13] he was not personally acquainted with the Lutheran leaders, the only one he met and disputed with being Bucer. His ministry was confined to Catholics, the low level of faith and morals among Catholics causing him more anxiety than the spread of new doctrines. His knowledge of Protestantism was to a large extent second-hand, a good deal of it acquired from Catholics who were about to leave the Church or who, having left, were returning.

At Worms, as has been seen, after having been refused permission to meet and speak with Melanchthon he wastes no time in regrets but says, 'I have enough to do to fulfil my vocation among the Catholics.' If he had been given the opportunity to meet Philip Melanchthon Favre would have been the first to concede that the Reformers' desire to purge the Church of abuses, to bring her back to the fervour of primitive Christian times, was in itself good. For he had seen with his own eyes to what a pass the Church had come, especially in Germany, and he was appalled: 'No priests at all in some places, no resident priest in others; priestly chastity abandoned by both secular and regular, higher and lower clergy. Our Lord permitting these defections and ruins which we see before our eyes. And on all sides abuses in civil and ecclesiastical administration. No wonder the Lutherans make such gains.'

It may be argued that his contacts in Germany were with worldly and immoral clergy and that his assignments in that country placed him in centres of controversy—Spires, Worms, Ratisbon, and Cologne—that his temperament inclined him to be over-optimistic before a Diet or Colloquy, over-despondent afterwards, and that this caused him to take too gloomy a view of the Catholic situation.[14] But the Venetian ambassadors, under orders to maintain good relations with Pope and Emperor, with all kings, princes and religious leaders, paint a darker picture than Favre's in their factual and objective despatches.

It is interesting to note the line Peter Favre's thinking followed between 1540, when he arrived in Germany, and 1546, when he advised Lainez how to deal with heretics. First he observes for himself, and not without grief, the numbers of Catholics, clerical and lay, living lives at variance with the faith they profess; he notes the defections from the Church, pastors and people going over to the new religion. He sets himself to discover the reasons for the laxity, the reasons for abandoning the faith of their fathers. He finds that the faith is not taught, not understood, not appreciated, not lived up to; he meets individuals who defend their moral lapses by choosing from Scripture or Tradition some text that conveniently justifies the action taken or contemplated. Experience convinced him that defection began not in the mind but in the heart, not in the intellect but in the will. Experience also convinced him that moral rehabilitation had to precede not follow the recovery of a lost faith, and that it, too, began not in the intellect but in the will. As time moves on we see him concentrating more and more on the clergy, and then on the higher and better educated clergy, the shepherds of the flock of God. Reformed prelates meant, in his estimation, a reformed clergy; and good priests meant good people.

He was not to live to see a completely different situation. After the 1540's it was no longer a case of Catholics abandoning the faith of their youth but of a generation reared and formed in a new faith, fashioned by new ideas. From then on there would be two blocs, one Catholic, one Protestant. New ways of thinking developed, ways for which Favre and his contemporaries were not prepared or trained. Yet this Savoyard, though limited in experience, though lacking in subtlety, in self confidence, in 'drive', had interior resources of faith and holiness and wisdom that enabled him to carry out—unobtrusively but efficiently—tremendously important work for God and souls in a time when the Church faced a great crisis.

In July he was sailing towards Italy, looking forward no doubt to a reunion with his dear friend and father, Ignatius. He was still praying for the Pope and the Emperor, the Kings of France and England, Bucer and Philip Melanchthon, the Grand Turk and the late Martin Luther. The Europe Peter was so soon to leave for ever was, in 1546, largely what these men had made it. If he could have seen the continent and its peoples spread out before him as he looked north from the Mediterranean, his heart would have sunk within him. The German princes, following their decision to oppose by force any decisions that might be taken at Trent, were arming. Their decision was followed by a military alliance between Paul III and the Emperor. The prelates at Trent, doing their best to concentrate on the subject being discussed—justification —wrote to the Pope explaining their difficulty: the Lutherans had captured a pass in the Dolomites not far from Trent and were assembling troops in the Grisons; there were Lutheran sympathizers in Trent itself. The assembled churchmen were in danger and completely defenceless if attacked; men in danger of their lives were not at their best when discussing so important a theological question as justification.

On Favre's list of people to be prayed for daily was the Pope. The Council started, Paul III did not allow his great age, the cares of office, or the dangers menacing the Church to overwhelm him:

Paul III cannot, on the whole, be acquitted of the charge that he himself often yielded to secular impulses little in accordance with the seriousness of the times. As in previous pontificates, luxury and pleasure were still displayed not merely in the palaces of Cardinals but in the Vatican itself. Musicians, improvisatores, female singers, dancers and buffoons appeared upon the scene. Now, as in earlier days, the chief pastor of Christendom was seen setting forth on clamorous hunting parties, receiving the ladies of his family as guests at his table, and taking part in the brilliant receptions of the younger Farnesi. A long time had yet to elapse before Popes would come to whom it would be impossible to attach the reproach of conduct so incongruous with their high office.[15]

Francis I, ostensibly at peace with the Emperor, was burning Waldensians in Provence and other heretics elsewhere. Cavalli,

Venetian ambassador to France, in a report on 1546 remarked that all these burnings 'were doing nothing to check the spread of the new religions in France. Whole towns like Caen, Poitiers, La Rochelle and many in Provence are silently united in living after the Protestant fashion.'

Henry VIII was blowing hot and cold; suggesting the abolition of the Mass after Easter, at Whitsuntide, 'in the midst of the New Men, great stirrers of heresy' that thronged his palace, making his will, arranging to have Masses said for his soul and burning those who denounced the Mass. 'If the Emperor should lose the war against the German princes,' wrote a shrewd observer, 'the King of England will take up the Gospel of Christ. Should the Gospel sustain a loss in this most destructive war, he will then retain this impious Mass, for which he has this last summer committed four respectable and godly persons to the flames.' Henry believed in taking out double insurance, Catholic and Protestant.

In Scotland Cardinal Beaton had been murdered. Ireland, under English rule, saw a new Church, 'Catholic, without the Pope, but with Henry as its Supreme Head on Earth', set up; abbeys and monasteries were wrecked and Church lands and goods confiscated; statues and relics were destroyed, among them the famous crozier of St Patrick, the legendary *Bachall Iosa*—the Staff of Christ—which was burned publicly in the centre of Dublin. The Scandinavian rulers, following the example of the English king and the German princes, had made Protestantism the State religion and enriched themselves while they wrenched their respective nations from the Church that had given them their culture and civilization. Poland began to lean toward the new teachings as did several Italian cities and states, notably Siena, Lucca, Modena and Naples. The Grand Turk, still supreme on the Danube, had troubles brewing between his sons and one of his wives, and thought of making a truce with the Christian rulers, so that he could attend to his domestic affairs.

At Ratisbon the Emperor, waiting during May and June for the Papal troops and his Italian and German mercenaries, relaxed a little. 'The Emperor and his Papists make merry,' reported a Lutheran observer in Ratisbon. 'There are banquets and dances every night; you would think that there is no war ahead.' Caesar's affair with Barbara Blomberg, mother of his son, Don Juan of Austria, ran its course during those weeks. Love affairs had not been a feature of his life. Even Melanchthon went out of his way to contrast the Emperor's personal conduct with that of contemporary rulers. 'In his private life he gives the most honourable example of continence, self-control and moderation. The strict moral standards that formerly held sway in the home life of German princes can now be found only in the household and among the retinue of the Emperor.' As Peter Favre's ship neared Italian waters Charles V was parading his soldiers, to the sound of kettle-drums and fifes, preparatory to taking the field.*

On 7 July Peter's ship sailed into Genoa. From there he wrote to the brethren in Madrid. The letter has not survived but is mentioned in a reply, a reply he did not live to receive. The Fathers were delighted to hear that he had a good voyage, especially since Monsignor the Nuncio had been more angry to hear of the 'wretched little craft' on which Master Peter sailed. It had taken all Araoz could do to appease His Excellency's 'holy anger'. Araoz had been so ill of 'a double tertian and *cencillas*' that his life was despaired of. But since the doctors had bled him twice and administered remedies for worms he was improving. The Nuncio called daily to see him as did his secretary; but now the secretary was down 'with what the medicos call arthritic gout, and all his members are swollen.' Doctor Ortiz, in Madrid on State business, had called and left his usual generous donation before returning to Galapager.

*Though he always trembled when his armour was buckled on, Charles V was calm and fearless in battle. When a general begged him not to ride out under gunfire he replied, 'This is not the time to set my sons a bad example.' His soldiers knew that he called them his sons and proclaimed their love and esteem for him in their marching songs. Strong in war and council, he was weak-willed at table. Oysters, crabs, lobsters, sardines, and herrings, liver pates and partridges, highly spiced sauces and sweets and above all, strawberries and cream, he could never resist. His faithful servant, Quijada, used to fling himself between Caesar and the salted eel-pies that inevitably brought on attacks of gout. His confessor used to reproach the Emperor for 'time-wasting, a passion for glory, and indulgence at table.' He hardly had to call him to order regarding his words, 'The Emperor wears a padlock on his heart', jibed Luther, 'I say more in one day than he does in a year.'

Ten days after landing at Genoa and some seven years after leaving for Parma Master Peter Favre arrived back in Rome. There is no account of the welcome he undoubtedly received, though a later record states that he returned safe and well. He arrived at a time of worry for Ignatius and the Rome community. That very week they received from Isabel Roser a bill for 465 *escudos*. Its items were the 'gifts', most of them 'almost new', which she had given them after transferring herself from Barcelona to Rome. Ignatius had come to regret the day this benefactress of his earlier years had insisted upon grafting herself and her companions on to the Society. The bill, dated 7 July, 1546, was for him and the brethren only the beginning of months of annoyance and embarrassing publicity.* When Peter Favre met Doña Roser in Barcelona early in 1542 and heard of her intentions, he had felt uneasy and had written Ignatius, 'I do not know what will come of this.' On his return to Rome he saw for himself how justified were his forebodings.

His first week back in Rome was spent in 'visiting and being visited, to the great joy of all'. On 23 July he wrote to Lainez and enclosed letters he brought from Spain not only for various prelates at the Council but for their servants. 'I meant to deliver these letters myself but since I have to defer my departure for Trent until the present heatwave in Rome abates, I beg you to take good care of them and see that they are delivered.' Peter told Lainez of how the latter's sister Maria had written him before he left Madrid to tell of her father's death. This news broken, he continues:

I wrote from Madrid to console your mother, your two sisters and young Cristobal. Write to them yourself at once and make your letter a long once since you have a spirit far removed from trouble and desolation. I waste time recommending his soul to your prayers or reminding a son such as you of his duty to a father such as yours. May he be in glory! I got the Fathers of the Roman house to say Masses and when I write to those in Portugal, Valladolid, Alcalá, Valencia and Barcelona I will ask them to do likewise. I made sure to ask prayers for him in places on my journey where there were people capable of feeling compassion for those who are bereaved . . .

May the Holy Spirit and the sentiments of all the Holy Fathers

*See pages 105–107 *supra*.

who attended Church Councils in times past be with you and all who are nominated to this holy Council in Trent.

From Rome, 23 July, 1546.

Your brother in the Lord,

Pedro Fabro.

To my brother in Christ our Lord, Father Master Lainez of the Company of Jesus in Trent.[16]

It was the last letter. Two days later, on the sixth Sunday after Pentecost, Peter went down with a fever that worsened daily. He knew that he was dying and looked forward to the end. On Saturday 31 July, he made his confession and the next morning heard Mass and received the Last Sacraments. 'Between noon and Vespers on 1 August, the day of St Peter's release from prison, all in our house and many friends being present, Master Peter Favre, of beloved memory, died.'[17]

In Trent, a little Tyrolean town peopled by Italians under imperial rule, the Council waited in vain for Master Peter Favre, the Paris theologian. That much-travelled man, his last frontier crossed, his earthly journeyings ended, had been called to a more glorious assembly.

Afterthoughts

THE legend that the Society of Jesus was founded to combat sixteenth-century heresies is widespread but groundless. From the time Ignatius, Favre and Xavier joined forces in the Ste-Barbe until they left Paris, Protestantism made little impact on them. When in 1534 they and the other *iniguistas* banded themselves together to work *ad majorem Dei gloriam* their intention was not to confute or convert Lutherans but to spend their lives in the Holy Land evangelizing the infidel.

For them, as for most of their fellow-students, the word *Reform* did not imply a radical overhaul of religious institutions, much less a re-statement of dogma. They thought of it as a reform within the Church, a movement like that of Meaux—where the diocesan clergy were reforming themselves preparatory to reforming their people—but on a scale as large as Christendom. Though standards of clerical morality were then low the faithful were not unduly scandalized by a state of affairs that provided them with excuses for their own lapses. Priestly chastity had come to be regarded as an external precept, theoretically good and possible but too difficult in practice for the majority; hence the numbers who dispensed themselves from its observance.

These priests were more deserving of compassion than blame. The special education and spiritual formation of aspirants to the priesthood, obligatory after the Council of Trent, did not then exist. There were no seminaries. Incidentally, those who now complain about how long it takes to translate conciliar decrees into action should remember that a century after Trent Vincent de Paul, Bérulle and others were working might and main to get the Tridentine decrees accepted and implemented in Catholic France. Priests who realized the need for personal holiness in men set apart for the service of God were few. Prelates, even pontiffs, who should have set a headline, were no models of priestly virtue. Many, raised to the episcopate as children, could not shepherd their flocks; their authority was unacknowledged and flouted. We need only recall the revolt of hundreds of Dominican and Franciscan student-novices in Paris against the papal legate sent to reform them* to realize the spirit of disobedience then abroad and to appreciate the importance of the obedience established by Ignatius and perfectly practised by Peter Favre—an obedience rooted in abnegation and the love of God.

During Favre's years in Paris, 1525–1536, he and the Companions seem to have regarded Lutheranism as a passing phase, an innovation hailed by those who hailed all innovations, certainly not as a movement with a future. Even after the shock of the Placards affair, even after the publication of Calvin's *Institution Chrétienne*, they did not know that they were living through a major religious upheaval after which things would never be quite the same again. Not until their journey from Paris to Venice at the end of 1536 did they begin to realize the strength and extent of Protestantism. So it is not surprising to find them in 1534 planning an apostolate in Palestine, not in Germany.

In the following decade Peter was the Jesuit who came into closest contact with the Reformation. He wasted no time in argument or recrimination but set about winning back to their earlier obedience priests and religious whose moral downslide had preceded their secession from the Church. He did not condemn Luther, Bucer or Melanchthon but wrapped them in the mantle of his prayer.

'From the entire sixteenth century not a single spark of tolerance can be struck', asserted the French lexicographer, Littré. Yet famous men like More, Erasmus, Melanchthon and the du Bellay brothers voiced strong objections against compulsion in religious matters, and thousands of lesser, humbler men also opposed it. Favre was one of these. Gentle and compassionate by nature, educated in a college with strong humanist leanings, he abhorred compulsion because it invaded

*See pages 20–21 *supra*.

man's most sacred citadel, the soul. He knew that it defeats its own ends; the making of martyrs, no matter what their cause, does not deter but draws followers. He saw the alliance of Church and state to compel religious adherence as productive of more harm than good. More than once he quoted Christ's injunction to his followers to abandon the intolerant methods of the Old Law for charity and patience, the spiritual weapons of the New.

It is sometimes forgotten that the medieval principle 'one faith, one law, one king' continued to permeate Renaissance Europe. Both Catholics and Protestants upheld this rigid, traditional principle. Neither Luther nor Calvin attempted to contravene it, rather they consolidated it by encouraging rulers to enforce religious unity within their domains; Luther, after some initial hesitancy, gave the prince the right to punish dissenters with death. The question that troubled each state, each ruler, was whether dissenting groups and their forms of worship could be tolerated within their frontiers without weakening the state.

The question is not asked today. We live in a secularized society, a society unconcerned with the problem of tolerance in matters of belief and worship because so many no longer believe or worship. Modern man tends to regard execution for one's beliefs as heroic but futile, partly because of his lack of faith but partly, too, because of the increasing and exclusive value now set on human life. Sixteenth-century man also valued life but, whatever his religious persuasion, he valued the after-life more. Death was for him a formidable accident but it had not the absolute finality it has for the latter-day secularist and unbeliever. The Lutheran burned on the Place Maubert, the Catholic hung, drawn and quartered at Tyburn went serenely to execution, his serenity born of fidelity to conscience; in the physical anguish he faced he saw not merely a passport to heaven but a witnessing to Christ.

Although in 1546, the year of Favre's death, the Reformation was already bringing about religious pluralism in states and further sundering of Christian unity, as various sects broke away from Lutheranism and Calvinism, there were to be found in all denominations men to whom unity was still precious, men who prayed like Favre for peace among Christians. Four centuries were to elapse before Pope John, echoing Peter Favre, said: 'Let us speak on things about which we agree and avoid discussing subjects that give rise to disagreement. But let us speak to one another. We are believers; we are brothers in Christ'. And straightaway men of faith and good will began to realize that we had been long suffering nostalgia for a lost unity, that unity so desired by Christ, so splintered by Christians.

—MARY PURCELL. Dublin. September 1967.

Appendix

PETER FAVRE was forty years old when he died. He was buried in the little church of our Lady of the Wayside on 2 August 1546, feast of the Joys of Mary. Six years later Francis Xavier died on an island off the coasts of China. In 1556 Ignatius followed his first two Companions to the grave. When, in the following decade, the Roman Jesuits decided to build the *Gesù* over their Founder's tomb they demolished the chapel of our Lady to make way for the new church. While every care was taken to identify and translate the body of Ignatius, no one remembered Peter Favre until it was impossible to distinguish his bones from others exhumed at the same time. He who had treasured the relics of so many holy people was not to leave posterity anything of himself for veneration. His remains, mingled with those of his brethren, were reinterred under the main door of the *Gesù*.

A new generation of Jesuits arose 'who knew not Joseph' and the memory of Favre faded in Rome. But in the Grand-Bornand the people he sprang from spoke his name by their hearths in the long winters and local priests collected what information they could about him. A little chapel was erected in Villaret to house his statue, locally carved, and Savoyards came to honour him there. On each anniversary of his death and every Christmas processions headed by the clergy would come through the mountains, 'bearing standards and crucifixes' to Villaret. Votive offerings were left at the shrine and stories were told of how 'holy Peter of Villaret' had saved a traveller who invoked him when he fell down a precipice, and of how the sick and injured who prayed to him were cured.

In 1607 another Savoyard, Francis de Sales, making a visitation of his Diocese, publicly consecrated an altar in the chapel at Villaret. In his *Introduction to the Devout Life* he cited 'the great Peter Favre, first priest, first preacher, first theologian of the Company of Jesus and first Companion of blessed Ignatius, Founder of that Company' as an example of a man devoted to the angels. 'I had the happiness last year,' continued St Francis, 'of consecrating an altar at that holy man's birthplace in the hamlet of Villaret which lies in the heart of our mightiest Alps.'

When in 1622 Ignatius and Xavier were canonized the Jesuits did not press Favre's Cause. They may have felt that sufficient honour had been paid to their comparatively young Society in the raising of two of its first members to the altar. They may have thought it wise, in view of the scandals associated with the name Borgia, to proceed with the canonization of Francis Borgia. Because of the new regulations governing Beatification and Canonization, which strictly forbade public cultus of a dead person until such cultus was sanctioned by Rome, they may have felt that Favre's Cause was lost in advance because of the honour paid him in his native place since his death. Just as the Dominicans allowed Albert the Great to be forgotten while his famous pupil Aquinas was canonized, so the Jesuits did nothing to promote the Beatification of the man who deserved, equally with Xavier, the title of co-Founder of the Society.

For two and a half centuries Peter Favre remained practically unknown outside Savoy. Then an able canonist pleaded his Cause, pointing out that the local cultus of Favre existed long before the new decrees became Church law and had the full approval of the then bishop of the Diocese, himself a saint. A new appeal, based on Peter's life and writings, was submitted and Pius IX declared Peter Favre Blessed on 5 September 1872.

Bibliography

PRIMARY SOURCES:

Monumenta Historica Societatis Jesu (MHSI) Madrid 1894 ff. and Rome 1932 ff.
A collection of, to date, ninety-four volumes of documents concerning St Ignatius Loyola, his first companions and the early history of the Society of Jesus. One of these volumes, devoted exclusively to Favre, is referred to throughout the Notes as MF. Favre is mentioned in several other volumes of MHSI. The following were used extensively in the preparation of the present work: (abbreviations in brackets.)

Bobadillae Monumenta. (Bob. Mon.) Madrid 1913.

Commentarium de Origine . . . Societatis Jesu. (Rod. Comment.) Madrid 1903.

Epistolae Mixtae (Epp. Mixtae) I. Madrid 1898.

Epistolae P. H. Nadal (Epp. Nadal) II Madrid 1899; IV Madrid 1905.

Epistolae et Instructiones S. Ignatii. (Epp. et Instructiones) I Madrid 1903.

Fabri Monumenta (MF) Madrid 1914.

Fontes Narrativi (FN) I. Rome 1943. II Rome 1951.

Polanco, Chronicon. (Pol. Chron.) I. Madrid 1914.

Scripta S. Ignatii. I. Madrid 1904.

BOOKS AND ARTICLES ON PETER FAVRE:

Bangert, W., *To the Other Towns; a Life of Blessed Peter Favre.* Baltimore 1959.

Certeau, M. de, *Bienheureux Pierre Favre: Mémorial.* Paris 1959.

Certeau, M. de, Articles on Favre in the quarterly Jesuit review, *Christus,* (No. 1, 2, 5, 6, and 45); also in RAM, *(Vol. 22) 1946.

Gilmont, J. F. *Les écrits spirituels des premiers Jesuites.* IHSJ Rome, 1961.

Guitton, G., *L'Ame du Bhx. Pierre Favre.* Paris 1934.

Guitton, G., *Le Bhx. Pierre Favre, premier prêtre de la Compagnie de Jésus.* Lyons 1959.

RAM = Revue d'Ascétique et de Mystique. Toulouse, 1920 ff.

Iparraguirre, I., Articles on Favre's character, spiritual teaching, and the spiritual influences discernible in his writings; in *Manresa* (Vol. 18) 1946, and (Vol. 19) 1947; *Razón y Fe* (Vol. 134) 1946; *Revista de Espiritualidad* (Vols. 20 and 21) 1946.

Orlandini, N., *Vita Petri Fabri.* Lyons 1617.

Plaza, C. G., *Contemplando en todo a Dios: Estudio ascetico-psicologico sobre el Memorial del Beato Pedro Fabro.* Madrid 1943.

Pochat-Baron, F., *Le Bhx. Pierre Favre.* Paris 1931.
A propos du Bhx Pierre Favre . . . Quelques notes sur sa paroisse natale . . . in the record of the *17ᵉ Congrès des Sociétés savantes savoisiennes.* Chambéry 1906.

Sola, J., Three articles on Favre in *Manresa:* two in (Vol. 18) 1946; one in (Vol. 19) 1947.

Other works:

Allen, P. S., cf. Erasmus.

Astrain, A., *Historia de la Compañía de Jesús en la Asistencia de España.* (Vol. 1) Madrid 1902.

Audin, J. M. V., *Histoire da le vie de Calvin.* (2 Vols.) Paris 1841.

Beatis, A. de, *Voyage du Cardinal d'Aragon.* Paris 1913.

Bernard-Maître, H., *Pierre Cousturier, dit 'Sutor'.* RAM (Vol. 32) 1956.

Bounaffe, E., *Voyages et voyageurs de la Renaissance.* Paris 1895.

Bourrilly, V. L., *Guillaume du Bellay, seigneur de Langey.* Paris 1905.

Bourrilly, V. L., (ed.) *Journal d'un Bourgeois de Paris sous le règne de François I.* Paris 1910.

Broderick, J., *The Origin of the Jesuits.* London 1940.

Broderick, J., *The Progress of the Jesuits.* London 1946.

Broderick, J., *St Peter Canisius.* London 1935.

Broderick, J., *St Francis Xavier.* London 1952.

Broderick, J., *St. Ignatius Loyola.* London 1956.

Cartier, A., *La Savoie et l'Orient.* Paris 1934.

Casanovas, I., *San Ignacio de Loyola . . .* Barcelona 1944.

Chambers, R. W., *Thomas More.* London 1935 and 1963.

Chatenay, L., (ed.) *Vie de Jacques Esprinchard et journal de ses voyages au 16ᵉ siècle.* Paris 1957.

Couderc, C., *Documents inédits sur Guillaume Fichet.* Paris 1900.

Coutin, F., *Quatrième centenaire de la Réforme et ses tristes conséquences pour le Diocese de Genève. in Mémoires et Documents publies par l'Académie salesienne.* (Vol. 54) 1936.

Dalmases, C. de., *Les idées de S. Ignace sur le Réforme Catholique. in Christus* (No. 18) 1958.

D'Auton, J., *Chroniques de Louis XII.* (Vol. 2) Paris 1891.

Dawson, C., *The Dividing of Christendom.* New York 1965.

Doumergue, E., *Jean Calvin, les hommes et les choses de son temps.* (7 Vols.) Lausanne 1899–1917.

Ducros, J. P., *Histoire Emmanuel-Philibert* . . . *précéde d'une notice sur le règne de Charles-le-Bon* (Charles III of Savoy). Paris 1838.

Dufayard, C., *Histoire de Savoie.* Paris 1922.

Erasmus, D., *Opus Epistolarum.* (ed. P. S. Allem) (11 Vols.) Oxford 1906–1947.

Falconnet, J., *La Chartreuse de Reposoir.* Montreuil-sur-Mer. 1895.

Frank, G., and Miner, D., *Proverbes en Rimes: Text and illustrations of the 15th century from a French Manuscript* . . . Baltimore 1937.

Freymond, J., *La Politique de François Ier à l'égard de la Savoie. Lausanne* 1939.

Febvre, L., *Au coeur religieux du 16e siècle.* Paris 1959.

Gachard, L. P., (ed.) *Trois années de l'histoire de Charles-Quint d'après les dépèches de l'Ambassadeur Venetien Bernard Navagero.* Brussels 1865.

Galtier, P., *La Confession et le Renouveau Chrétien.* RAM. (Vol. 22) 1946.

Guichonnet, P., *Savoie.* Paris 1960.

Guy, L., *Les Grands Faucignards.* Bonneville 1938.

Hackett, F., *Henry the Eighth.* London 1929.

Hackett, F., *Francis the First.* London 1934.

Hughes, P., *A Popular History of the Reformation.* London 1957.

Hughes, P., *The Church in Crisis.* London 1961.

Jeanne, A., *Geographie* . . . *des 89 Départments.* (6 Vols.) Paris 1868–1882.

Laemmer, H., *Monumenta vaticana historicum ecclesiasticum saeculi XVI.* Friburg 1861.

Lancisius, N., *Opuscula* (II) Antwerp 1550.

Lecler, J., *Toleration and the Reformation.* (2 Vols.) London 1960.

Lefranc, A., *La vie quotidienne au temps de la Renaissance.* Paris 1958.

Lewis, D. B. W., *The Emperor of the West: Charles the Fifth.* London 1932.

McElwee, W. L., *The Reign of Charles V.* London 1935.

Madariaga E. de, *Hernán Cortés, Conqueror of Mexico.* London 1942.

Merriman, R. B., *The Spanish Empire.* (4 Vols.) Vol. III. New York 1943.

Mignet, F. M. A., *Rivalité de François Ier et de Charles-Quint.* (2 Vols.) Paris 1875.

Moureau, E. de, *La Crise Religieuse du 16e siècle.* (Vol. 16 of *l'Histoire de l'Église*) Paris 1950.

184 *Bibliography*

Naz, R., *L'Ame de la Savoie*. Chambéry 1961.

Pastor, L. F. Von, *History of the Popes*. (40 Vols.) Vols. XI, XII and XIII. London 1925–1933.

Pérouse, G., *La Savoie d'autrefois*. Lyons 1933.

Pérouse, G., *Vielle Savoie*. (3 Vols.) Chambéry 1937 ff.

Pochat-Baron, F., *Les Paroisses de la Vallée de Thônes* . . . in *Mémoires et Documents* de l'Academie salesienne. (Vol. 60) Bellay 1942.

Pochat-Baron, F., *Histoire de Thônes depuis ses origines* . . . (2 Vols.) Annecy 1925–26.

Poncelet, A., *Histoire de la Compagnie de Jesus dans les Anciens Pays-Bas*. Brussels 1927.

Quicherat, J., *Histoire de Ste-Barbe*. (3 Vols.) Paris 1860–1864.

Retaña, L. F. de, *Doña Juana de Austria*. Madrid 1955.

Ricard, R., *La place de Saint Ignace dans la spiritualité espagnole*. RAM. Vol. 33 Toulouse 1957.

Rouquette, R., *Ignace de Loyola dans le Paris intellectuel du 16e siècle*. *Etudes* Vol. 290. Paris 1956.

Schurhammer, G., *Franz Xaver, sein Leben und seine Zeit* (Vol. I.) Fribourg-en-Brisgau 1954.

Tacchi-Venturi, P., *Storia de la Compagnia di Gesù in Italia*. (2 Vols.) Rome 1930–1, 1951.

Tandonnet, R., (ed.) *Memorial 1555—Louis Gonçalves da Câmara*. Paris 1966.

Tirsot, J., *Chansons populaires des Alpes Françaises*. Grenoble 1903.

Vallée, J., *Voyage dans les Departments de France*. (10 Vols.) Vol. III. Paris 1892.

Van-Gennep, A., *La Saint-Jean dans les croyances et coutumes de la Savoie*. in *Journal de Psychologie*. (Vol. 24) 1927.

Villoslada, R. G., *La Universidad de Paris durante los estudios de Francisco de Vitoria*, O.P., 1507—1522. Rome 1938.

NOTES

(ABBREVIATIONS)

MHSI = *Monumenta Historica Societatis Jesu.* The 94 volumes referred to on page 135. Abbreviations for different volumes used are also given on page 135.
(—) A numeral in brackets indicates the paragraph of Favre's *Memorial* or spiritual journal as given in the MHSI volume MF pp. 489—696.

INTRODUCTION
1. MF 400.
2. MF 399–402.
3. MF 414.
4. (23).

CHAPTER I
1. Naz, R. *L'Âme de la Savoie.* (Chambéry 1961).
2. Falconnet, J. *La Chartreuse de Reposoir* . . . (Montreuil-sur-Mer 1895) 593–4.
3. Vallée, J. *Voyage dans les Départments de France.* 10 vols. (Vol. III, Paris 1892).
   Jeanne, A. *Géographie, etc des 89 Départments.* 6 vols. (Paris 1868–1882).
4. Guichonnet, P. *Savoie.* (Paris 1960) 51–2.
5. (1), (4).
6. (29).
7. Pérouse, G. *La Savoie d'autrefois.* (Lyon 1933) 195.
8. Pochat-Baron, F. *Le Bhx. Père le Fèvre ou Pierre Favre.* (Paris 1931) 178–9.
9. (3).
10. Hanotaux, G. et le Duc de la Force. *L'Histoire du Cardinal de Richelieu.* 6 vols. (Paris 1895–1899) Vol. 1, 82–84.
11. MF 777—8, 804.
12. (5).
13. (244).
14. Couderc, C. *Documents inédits sur Guillaume Fichet.* (Paris 1900) 8 ff. Guy, L. *Les Grands Faucignards.* (Bonneville 1938) 33–47.
15. (3).
16. MF 775–6.
17. (11).
18. (401).
19. Pérouse, G. *op. cit.,* 195.
    Tirsot, J. *Chansons Populaires des Alpes Françaises.* (Grenoble and Moutiers 1903).
20. MF 774.
21. (244).
22. Pochat-Baron, F. *Histoire de Thônes* etc., 2 vols. (Annecy 1925, 1926) Vol. II, 55–6, 59.
23. (4).
24. (3), (4).
    MF 491.
    Pochat-Baron, F. *À propos du Bhx. Pierre Favre* . . . *sa paroisse natale etc,* in XVIIe *Congrès des Sociétés savantes Savoisiennes* (Chambéry 1906) 461–487.

Iparraguirre, I., S.J., *Influjos en la espiritualidad del B. Pedro Fabro*, in *Revista de Espiritualidad*. vols. XX and XXI (Madrid 1946) 438–452.

25. Pérouse, G. *Vielle Savoie*. 3 vols. (Chambéry 1937 ff.) vol. III, 55, ff.

Ducros, J. P. *Histoire d'Emmanuel Philibert* . . . *précéde d'une notice sur le règne de Charles-le-Bon*. (Paris 1838) VII ff.

CHAPTER II

1. (6).
2. MF 151.
3. Lescure, C. *Joseph de Maistre et sa famille*. (Paris 1892) 15. (Letter written by de Maistre 14 February 1905).
4. Dante. *Paradiso* X, 137.
5. D'Auton, J. *Chroniques de Louis XII* (Paris 1891) vol. II, 220 ff.
6. *ibid.*
7. Quicherat, J. *Histoire de Ste-Barbe*. 3 vols. (Paris 1860–64) vol. I, 16, 126 ff.
8. Villoslada, Ricardo G. *La Univerlidad de Paris* ... 1507—1522. (Rome 1938) 442.
9. Quicherat, *op. cit.*, 163–4
10. Villoslada, *op. cit.* 81.
11. Quicherat, *op. cit.*, 145 ff.
12. Erasmus, *Opus Epistolarum* 11 vols. ed. P. S. Allen (Oxford 1906–1947) vol. II, 85.
13. *ibid.* vol. IV, 101, 102, 106
14. *ibid.* vol. XI, 62
15. (14)
16. Casanovas, I. *San Ignacio de Loyola* etc (Barcelona 1944) 193
17. (9)
18. (8) (10) (11)
19. (418)
20. Bernard-Maître, H. *Pierre Cousturier, dit 'Sutor'* in *Revue d'Ascétique et de Mystique* (Toulouse) vol. 32, (1956) 174–195
21. Orlandini, N. *La Vie du R. Pierre Favre.* (Bordeaux 1618) 163. (He is quoting Araoz, one of the first Jesuits who spent a long time with Bl. Peter Favre in Spain). Orlandini's work was first published in Lyons 1617 as *Vita Petri Fabri.*
22. Pérouse, G. *op. cit.*, (*Vielle Savoie*) vol. III, 66 ff.
23. Ducros, J. P., *op. cit.*, VIII ff.
24. (13)
25. FN (I) 704–5
26. *ibid.* (I) 658

CHAPTER III

1. $\frac{5}{4}$(14)
2. (15)
3. $\frac{3}{4}$(15)
4. Lecler, J. *Toleration and the Reformation* (Trans. T. L. Westow) 2 vols. (London 1960) II, 18
5. Bourrilly, V. L. *Guillaume du Bellay, seigneur de Langey 1491–1543.* (Paris 1905) 173

6. *Journal d'un Bourgeois de Paris sous le règne de François I.* (ed. V. L. Bourrilly) (Paris 1910) 359–60
7. Audin, J. M. V., *Histoire de la vie de Calvin.* 2 vols. (Paris 1841) I, 35
8. FN I, 480–482
9. *ibid.*, 104
10. MHSI: *Epp. 1*, 90–92
11. de Certeau, M. *Bienheureux Pierre Favre: Memorial* (Paris 1960) 19
12. *ibid.*, 20
13. *ibid.*, 25–26
14. Lecler, *op. cit.*, II, 20–21
15. Doumergue, Emile. *Jean Calvin, les hommes et les choses de son temps.* 7 vols. (Lausanne 1899–1917) II, 147—148
16. MHSI: *Epp. I*, 109–110
17. (16)
18. FN I, 106–108
19. Dudon, Paul. *St Ignatius Loyola* (trans. W. J. Young S.J.) (Milwaukee 1949) 189
20. MHSI: *Epp. I*, 118–122
21. (18)
22. MHSI: *Chron. Pol.* 69
23. MHSI: *Documenta Indica* (I) 750
24. MHSI: *Bob. Mon.* 616

———

CHAPTER IV
1. FN I, 212–213
2. MF 25
3. *ibid.*, 252
4. *ibid.*, 23–24
5. (159)
6. FN I, 658
7. *ibid.*, 212–214
8. MF 17
9. *ibid.*, 18–19
10. *ibid.*, 29–30
11. *ibid.*, 34
12. de Certeau, *op. cit.*, 60
13. *ibid.*, 60–61
14. Lancisius, N. *Opuscula* (Antwerp 1850) II, 518–519
15. MF 84
16. *ibid.*, 91–92
17. Laemmer, H. *Monumenta vaticana historicum ecclesiasticum saeculi XVI* (Friburg 861) 301
18. Chatenay, L., (ed.) *Vie de Jacques Esprinchard et journal de ses voyages au XVIᵉ siècle.* (Paris 1957)
19. Laemmer, *op. cit.*, 302
20. MF 45–48
21. *ibid.*, 48–49
22. *ibid.*, 55–57: 59–60
23. *ibid.*, 62.
24. *ibid.*, 65: 67–68

25. *ibid.*, 69
26. (21) and (22)
27. MF 80–81
28. *ibid.*, 96
29. *ibid.*, 105
30. de Moreau, E.S.J. *Histoire de l'Église* Vol. *16.* (Paris 1950) 118
31. Pastor, L. F. Von, *The History of the Popes,* (*40 Vols.*) (London 1891–1953) XII, 125.

———

CHAPTER V

1. Guichonnet, P. *La Savoie* (Paris 1960) 49.
2. MF 776; Schurhammer, G. *Franz Xaver, sein Laben, und seine Zeit* (2 vols.) Fribourg-en-Brisgau 1954. I, 102, n. 1
3. MF 773–779
4. *ibid.* 793–795
5. Pérouse, G. *La Savoie d'autrefois* (Lyon 1933) 276–277
6. (28)
7. MF 131
8. *ibid.*, 130
9. *ibid.*, 132–133
10. de Certeau, *op. cit.*, 62–63
11. (25)
12. MF 140
13. de Retaña, L. F. *Doña Juana de Austria* (Madrid 1955) 43
14. (29)
15. MF 143
16. MI, IV (2) 92, 275, 289 ff, 309, 348, 397
17. MF 156
18. (see note 16 also MI, IV (1) 653 and Tacchi-Venturi, P. *Storia de la Compagnia de Gesù in Italia* (2 vols) (Rome 1930–1950) II (2) 79 ff
19. MF 156–157
20. (33)
21. de Certeau, *op. cit.* 136–137
22. MF 159
23. *ibid.*, 160

———

CHAPTER VI

1. Von Pastor. *op. cit.* XI, 206–207
2. MF 162–163
3. *ibid.*, 187
4. *ibid.*, 176–177
5. Ricard, R. *La place de saint Ignace dans la spiritualité espagnole.* Revue d'Ascétique et de Mystique. (Toulouse,) Vol. 33. 1957 pp. 130–133
6. MF 185
7. (176) (177)
8. Von Pastor, *op. cit.*, XI, 482
9. *ibid.*, 486–487

10. *ibid.*, 492, 499–500
11. (117)
12. (118) (120) (123) (124) (129) (130)
13. (134)
14. *de Certeau, op. cit.*, 219–220, n. 3
15. MF 186
16. (435)
17. Beatis, A. de, *Voyage du Cardinal d'Aragon* (Paris 1913) pp. 71–72
18. MF 189–190
19. *ibid.*, 192–193
20. (282) (283) (284)
21. MF 198–199
22. MHSI: *Epp. Can* (1) 76–77
23. MF 447–448
24. *ibid.*, 202
25. *ibid.*, 202
26. (385) (386)
27. MF 459–461
28. *ibid.*, 253–255

CHAPTER VII

1. MF 236–239
2. Gachard, L. P. *Trois années de l'histoire de Charles-Quint d'après les dépêches de l'ambassadeur Venitien Bernard Navagero.* (Brussels 1865) 29–30
3. MF 415
4. MHSI: *Epp. Nadal* (II) 61
5. Broderick, J., *The Progress of the Jesuits.* (London 1946) 35–36
6. MHSI: *Scripta San Ignacio* (I) 709
7. MF 280–284
8. MHSI: *Epp. Mixtae* (I) 173
9. (380)
10. MF 305
11. (401) (402)
12. MF 311
13. de Certeau. *op. cit.*, 29–30
14. de Retaña, *op. cit.*, 48–49
15. Von Pastor, *op. cit.*, (XI) 38–39
16. de Madariaga, S., *Hernán Cortés, Conqueror of Mexico.* (London 1942) 481–482
17. *ibid.*, 480
18. (412)
19. (421)
20. (427)
21. (429)
22. MF 471–472
23. *ibid.*, 331–332
24. de Certeau, *op. cit.*, 53
25. (433)
26. MF 365
27. MHSI: *Epp. Mixtae* (I) 231–232

CHAPTER VIII

1. MF 384
2. *ibid.*, 382
3. MHSI: *Epp. Mixtae* (I) 262
4. MF 398
5. Tandonnet, R., (ed.) *Mémorial 1555:* Louis Gonçalvez da Câmara (Paris. 1966) pp. 53, 63
6. Dawson, C., *The Dividing of Christendom.* (New York 1965) 157
7. MF 422
8. MHSI: *Epp. Mixtae* (I) 272–273
9. MF 399–402
10. *ibid.*, 414
11. MHSI: *Epp. et Instructiones* (I) 386–389
12. de Certeau, *op. cit.*, 142–3, n. 3
13. MF 80
14. de Certeau, *op. cit.*, 72
15. Von Pastor, *op. cit.* (XI) 357–358
16. MF 434–437
17. *ibid.*, 840

INDEX